# THE LITERARY LEGACY OF REBECCA WEST

# Carl Rollyson

# THE LITERARY LEGACY OF REBECCA WEST

A15015 915976

# Carl Rollyson

International Scholars Publications
San Francisco - London - Bethesda
1998

*Library of Congress Cataloging-in-Publication Data*

Rollyson, Carl E. (Carl Edmund)
    The literary legacy of Rebecca West / Carl Rollyson.
       p. cm.
    Includes bibliographical references and index.
    ISBN 1-57309-182-0 (hc : alk. paper). -- ISBN 1-57309-181-2 (pb :
    alk. paper)
    1. West, Rebecca, Dame, 1892-  --Criticism and interpretation.
    2. Women and literature--England--History--20th century. I. Title.
    PR6045.E8Z84          1998
    828'.91209--dc21                                   97-33532
                                                          CIP

Copyright 1998 by Carl E. Rollyson

*Editorial Inquiries:*
International Scholars Publications
7831 Woodmont Avenue, #345
Bethesda, MD 20814

*To order: (800) 55-PUBLISH*

To Michael Millgate

# CONTENTS

## ACKNOWLEDGMENTS

Grateful acknowledgment is made to:

Scribner and Hodder & Stoughton to quote from *Rebecca West: A Life* and *Rebecca West: A Saga of the Century*.

Viking Penguin to quote from *Black Lamb and Grey Falcon*.

Peters Fraser Dunlop to quote from *Black Lamb and Grey Falcon*, *The Thinking Reed*, and the unpublished writings of Rebecca West.

# INTRODUCTION

*The Literary Legacy of Rebecca West* is the first book to explore the entire corpus of her extraordinary seventy-one year writing career.[1] Peter Wolfe published the first monograph on West. His short book is a competent but very selective study of West's writings; he tends to emphasize the importance of her nonfiction, and he organizes his chapters around the themes of her most significant books. Motley Deakin provides a more straightforward introduction to the range of West's work. His book contains a chronology of West's life and career, and chapters on her as feminist, critic, journalist, historian, and novelist. He also includes a selected bibliography. Finally, Harold Orel complements Deakin's introductory study, but his work appeared before the posthumous publication of several West novels and a memoir.

These books tend to chop West up into categories and genres. I propose, instead, to follow the evolution of her career, demonstrating how the fiction and nonfiction relate to each other, and drawing on her unpublished

---

[1]Rebecca West is the pen name of Cicily Fairfield (1892-1983), a name she took from Henrik Ibsen's feisty heroine in *Rosmersholm* as a way of asserting a personality at odds with her genteel family name but also of saving her straitlaced mother the embarrassment of an association with a political and literary radical. It is characteristic of West's divided personality that she should want to respect her mother's sense of propriety even as she attacks the conventions of her time. For more discussion of this pen name, see Carl Rollyson, *Rebecca West: A Life* (New York: Scribner, 1996), 35-36.

manuscripts and letters in collections at the universities of Texas, Tulsa, Yale, and in other archives.[2]

West began publishing at the age of nineteen in 1911. An ardent feminist journalist, already an accomplished stylist, she astounded her contemporaries with her astringent wit and iconoclastic judgments. Her mother, Isabella Fairfield, trained as a concert pianist, guided her precocious child's intellectual and esthetic development--as did her two older sisters, Letitia (who would become a doctor and a lawyer) and Winifred (a lifelong unpublished poet). West seemed to begin writing poetry and fiction almost immediately, attributing her early literary beginnings to nurturing in a family that loved to write and to argue. Her father, Charles Fairfield, a brilliant journalist with decidedly conservative opinions, brought home many of his intellectual friends to debate politics, literature, and the arts. West cherished the story (unverified) of her father's winning a debate against Bernard Shaw.[3]

Charles Fairfield presided over his family as though it were a court in which males were sovereign. In many ways a man of another age, he longed for a loftier station than he was ever to achieve, and he lifted his daughters to his high level of expectation, never talking down to them, always presuming that they would understand that the word, like his authority, was sovereign. The result, especially for his youngest daughter Cicily (a name she never abandoned among certain friends and family), was that she would come to have a remarkable affinity for royalty, for seeing life in terms of dynastic disputes, tracing her own troubles in family history, ferreting out treachery at

[2]*Rebecca West: Artist and Thinker* (Carbondale: Southern Illinois University Press, 1971); *Rebecca West* (Boston: Twayne, 1980); *The Literary Achievement of Rebecca West* (New York: St. Martin's Press), 1986. Tony Redd, "Rebecca West: Master of Reality" (Ph.D. diss., University of South Carolina, 1972), is a chronological, developmental approach to West's writing that won West's approval. See Rollyson, 388.

[3]Rebecca West, *Family Memories: An Autobiographical Journey*, ed. Faith Evans (New York: Viking, 1988), 194. In her notes, Evans points out that Shaw's biographer, Michael Holroyd, believes the story is probably apocryphal.

home and abroad, in the annals of Central European monarchies she commands so brilliantly in *Black Lamb and Grey Falcon* and in the spy trials after World War II. When things went to pieces, she would often think of what to her was the supreme work of literature, *King Lear*, which presented the world as a court and a family gone awry, a father fallen among three daughters whom he would have serve as caretakers of his legend.

Nearly sixty years later, when West set down her mature reflections on the literature that meant most to her, she titled her critical masterpiece *The Court and the Castle*, thus bounding literature as she had bound her life-- between the politics of public and private interests, between kings (fathers) and children (subjects), who owed allegiance to authority, even though authority always compromised itself as something less than the majesty Lear required his daughters to revere. The flaw in human relations, as Hamlet discovered at court, was that they were corruptible, and that the castle could not stand as an abiding principle of loyalty and service to the king, his father. West insisted that Hamlet's inability to reconcile the ideal of kingship and of family proved his undoing--not the fact that he could not steel himself to avenge his father. Hamlet was perfectly capable of violence (witness his murder of Polonius), she pointed out in *The Court and the Castle*, but not of remaining both a dutiful son and lawful subject of the state. Shakespeare knew kings governed badly, West averred, but without the principle of sovereignty society would disintegrate, since it could not, in itself, sustain its authority. Rejecting its king, the body politic lost its head. When Charles Fairfield left home and abandoned his family, he inflicted a dynastic wound and bequeathed to eight-year-old Cicily a lifetime's search for sovereignty. In *1900*, her last completed book, she affirmed:

> The idea of a king who can save all his subjects from all enemies has the deep roots of a fairy tale. It also has the relation to reality that converts a mere fairy-tale into a lasting

myth. A strong king can certainly make life safer for his subjects; history tells us that.[4]

When Charles Fairfield left home (never to return) his eight-year-old daughter penned a painful poem of longing, addressed to him as her soulmate, her twin.[5]

From her earliest age, West associated writing with self-expression, rebellion, and a search for authority. On the one hand, she admired her father's articulate and controversial opinions (he was said to have lost a job in Australia defending the rights of Catholics to have their own schools). On the other hand, part of her writer's task derived from combating his low opinion of unions, women's rights, and socialism. She joined her sisters in suffragist campaigns, and she despised what she deemed her father's arrogant Anglo-Irish, aristocratic attitudes--a fact she made plain to Bernard Shaw-- when she called her father a "Dublin snob."[6] In later years, West's attitude toward her father would soften, just as her critical views of the monarchy and of the modern, capitalist state would moderate as she assessed the threats to civilization posed by the two world wars and revolutionary movements.

How West came to adopt a position somewhere between left and right is not well understood. When feminist scholars rediscovered her in the 1970s, they tended to extol her earliest writing,[7] neglecting the evolution of her politics--which is inseparable from the development of her literary career.

---

[4]*1900* (New York: Viking, 1982), 178.

[5]For the details of West's childhood, see Rollyson, 22-30, and Victoria Glendinning, *Rebecca West: A Life* (New York: Knopf, 1987), 9-35.

[6]RW to GBS, n.d., George Bernard Shaw papers, British Library.

[7]See especially, Jane Marcus, ed. *The Young Rebecca: Writings of Rebecca West 1911-1917* (Bloomington, Indiana University Press, 1982).

Her primary intellectual guide was Edmund Burke, whom she also claimed as a family ancestor.[8]

A full understanding of West's literary development has been hindered by opposition to her fierce anti-Communism, and by an academic world that has not known how to interpret a writer whose work cuts across so many different genres. Fortunately, a new generation of scholars is providing a more nuanced and comprehensive appreciation of West's career. This study contributes to their efforts by supplying the first organic account of her esthetic.[9]

---

[8]RW to Emanie Arling, December 29, 1953, Yale: "Burke, by the way, was a collateral ancestor of mine - a great-great-grandfather of mine had a mother who was a Miss Cuppidge, descended from a sixteenth century soldier of fortune, German, called Eustus Cuppich, and his sister was mother of Edmund Burke, and our family were his only respectable relatives."

[9]Bonnie Kime Scott, ed., *The Gender of Modernism: A Critical Anthology* (Bloomington: Indiana University Press, 1990) and *Refiguring Modernism* (Bloomington: Indiana University Press, 1995); Margaret Diane Stetz, "Drinking 'The Wine of Truth': Philosophical Change in West's *The Return of the Soldier,*" *Arizona Quarterly* 43 (1987):63-78 and "Rebecca West and the Visual Arts," *Tulsa Studies in Women's Literature* 8 (1989):43-62; Ann Norton, "Paradoxical Feminism: The Novels of Rebecca West" (Ph.D. diss., Columbia University, 1992); Loretta Stec, "Writing Treason: Rebecca West's Contradictory Career" (Ph.D. diss., Rutgers University, 1993).

# CHAPTER ONE

## 1900-1916

In 1982, shortly before her death, Rebecca West published a memoir/history of the turn of the century. *1900* retains all of her sparkling style, and it is a fitting companion to *The Young Rebecca*, a collection of her early, irreverent journalism, also published in 1982. Indeed, the continuity between the nineteen-year-old upstart who rocked the literary and political world of Edwardian London and the ninety-year-old doyenne of Margaret Thatcher's first years in power is extraordinary:

> *Woman Adrift* is a respectable piece of journalism, illuminated towards the end by some passages of meteoric brilliance, which starts out to prove that men are the salt of the earth, and women either their wives or refuse. . . "Woman is wholly superfluous to the State save as a bearer of children and a nursing mother." There is a kind of humour in the way these things work out. Just as Napoleon proved in his latter end that no man dare be a despot, so Mr Owen finishes by showing that all men are fools and a great many of them something worse.[1]

> It looked as if society disapproved of homosexuality, since it was for long a capital offence, but on the other hand here in every generation were fathers sending their sons to the schools they themselves had attended, well knowing that what had happened to them within the ivied walls would happen to their children, and making no effort to change the pattern. Do not try to work this out. It is simply an illustration of the tropism

---

[1]Jane Marcus, ed., *The Young Rebecca: Writings of Rebecca West 1911-1917* (Bloomington: Indiana University Press, 1982), 28. Page numbers for subsequent quotations will be cited in the text within parentheses.

by which male minds feel an instinctive desire to defend any unreasonable proposition.[2]

West's sweeping judgments and sardonic tone owe much to her father's scornful sendups of the status quo. Writing as "Ivan" for a Melbourne newspaper, *The Argus*, he excoriated the governing class:

> To-day, greatly given to cigarette-smoking, pigeon-shooting, dry champagne, and new ways indescribable, that class no longer believes in itself: if it still possesses the genius of command, it has more than once shown itself wanting in the loyalty to follow a capable leader, and courage to assert its constitutional position.[3]

Charles Fairfield leveled his criticisms from the right, whereas West, following the lead of her sister Letitia, castigated society from the left.

Father and daughters agreed, however, on what Letitia termed "liberal imperialism," a concept championed by Edward Fairfield (Charles's brother) in the Colonial office. He believed that the empire could be a civilizing influence, expanding trade and improving living conditions throughout the world--even if certain imperialists corrupted the system and cheated colonials. Not to understand this fundamental attitude toward the Empire is to misunderstand much of what Rebecca West stood for politically, and it is an attitude that she and her sisters absorbed in their infancy from their father.[4] Of imperialism, West writes in *1900*: "In certain times and places it engendered such costly tragedy as the Boer War; in other times and places it abolished such accomplishments as head-splitting by sword. It has resembled

---

[2]Rebecca West, *1900* (New York: Viking, 1982), 124. Page numbers for subsequent quotations will be cited in the text within parentheses.

[3]Quoted from scrapbooks of Charles Fairfield's journalism (some of it undated), Tulsa.

[4]Letitia Fairfield's explanation of liberal imperialism is contained in unpublished interviews with her supplied to me by her niece, Alison Macleod, whose private collection will be hereafter cited as AM.

parenthood as its most enlightened, and parenthood hostile and perverted" (108-09). As always, her metaphor had to be a familial one.

In an essay on Rudyard Kipling, West fondly remembers that during the Diamond Jubilee she had been petted by "dark men from the ends of the earth." To be part of an empire seemed indeed like having a charming and exotic extended family: "They were amiable, they belonged to our Empire, we had helped them to become amiable by conquering them and civilizing them. It was an intoxicating thought," and it gave the population of England, which had "slowly lost touch with their traditional assurances throughout the nineteenth century" a "new sense of religious destiny. Since they were subjects of the British Empire they were members of a vast redemptory force."[5]

West turned to journalism in the autumn of 1911 after a disappointingly brief career in the theater (studying at the Academy of Dramatic Art in London and taking roles in regional productions). A bout of tuberculosis ended her formal education; there was no money to send her to college-- which she seemed not to want anyway, since she chafed at the formal requirements of the school curriculum and saw little to emulate in the careers of the educated women who had taught her at The George School in Edinburgh.[6] She regretted that her mother's concert career had been hampered by lack of equal opportunity and then cut short by marriage and child rearing. Isabella Fairfield, a bright, articulate artist should have dedicated herself to music, West believed.[7] Instead Isabella had relied on an adulterous husband who

---

[5]*Rebecca West: A Celebration* (New York: Viking, 1977, 442.

[6]Rebecca West, "The World's Worst Failure II: The Schoolmistress," *The New Republic*, January 22, 1916, 300-02.

[7]Rebecca West, *Family Memories* (New York: Viking, 1988) and *The Fountain Overflows* (New York: Viking, 1956) contain the most vivid portraits of Isabella Fairfield as musician and mother. Recently Margaret Diane Stetz has discovered a West story that has escaped the attention of critics and bibliographers and that deals rather directly with her feelings about her mother. See "Rebecca West's 'Elegy': Women's Laughter and Loss, *Journal of*

gambled away his salary, abandoned his family, and died destitute in Liverpool when West was only thirteen.

Although Isabella did not approve of radical politics, she had a critical and esthetic temperament that her daughter emulated.[8]   Isabella took her young daughter to concerts and to political meetings. But West could not "remember a woman asking a politician a question at any meeting, though this was in Edinburgh, where women were given more leash as intellectuals than they were in London" (*1900*, 79). On one occasion, she observed a trembling woman stand up to put a question that took issue with a Protestant clergyman, who rebuked her: "Madam, you are dressed as a lady. Please behave as one" (*1900*, 79).

West believed that the structure of a male dominated society enforced the injustice that her mother and millions of other women suffered. British society, West later avowed in *1900*, was like

> a huge nesting-box containing many compartments which were designed according to a number of patterns; one was expected to behave in different ways, according to the type of compartment in which one had come out of the egg. One knew what one could and could not do, and everybody one met shared one's knowledge of the pattern laid down for one; if one performed unusually well, or unusually badly, one moved into another type of compartment, and found oneself following another pattern. (113-14)

Only through political action and the power of the pen could the nesting-box be changed. In West, writing--the search for new metaphors--was a political act, a way of altering human consciousness and actions.

"Indissoluble Matrimony," one of West's first accomplished works of fiction evoked the fluid world of human consciousness a la D. H. Lawrence,

---

*Modern Literature* 18 (Fall 1993): 369-80.

[8]For the best description of Isabella Fairfield's critical sensibility, see Rebecca West, "I Regard Marriage with Fear and Horror," *Heart's International*, November 1923, 66.

whose writing she would champion in reviews and articles throughout her career. George Silverton is married to a woman with "black blood in her," with "great humid black eyes," a "mass of large hair," and a large mouth. Evadne attracts and repels him--a goddess of sex, he hates her because she holds him in thrall. "The disgust of women," he thinks, "the secret obscenity of women!" He feels demeaned and inadequate beside her ease of movement, comparing her to a cat and also to a "grotesquely patterned wild animal" as she runs down to the lake for a swim, her white flesh reflected brilliantly in the moonlight. So powerful is her sexuality that in spite of all evidence to the contrary, he suspects her of being unfaithful, for he can only suppose that such voluptuousness must seek out male lovers. The quarrel between them, however, is provoked by her insistence that she will accept an invitation to speak at a public meeting, for she is much in demand as a passionate socialist journalist, and he cannot abide this additional sign of her superiority. At the lake, an angry husband and wife are about to strike each other, but Evadne hesitates:

> There entered into her the primitive woman who is the curse of all women: a creature of the most utter femaleness, useless, save for childbirth, with no strong brain to make her physical weakness a light accident, abjectly and corruptingly afraid of man, A squaw, she dared not strike her lord.

Her lord, having "no instinct for honourable attack," strikes her in the stomach, and she pulls him into the water with her. After a struggle he drags himself on to a rock and then forces the head of his struggling wife down into the water, exulting in her death: "I must be a very strong man." In fact, she has swum away from the pressure of his hands, and on his return home, an exhausted Silverton finds his wife soundly sleeping and "distilling a most drunken pleasure." Admitting that he is "beaten," he "had thought he had had what every man most desires: one night of power over a woman for the business of murder or love." He undresses and goes to bed, "as he would every night until he died. Still sleeping, Evadne caressed him with warm arms" (Marcus, 267-89).

In physical appearance--"I should love to be a cat," she divulged in one of her *Clarion* articles (Marcus, 170)--in sensuality and intellectuality, West and Evadne are coevals, and the story is an early dramatization of what West would call in her feminist book reviews "sex-antagonism" (Marcus, 97-101). The conflict between George and Evadne is so melodramatic that it verges on the comic, an effect West apparently intended, for she could not help fancying her story as a "jest," she confided to novelist Violet Hunt.[9] Yet the ironic reference to George as "lord" also evokes West's ambivalence about the male prerogative.

The young Rebecca West favored a radical tone: "There are two kinds of imperialists - imperialists and bloody imperialists," she declared on November 30, 1911 in her first article in *The Freewoman*, a journal dedicated to furthering the equality of women in all realms of society (Marcus 12-14). In her second, an attack Mrs. Humphrey Ward, the reigning female novelist of the Edwardian period, West observed that the "idea of Christ is the only inheritance that the rich have not stolen from the poor" (Marcus, 14). She reviewed literature, drama, social theory, and political tracts. In less than a year (from late 1911 to the autumn of 1912), she established her reputation as a witty and formidable critic.

As literary editor of *The Freewoman*, West strove to create a journal whose political and literary program coalesced. As she wrote to the journal's founder, Dora Marsden: "I don't see why a movement towards freedom of expression in literature should not be associated with and inspired by your gospel."[10] West's own writing constantly melded the esthetic and the

---

[9]RW to VH, n.d., Cornell.

[10]Quoted in Bruce Clarke, *Dora Marsden and Early Modernism: Gender Individualism, Science* (Ann Arbor: University of Michigan Press, 1996), 96.

political, demonstrating how character development in a novel, for example, reflected political judgments. Praising novelist Rose Macaulay's "exquisite" style, West nonetheless chides her for creating Louie in *Views and Vagabonds* as a "representative of the poor." Macaulay equates, in West's judgment, decreasing vitality with lowered social position, implying that Louie's weak grip on life is what makes her a typical peasant. "If this were so it would be an excellent thing to form immediately an oligarchy with the proletariat in chains. But the proletariat isn't like that. Even the agricultural labourers have shown in their peasant revolts that they have courage and passion" (Marcus, 27).

West herself was struggling to find a form for the novel that would do justice to both literary values and politics, shaping a vision of history that would transcend her work as a journalist and critic. Her most significant effort, "The Sentinel," an abortive novel written sometime between 1911 and 1912, concerns a troubled science teacher, Adela Furnival, who feels the lack of art in her life.[11] Her school work exhausts her, and she comes under the spell of a staunch Tory, Neville Ashcroft, an architect whose principles repel her and yet who exerts a narcotic and sexually arousing influence on her. She succumbs to his advances--in part because he is an artist whose style she finds irresistible. Instead of feeling fulfilled, she feels defiled and turns to a fierce involvement in the feminist cause, now that an inheritance releases her from the drudgery of teaching. In Robert Langlad, a Labor M.P., she glories in the principle of opposition, in joining an army of women fighting for the vote and for, as she sees it, the "earth's redemption." Life is not worth living without a protest, she affirms.

---

[11]West scholar Kathryn Laing recently discovered the manuscript of this novel at Tulsa. It had been mistakenly catalogued among works by other writers because West had written the name Isabel Lancashire on the manuscript. See Laing's forthcoming article, "'The Sentinel' by Rebecca West: A Newly Discovered Novel" in *Notes and Queries*, June 1998.

Yet Adela cannot give herself to Langlad any more than she can to Matthew Race, a robust Labor candidate for Parliament. She shies away from both men because she feels she is unworthy, having submitted to the erotic yearning that Ashcroft had excited. Instead, she takes on the most punishing protest assignments, getting herself arrested, beaten, and brutally force fed in prison. It is as if she is punishing the body that once betrayed her in an act of pleasure with a man she wanted but did not love. For Adela, as for Rebecca West, the personal and the political are one. Or as Adela asserts, "politics is minding the baby on a large scale." By having given into her body's craving once, Adela fears she has conceded the anti-feminist argument that women are primarily bodies, not minds.

The mind/body split, like the art/politics split, remains in tension in this uncompleted novel and would become the central theme of much of West's fiction and nonfiction. It is at the heart of the book review that brought her to H.G. Wells 's attention on September 19, 1912. She attacked the famous novelist on the very ground he thought himself most advanced: the emancipation of women. While she conceded that too many women had been encouraged to please and prey on men, she rounded on Wells for his failure to conceive of a thinking woman. Marjorie Trafford, the heroine of *Marriage*, dislikes her scientist husband's work and overspends him into a domestic crisis. Why can Wells only think of women as drags on men's souls? West wonders. Has he taken a good look lately at his male fellow passengers on the tube? He would find them no more prepossessing than unimaginative women, West assures him. In effect, then, Wells was merely perpetuating a feminine stereotype that surely existed but that was unworthy of a writer who also claimed that women were as capable as men and ought to be treated as equals.

If West's critique had gone no further, Wells might not have invited her to his home or begun an affair with her several months later. But she gave evidence of a sensibility not only like his own but of one from whom he could learn. She pinpointed a scene in which a cold, self-pitying Marjorie called for tea:

> That repulsive desire for tea is a masterly touch. It reminds one of the disgust one felt as a healthy schoolgirl when one saw the school mistresses drinking tea at lunch at half-past eleven. It brings home to one poignantly how disgusting the artificial physical weakness of women, born of loafing about the house with only a flabby mind for company, must be to an ordinary, vigorous man. (Marcus, 67)

In effect, West was presenting herself as the thinking woman whom Wells had failed to create in his fiction, a woman with literary and political insights on a par with any man's, and a woman unafraid to assess her own sex in terms that acknowledged Wells's but showed that he had not gone far enough in conceiving a liberated female mind.

At their first meeting Wells found West's aggressive and forthright personality attractive, though he believed that she was still unformed and did not know quite as much as her confident reviews suggested. He was also wary. He had already had one scandalous affair with a young woman, Amber Reeves, and fathered an illegitimate child. He had a wife, two children, and a cozy life in a country home--not to mention the attentions of a mistress, the novelist Elizabeth von Arnim. He wanted a hand in West's career, but his first impulse was to deflect her obvious interest in having an affair. The evidence of her letters shows that she thrilled at Wells's attention.[12]

Later in 1912, the novelists Ford Madox Ford and Violet Hunt took West up after her review of a Ford novel, *The New Humpty Dumpty*. Just as she skewered *Marriage*, she excoriated Ford's stodgy championing of an aristocratic hero--hardly a replacement for the roguish radicalism of Wells's *The New Machiavelli*, the novel Ford was satirizing. West surveyed both men and found them somewhat wanting, but in such a deft way that each literary

---

[12]See Carl Rollyson, *Rebecca West: A Life* (New York: Scribner, 1996), 43.

lion sought a share in her budding success. Wells kept up a steady drumbeat of letters to West about her articles, and Ford commissioned her to review books for his prestigious journal, *The English Review*.[13]

When *The Freewoman* lost its financial backer in the middle of October 1912 and ceased publication, West was already working for *The Clarion*, a feisty socialist paper that allowed her to write about sex-antagonism, the conditions of women workers, the Labor Party, the women's movement, socialists and feminists, and the Church. She seemed to take on every major institution of society in a heady prose that brought Wells round to make love to her after his liaison with Elizabeth von Arnim soured. Wells saw in her not just an attractive young woman (she was twenty and he forty-six when their lovemaking began) but his "lover-shadow," a kind of female twin with whom he could debate any subject. Like him, she had a gift for fables and exuberant play and soon the couple took to calling themselves Panther and Jaguar. Their lovemaking was like her writing--robustly physical and metaphorical, a give-and-take like the tussling of two jungle cats. West's lack of cant and gift for the arresting image enchanted Wells as much as it did her readers. The personal and the political came to vivid life in her prose:

> At its best the Liberal Party is a jellyfish. Sometimes the milk of human kindness which flows through it, instead of blood, gets heated, and then it flops about and tries to do good. This warm milk enthusiasm soon evaporates, and it lies inert. At present it is lying on top of the Labour Party. Through the transparent jelly one sees dimly the programme of socialist ideals which those who have gone before wrote in their heart's blood. To be wiped out by the Liberal Party is a more inglorious end than to be run over by a hearse. (Marcus, 110)

Ideas and political movements are not abstractions to West but concrete phenomena to be described with a novelist's gift. As she would late argue in

---

[13]See Wells's reminiscence of his first meeting with West in *H. G. Wells in Love*, ed. G.P. Wells (London: Faber & Faber, 1984). For West's relationship with Ford and Hunt, see Carl Rollyson, *Rebecca West: A Life* (New York: Scribner, 1996), 53-54.

defense of Wells--replying to critics who chided him for dwelling so much on ideas in his novels--life exists on several levels at once, and the best writers try to capture the continuum of thoughts and feelings rather than separating them into concepts and characters.[14]

West's writing never lost its organic quality, or its humorous yoking of the physical and mental. In *1900*, she explains that Colonial Secretary Joseph Chamberlain's family had moved from poverty to modest prosperity in three generations by the shrewd management of a boot and shoe factory, "and by a curious coincidence he himself looked like a single highly polished boot, with a monocle in one of its eyelets, and not at all unlikeable" (62). History, biography, social class, physical characteristics, mental tics--an extraordinary array of observation and learning--inform a Rebecca West sentence. Witness her devastating dismissal of Liberal Leader Herbert Asquith:

> There can be no more damning indictment of the nation than the fact that it allows Mr Asquith to decide the question of woman suffrage. Is not the idea of letting Mr Asquith decide anything on earth not enough to blot out the sun in heaven? He would make an excellent butler. I can imagine that owlish solemnity quite good and happy polishing the plate or settling a question of etiquette in the servants' hall. Such flunkey minds, afflicted at birth with an irremedial lack of dignity, must inevitably be attracted by the elaborate insincere ceremony of party politics. (Marcus, 193)

By the end of 1913, West had left *The Clarion* and her primarily socialist audience, and moved to Fleet Street, writing book reviews of fiction, literary studies, and political tracts for the *Daily News & Leader*. She also begin in 1914 to publish a series of articles in *The New Republic* asserting that "it is really art which governs the world." Art and criticism were absolutely essential to the survival of civilization; a life that was not self-critical was no life at all. A humanity that forgets its art also forgets its collective memory

---

[14]"The Novel of Ideas," *The New Republic*, November 20, 1915, 3-5.

of what holds humanity together and is amnesiac. West used *The New Republic* as a forum for harsh criticism which cut through the complacency of English men of letters, who were content to edit each other's papers and publish "platitudinous inaugural addresses like wormcasts." Even the greatest writers of the day, Shaw and Wells, required correction. Shaw believed "too blindly in his own mental activity," and Wells brooded over the future while failing to notice that his stories were falling in "ruins about his ears."[15]

In her first book, *Henry James* (1916), West calls for an attachment to ideas as passionate as what the majority of people reserve for personal relationships, so that a concept could be felt with the "sensitive finger tips of affection."[16] In *Henry James*, West extended her critical insights beyond those of her reviews and articles, but because her book constituted part of a series of short studies of authors, she felt hemmed in. As she said of a brief book on Hardy, "one cannot erect any majestic tower of criticism on the narrow basis of twenty thousand words" (Marcus, 312) She chafed under the constraint, commenting to novelist Arnold Bennett: "I'm sending 'Henry James' but shamefacedly. Remember how hampered I was by lack of space."[17] Actually, the cramping of her form led to virtues as well as vices. With her power to pack wit into a sentence, she could economically encompass the divide between the Master's early and late styles: "*The Europeans* (1878) marks the first time when Mr James took the international situation as a joke, and he could joke very happily in those days when his sentence was a straight young thing that could run where it liked, instead of a delicate creature swathed in relative clauses as an invalid in shawls" (41). Unfortunately, she also took refuge in grand but empty rhetoric, when she could not

---

[15]"The Duty of Harsh Criticism," *The New Republic*, November 7, 1914, 18-20.

[16]*Henry James* (New York: Henry Holt & Co., 1916), 53. Page numbers for subsequent quotations will be cited in the text within parentheses.

[17]RW to AB, July 4, [1916], Arnold Bennett Collection, University College (London).

compact her meaning into short form. Of *The Wings of the Dove*, she concludes: "One just sits and looks up, while the Master lifts his old grief, changed by his craftsmanship into eternal beauty as the wafer is changed to the Host by the priest's liturgy, enclosed from decay, prisoned in perfection, in the great shining crystal bowl of his art" (104).

Wells detested this kind of quasi-religious rhetoric in James and began to deplore its impact on West's work. Eventually her Jamesian style would cause a rupture between them during the writing of her second novel, *The Judge* (1922). Wells had published an attack on what he called the "James cult" in *Boon* (1915) that had influenced West, although she later told biographer Gordon Ray "I was all against Wells in his view of James." Yet she qualified the absoluteness of her assertion by adding: "it seemed to me as an earnest young Socialist that his [James's] involvement in the drawingroom was excessive and that a tea-party manner took away the impressiveness of some of his subjects."[18]  *Boon* argues that "literature is something tremendously comprehensive, something that pierces always down towards the core of things, something that carries and changes all the activities of the race."[19] West shared Wells's capacious imagination, believing that literature should be redemptive.  Dostoevsky, for example, was "celebrating the glory of the universe by reasserting, more hopefully than Schopenhauer, that there is a Will-to-Live which sustains and guides humanity with blind genius." Dostoevsky had shown the complex human canvas of Russian life so palpably that it made the wartime alliance with England possible, an extension of a "literary friendship" she lauded because the "wonder of Russian literature is

---

[18]HGW to Hugh Walpole, n.d., Yale; RW to GR, March 16, 1958, PML.

[19](New York: Doran, 1915), 101. Page numbers for subsequent quotations will be cited in the text within parentheses.

now as indisputable as the glory of Rome."[20] James, Wells contended, "seems to regard the whole seething brew of life as a vat from which you skim, with slow, dignified gestures, works of art. . . . Works of art whose only claim is their art." In other words, James had removed art from life, not realizing "a novel isn't a picture. . . . That life isn't a studio." James valued unity and homogeneity, but the result was sterility. One never got anywhere in his fiction. "He doesn't find things out. He doesn't even seem to want to find things out. You can see that in him; he is eager to accept things-- elaborately" (104). Similarly, West protested that James had no sense of the past, and therefore no sense of history:

> He was always misled by such lovely shells of the past as Hampton Court into the belief that the past which inhabited them was as lovely. The calm of Canterbury Close appeared to him as a remnant of a time when all England, bowed before the Church, was as calm; whereas the calm is really a modern condition brought about when the Church ceased to have anything to do with England. He never perceived that life is always a little painful at the moment, not only at this moment but at all moments. (27)

Wells and West sensed in the Master too much of an affection for the upper class and the Establishment. He was, in a way, a figurehead for their lambasting of "dons and prigs, cults of the precious and cults of style" (*Boon*, 276). They both lamented what Wells called the lack of a "common purpose" and "sense of a whole community." The world of letters was filled with "posturing and competition and sham reputations." For a moment, at the outset of the war, "people seemed noble and dignified," but "what the devil do *we* stand for?" Boon asks. "Was there anything that amounted to an intellectual life at all in our beastly welter of writing, of nice-young-man poetry, of stylish fiction and fiction without style, of lazy history, popular philosophy, slobbering criticism?" (276) Among the younger novelists West held out hope only for

---

[20]"Redemption and Dostoevsky," *The New Republic*, July 10, 1915, 249-52.

D.H. Lawrence; the rest, she remarked, were "unanimously unaware of the existence of style (in all the work of Mr. Hugh Walpole, for instance, one could find hardly one sensitive phrase)." Yet even the great James had overlooked Lawrence in favor of Walpole in his criticism.[21]

When West returned to the subject of Henry James in *1900*, she deplored his butler-like attendance to the status quo and his static, ahistorical view of social reality, which bothered a writer with an exquisite command of history. Yet in her usual grasp of the concrete metaphor, she concluded: "But we cannot do without him; he diagnosed the world's sickness, though that hardly excuses the too pliant knee of his nature. A great, great genius" (100).

In the first two decades of the twentieth century, West reported on and analyzed the crisis of a patriarchal society. She had cherished and rejected her father's authority, seeing in him the promise and the failure of the paternal ideal--a subject she would return to over and over again in her fiction and finally set at rest in *1900*. The events that resulted in the First World War also signified to her the death of the nineteenth century. Losing her father at such a young age was, in fact, a precursor of what the new generation would experience--some young people losing their fathers in the war, and others losing that certitude that had strengthened Victorian values. Characteristically, West dramatized the collapse of the nineteenth century in a scene with her father. In 1898, when West was five-years-old, England's great Prime Minister, William Ewart Gladstone, had died--a tragic event West was made to feel acutely by her father's encomium:

> Gladstone looked like the stern and wise and honoured father everybody would like to have. Where are we to find another like that? It does not matter on which side he is. Things are better for a country when they have an elder statesman who

---

[21]Marcus, 346; "Reading Henry James in War Time," *The New Republic*, February 27, 1915, 98-100.

looks as if he could save one from any sort of drowning. But I don't see it happening in England today. (6)

In *1900*, reviewing the list of prime ministers succeeding Gladstone, West fails to find another father figure. "Since 1900 we have had no certainty at any time that there was somebody who would take care of us. We were going to have to look after ourselves" (8).

## CHAPTER TWO

### 1914-1922

Life for Rebecca West became considerably more complicated with the birth of her son Anthony by Wells on the day Britain declared war. She managed to continue writing for periodicals, but it proved difficult to find the time to concentrate on a major work. American publisher Alfred A. Knopf wrote to her about turning her *New Republic* series, "The World's Worst Failure," into a book, but she replied that she had not finished it. It would have to contain the "ultimate wisdom about feminism" which she had had to acquire slowly, "by fletcherising my experience"--that is, masticating it hundreds of times so that it could be digested.[1]

Although West had a nurse to help with her infant son, she felt harried by housekeepers who saw through the fiction of married life she and Wells tried to maintain throughout a decade of a passionate on-again, off-again affair. He was a fitful father who took several journalistic jaunts outside England when he was not shuttling between his country home and the various domiciles he established for West and her son that kept them out of London and thus out of range of the literary gossips. Wells, whose only birth control method had been withdrawal prior to ejaculation, admitted that Anthony had been an accident. Neither he nor West were prepared for the consequences and had to make do--in her case perpetuating humiliating ruses that had Anthony calling her auntie and his father Wellsie. Her days as an unfettered

---

[1]RW to AK, June 12, 1917, Texas.

feminist were over, and West struggled to reconstruct her vision of a literary career.

West finally found her inspiration in Ford Madox Ford's masterpiece, *The Good Soldier*, which she reviewed in the *Daily News* on April 2, 1915. She hailed his work as "clever, as the novels of Mr Henry James are clever, with all sorts of acute discoveries about human nature; and at times it is radiantly witty." She marveled at Ford's union of passion and technique and set aside her youthful socialist dismissal of the rich:

> For the subject is, one realises when one has come to the end of this saddest story, much vaster than one had imagined that any story about well-bred people. who live in sunny houses with deer in the park, and play polo, and go to Nauheim for the cure, could possibly contain.

What intrigues West is the story of Edward Ashburnham, a handsome member of the governing class with a "fatal touch of the imagination," a romantic, in fact, with the sensibility of a creative artist. She had been seeking to create just such a character in her abortive novel, "The Sentinel," but she had failed to achieve a vision of a male with Ashburnam's degree of nobility, or to imagine a plot in which a woman might fail such a man--as Ashburnam's wife, Leonora, fails him, not understanding, in West's words, that "marriage meant anything but an appearance of loyalty before the world and the efficient management of one's husband's estate." Starved for a love that Leonora cannot provide, Ashburnam develops a sentimental innocent passion for a "quite innocent young girl," as West puts it. The denouement is a "beautiful and moving" tragedy told by an "intervener not too intimately concerned in the plot," who manages to convey an exquisite "effect of effortlessness and inevitableness." West's concluding sentence sounds a reverent note not heard before in her reviews: "Indeed, this is a much, much better book than any of us deserve."[2]

West's review is virtually a sketch of her first published novel, *The Return of the Soldier* (1918). At the center of her work is Chris Baldry, a handsome member of the governing class with a romantic sensibility. Indeed he is a Wordsworthian child who "was not like other city men," for he had always shown a "great faith in the improbable," really thinking that a birch tree would "stir and shrink and quicken into an enchanted princess," and that a tiger would show its fangs in the bracken.[3] Like Ashburnam, Baldry has a polished wife, Kitty, who observes the proper forms and is a neo-classical doll-like lady who cannot fathom his intensity. She substitutes "gracious living" for his "lack of free adventure" (21). Also like Ashburnam, Baldry is an innocent--an amnesiac victim of shell shock returning from war in the mental mood of a twenty-year-old, having obliterated any memory of his marriage to Kitty and yearning for an earlier liaison with Margaret, a lower class woman he courted but then spurned in a fit of jealously and misunderstanding (he concluded she would not answer his letters when in fact they were never forwarded to her). Baldry can think only of Margaret, crying out to the cold Kitty that he will die if he does not see her. Mediating between Chris and Kitty, between these romantic and neoclassical temperaments, is Jenny, the novel's narrator--or intervener--who is obviously in love with Chris and yet who is removed enough from the action to see clearly the dilemma that the Kitty-Chris-Margaret triangle presents.

At first, Jenny rejects Margaret, who has grown dowdy and worn from work in the years separating her from Chris. To Jenny, Chris's craving for

---

[2]Jane Marcus, ed., *The Young Rebecca* (Bloomington: Indiana University Press, 1982), 298-300. Page numbers for subsequent quotations will be cited in the text within parentheses.

[3]Rebecca West, *The Return of the Soldier* (New York: Carroll & Graf, 1990), 19. Page numbers for subsequent quotations will be cited in the text within parentheses.

Margaret shows Baldry Court for the sham it is; it is only a facade of happiness that she and Kitty have conspired to construct. Chris, Jenny realizes, never reconciled himself to the compromises of adulthood, to marrying a beautiful woman of his class who could make life tidy and comfortable but not exciting. It is Jenny who gradually comprehends the inevitableness of Chris's unhappiness even as Kitty accuses him of counterfeiting amnesia and of secretly wanting a mistress. Dr. Anderson, the psychiatrist called in to cure Chris--that is, to return him to adulthood and to his marriage to Kitty--has his doubts about restoring Chris to an ordinary life. For Dr. Anderson points out to Kitty that there is all the difference in the world between the "deep self in one, the essential self, that has its wishes . . . and the superficial self" which suppresses those wishes and puts on a "good show before the neighbours" (163-64). Chris has had enough of good shows. But for Kitty, there is only self-control, good breeding and manners. It comes as a shocking revelation to her when Margaret confides to Dr. Anderson that Chris has always been "very dependent." Margaret is confirming the doctor's speculation that Chris turned to sex with a "peculiar need" (167). The maternal Margaret, Anderson implies, is a substitute for Chris's cold mother and--though no one actually says so--an antidote to the icily correct Kitty.

Although it is tempting to Jenny and to Dr. Anderson to allow Chris to remain in his youthful, ever-hopeful state, that apparent bliss would also demean him, divorcing him from reality and dwarfing his manhood. A reluctant but resigned Margaret is delegated the task of taking to him some of his dead child's possessions as a means of shocking him back into his sense of fatherhood and adulthood. For Margaret, Chris's return to reality is particularly painful because she too has lost a child--at almost the same time that Chris and Kitty lost theirs. As Margaret observes, it is as if each child had half a life, or as if, one might speculate, the child in Margaret and Chris-- the innocence of their early love affair--must give way to a recognition of maturity and death.

What Chris needs, what Margaret gives, and what Kitty does not know is missing is a love that confirms the deep self, a love that West understood from her reading of *The Good Soldier*, particularly the passage in which the narrator observes that the

> the real fierceness of desire, the real heat of a passion long continued and withering up the soul of a man, is the craving for an identity with the woman that he loves. He desires to see with the same eyes, to touch with the same sense of touch, to hear with the same ears, to lose his identity, to be enveloped, to be supported. For, whatever may be said, of the relation of the sexes, there is no man who loves a woman that does not desire to come to her for the renewal of his courage, for the cutting asunder of his difficulties. And that will be the mainspring of his desire for her. We are all so afraid, we are all so alone, we all so need from the outside the assurance of our own worthiness to exist.[4]

Margaret is Chris's lover-shadow. When she comes to him at his urgent request, he buries himself in her bosom, feeling the need of an absolute envelopment in order to live. Both Kitty and Jenny suppose that he will be repelled by Margaret's spoiled looks, her reddened, seamed hands. But they overlook his powerful imagination and his desire to identify with his love. And Margaret never for a moment doubts that she will be attractive to Chris, for the memory of her love is as sacred to her as it is inviolable to him.

In "The Sentinel," Adela Furnival struggles to reconcile her sexual cravings with her feminist principles. She holds herself back from men because she believes that her indulgence in her animal appetites has corrupted her. She would like to give herself with love, yet she feels that she has ruined her innocence--a concept West finds of supreme importance in *The Good Soldier* and emulates in her novel. As Victoria Glendinning observes, West is celebrating "goodness, the creative, life-giving goodness that is

---

[4]Ford Madox Ford, *The Good Soldier* (New York: Vintage Books, n.d.), 114-115. Page numbers for subsequent quotations will be cited in the text within parentheses.

independent of intellect, or of art as it is usually understood."[5]  Margaret
embodies an ideal that eludes Adela, an ideal that would seem, as Glendinning acknowledges, unlikely for a young, independent feminist like Rebecca
West to embrace, and yet embrace it West does when she evokes Margaret
as the woman who has "gathered the soul of the man into her soul and is
keeping it warm in love and peace so that his body can rest quiet for a little
time. That is a great thing for a woman to do" (144). There are many ways
to be creative, Jenny suggests, as she observes Chris sleeping peacefully beside
Margaret:

> I know there are things at least as great for those women whose
> independent spirits can ride fearlessly and with interest outside
> the home park of their personal relationships, but indepen-
> dence is not the occupation of most of us. What we desire is
> greatness such as this which has given sleep to the beloved.
> (144)

*The Return of the Soldier* may help to explain why West never did complete
the book on feminism that Knopf wanted to publish. For the novel surely
suggests how difficult it would be to attain the "ultimate wisdom about
feminism" that West sought from fletcherising her experience.

Echoing the famous phrase of Ford's narrator, "the saddest story" (115)
Jenny remarks "This was the saddest spring" (132). The transition from "The
Sentinel" to *The Return of the Soldier* is from social protest to tragedy, which
drove West deeper into herself and estranged her from Wells, who wanted
her to pursue her gift for social criticism and comedy in a new novel, *The
Judge*, she was beginning to write, instead of miring herself in the "steamy rich
jungle of her imaginations."[6]

---

[5]Introduction to *The Return of the Soldier*, 3.

[6]*H. G. Wells in Love*, ed. G. P. Wells (London: Faber & Faber, 1984), 101. Page numbers
for subsequent quotations will be cited in the text within parentheses.

*The Return of the Soldier* sparked a reconsideration of where West stood esthetically and politically. She had written a novel closer in temperament to the conservative Ford than to the radical Wells. Her concern with point of view reflected not only her immersion in James but her reading of Freud. To be sure, she remained a staunch supporter of the Labor Party, the only political party pledged to support women's rights and the general welfare, especially the education of the entire populace. But the new Bolshevik government in Russia gave her pause. Unlike many on the Left, she did not hail its coming, and soon she would be siding with those who deplored its tyranny.[7]

Wells admired West's protests at injustice and hoped they would become the focus of her new novel, in which she intended to tell the story of a judge who picks up the wife of a man he had sentenced to death a decade earlier. She recognizes him immediately and leads him unsuspectingly home to her bed; there he suddenly dies of heart failure as she threatens him with a knife. West had conceived this story, Wells later remembered, after turning away in distaste from the sight of a judge "on his way to the Assizes. He was going to his job with an old fashioned stateliness, preceded by officials with silver staves" (101). It was this kind of pompous figure she would expose in her novel. She knew that something like this story had actually occurred, involving an English judge who had died of a seizure in a brothel.

West soon realized that in order to make the woman's actions comprehensible, she had to explain that the husband had committed murder out of a tragic necessity that had earned the sympathy of his loving wife. That tragic husband became Richard Yaverland and his sympathetic wife,

---

[7]For West's early skepticism of the Bolshevik government see her letter to S. K. Ratcliffe, March 12, 1918, Yale. For her support of the Labor Party see "Women as Brainworkers," *Women and the Labour Party*, ed. Dr. Marion Phillips (London: Headley Brothers Publishers, 1918).

Ellen Melville. It would become a "whale of a book," Wells complained, formless and self-indulgent (101).

Journalistic assignments interrupted West's concentration on the novel, but they paid her way and "kept the wolf from the door," as she told Eric Pinker, her agent.[8] Her articles also bolstered her reputation as a leading critic. Besides reviewing plays for *Time and Tide*, she produced (between April 1920 and December 1922) fifty-five two-thousand word reviews of 136 novels for *The New Statesman*. It was primarily this latter achievement that prompted critic Frank Swinnerton to remark in his classic study, *The Georgian Scene (1934)*: "I doubt whether any such brilliant reviews were ever seen before; they certainly have not been seen since. . . . She amused, she stung; but she held fast to her own standard of quality."

One of the stung, novelist Hugh Walpole, wrote to West protesting her "public scalpings" of him. She replied wondering why he listened to unfounded gossip. It was true that she did not hide her contempt for nonsense, but there were numerous instances in which she had praised beautiful writing. Taken as a whole, the body of her criticism resembled a "mixed grill." Why did he blame her if people chose to remember her negative reviews? She admitted she thought his work "facile and without artistic impulse." But there was no personal animus; in fact, she had liked him the only time they had met, but she could not accept his suggestion that she should not review his work if she did not like it. Why should she tolerate his being swallowed whole by the British public? She concluded her argument with a flourish: "Really, Mr. Walpole! I probably shall leave you alone as I am less keen than ever in reviewing novels now - but I am appalled by the theoretical aspects of your demand. Really, Mr. Walpole!" He had evidently mentioned a breakdown and she appended a sympathetic note: "I hope you will be better soon. And I apologise for anything I've added to your discomfort by my

---

[8]RW to EP, September 25, 1921, NYPL.

literary offensiveness." Walpole's biographer, Rupert Hart-Davis, reports that Walpole was crushed by her retort and thereafter "more than a little frightened of Rebecca West."[9]

In *The New Statesman*, West honed her gift for literary jousting and intellectual *jeu d'esprit*. She calls a character in a E. M. Delafield novel "a certain kind of female fool who is perhaps the penalty we pay for the Reformation," and then she adds an aria that goes well beyond the subject of the work at hand:

> Only in Protestant countries do we see this type allowed to draw on its vast stores of natural gases as freely as it would wish. In America it has its Paradise; there it founds new religions which, in their lack of any intellectual skeleton and their flabby, pellucid substance of characterless amiability, are as plainly beneath the level of the classic religions of the world as a jellyfish is beneath the level of a mammal.

West reviewed friends like Violet Hunt and G.B. Stern, and they did not escape unscathed. Neither did Somerset Maugham, an early supporter of hers, whose collection of short stories she termed "technically admirable," but marred by a "cynicism he stuffed into them to conceal his lack of any real philosophy." West had not met Virginia Woolf when she reviewed *Jacob's Room* which "has again provided us with a demonstration that she is at once a negligible novelist and a supremely important writer." West would revise her view of Woolf the novelist upward by the end of the 1920s.[10]

West discussed modern fiction's tendency to concentrate on increasingly less dignified subjects and concluded: "No doubt some young man of

---

[9]Walpole's letter is quoted in Rupert Hart-Davis, *Hugh Walpole: A Biography* (New York: Macmillan, 1952), 172-73. West's replied, July 16, 1918, Texas.

[10]"Notes on Novels," July 31, 1920, 477; October 16, 1920, 50; November 5, 1921, 142; November 4, 1922, 142. See Kathryn S. Laing, "Addressing Femininity in the Twenties: Virginia Woolf and Rebecca West on Money, Mirrors, and Masquerade" in *Virginia Woolf and the Arts: Selected Papers from the Six Annual Conference on Virginia Woolf*, eds. Diane F. Gillespie and Leslie K. Hankins (New York: Pace University Press, 1997), 66-75.

talent will some day startle us all by a long novel about a slag-heap in Leeds."
She did not, however, deprecate an interest in extreme subjects; indeed, she
lauded artists such as Velazquez, Rembrandt, Titian, and Goya who "loved
the life of their time wholeheartedly, from extreme to extreme." Sometimes,
of course, West lost patience. She dispatched one writer in two sentences:
"Mr. S. P. B. Mais has produced another novel. How long, O Lord, how
long."[11]

West's own labors on *The Judge* had been protracted beyond anything
she had imagined possible. The book went on "for ever and ever," she wrote
to one of her friends.[12] Its long gestation involved confronting issues that
remained unresolved in "The Sentinel," and in three other aborted narratives
centering on ambitious female figures struggling in a corrupt society for
autonomy and for relationships of equality with men.

In "Adela," clearly a reworking of "The Sentinel," West essayed a
portrait close to herself on the verge of a career: seventeen, with brown eyes
"as melting as the antelope's" and the "face of a young panther." She is a
"whirlpool of primitive passions" with a "ravenous intellect" and a "hunger for
academic fame." She has won a scholarship to study science in the university,
but she and her mother, deserted by the father, are so poor that they must
apply to a rich male relative, the industrialist Tom Motley, for additional
financial support, which he refuses them. Like Mrs. Fairfield during West's
formative years in Edinburgh, Adela's mother works as a typist to support the
family. Other than accepting employment from Motley or marrying a rich,
older man, there seems no way for Adela to achieve security. But she
disdains these solutions. She has a "passion for work. She was abandoned to
it as any nun to prayer: the inkstains on her fingers were her stigmata." She

---

[11]"Notes on Novels," September 30, 1922, 690; July 8, 1922, 390.

[12]RW to Henry James Forman, November 27, 1919, NYPL.

believes that not to be a scientist is tantamount to not living, and as a "secret member of the Saltgreave branch of the British Socialist Party," she scorns her wealthy, snobbish relatives, and feels humiliated by asking for their help. What is worse, her derelict father, who has "gambled away his patrimony in the pursuit of copper-mines," returns home to a forgiving wife who expects her daughter to forsake her education and help support him:

> Adela felt as if she had suddenly become ten years old again. That delicate voice with its perpetual undertone of offended taste had terrorized her childhood into unnatural quietness. From the moment of her birth she had been warned that any rough word or gesture might bring upon her plebeian mother and herself the appalling spectacle of an aristocrat repelled to tears and shame.[13]

Determined to desert her home's stifling atmosphere, Adela visits her Aunt Olga, whose family holds stuffy middle class ideas that are no improvement on Motley's demeaning offer to hire her. Here the novel ends, a promising work with sharp observations and a surprisingly mature style.

This version of Adela is quite different from her namesake in "The Sentinel," although both characters work for the Salgreave branch of the British Socialist Party. Adela in "The Sentinel" is remarkably free of family history, especially of the dominating father who looms over "Adela" and much of West's later fiction. "Adela," a much shorter narrative than "The Sentinel," is less documentary and contains nothing like the harrowing forced feeding scenes of "The Sentinel." Both narratives, however, seem stymied by West's inability to imagine Adela's escape route or to project a future for her.

West essayed at least two other less polished pieces of fiction before attempting *The Judge*.[14] Perhaps the earliest piece is "The Minx," by "Anne Telope," a story of sixteen-year-old Veronica Fawcett. She craves success,

---

[13]"Adela" was printed for the first time in Rebecca West, *The Only Poet and Short Stories*, ed. Antonia Till (London: Virago Press, 1992), 17-59.

[14]Manuscripts of West's early, uncompleted fiction are at Tulsa.

spurns a two hundred pound bursary and rejects her family. She swings down an Edinburgh street colliding with the young English architect, Arnold Ivory, who has a considerable reputation as a roue. He is dark-browed and slim, with the smirking assurance West attributes to her father in *Family Memories* (204). Veronica is susceptible to Arnold's charms but ultimately rejects him: "She glared at him savagely and pushed past into the chilled twilight. In the fraction of a second they had stood face to face he had not noticed her: she knew and loathed everything in him." Arnold is clearly a patch on Richard Yaverland, the hero of *The Judge*. Indeed, West's second unfinished and untitled early piece of fiction portrays Ellen Yaverland, a seventeen-year-old beauty in love with Richard (no last name is given). Ellen admires the stage actress, Emmy Marchant, the type of artist who had "all the virtues she lacked as a woman. On the stage her body was pure and supple and disciplined, an instrument of the soul . . . . On the stage she was without vanity - without class. Across the auditorium she spoke with another voice, an index of the spiritual splendour that she possessed in the field of her life's adventure." This florid evocation of an actress foreshadows the presentation of West's actress alter ego in yet another abortive novel, *Sunflower*, begun ten years after *The Judge*.

West was not able to quite transform her autobiographical Adelas/-Ellens into the stuff of living fiction until *The Judge*. Not only was she still finding her footing in fiction in those early works, she was also trying to create characters confronting conflicts that West had yet to settle in her own life. These apprentice narratives all seem to predate her involvement with Wells, and they reflect a theoretical or imaginative projection into what would happen when her heroines engaged with a dynamic, sexually active man. "Adela" and "The Sentinel" swathe their heroines in lucubrations; there is not enough dialogue to give these young women the spunk they deserve.

When West began *The Judge*, she had been tested by Wells and proven her mettle as a journalist and novelist. Her budding career had released extraordinary energy--as well as a darker view of family life and the relationships of the sexes. The exuberant Ellen in *The Judge*, springs off the page. She is romantic, funny, and unbowed by her lowly position as typist in a law firm:

> "I want to go somewhere right far away. . . . And I--I'll die if I don't get away."
> "Och, I often feel like this," said Mr. Phillip. "I just take a week-end off at a hydro."
> "A hydro!" snorted Ellen. "It's something more like the French Revolution I'm wanting. Something grand and coloured. Swords, and people being rescued, and things like that."[15]

Ellen wants people to be as splendid as her Scottish countryside. Like the young Rebecca West, she is galvanized by Sarah Bernhardt's acting and campaigns against the Liberal Party as a suffragist. Also like West, Ellen is attracted to powerful men even as she distrusts them. Her ambivalent feelings about her absent father (an Irishman who was "just an expense" [98]) are aggravated by the care she has to take of her ailing mother--a situation all too familiar to Ellen's author, whose ailing mother died while West was completing her novel.

When Richard Yaverland enters the law office, Ellen is struck by his regal bearing. Not only does he have the carriage of Charles Fairfield, he is a traveled man who sees in Ellen what West believed her romantic father saw in Isabella Fairfield.[16] Yaverland, like Wells, is looking for his "lover-shadow," the twin West felt she had lost when her father left the family forever. Yaverland seeks the vigorous woman that West in her reviews of Wells's novels insisted could be created if Wells had not been such an "old

---

[15]*The Judge* (New York: The Dial Press, 1980), 19. Page numbers for subsequent quotations will be cited in the text within parentheses.

[16]See *Family Memories*, ed. Faith Evans (New York: Viking, 1988), 126-30, 173-174, for portrayals of Charles Fairfield that are reminiscent of Richard Yaverland. Page numbers for subsequent quotations will be cited in the text within parentheses.

maid" in his conception of the sexes (Marcus, 64). Yaverland realizes that his vision of the ideal woman is taking shape in form of Ellen Melville:

> A woman who would not be a mere film of graceful submissiveness but real as a chemical substance, so that one could observe her reactions and find out her properties; and like a chemical substance irreducible to final terms, so that one never came to an end. A woman who would get excited about life as men do and could laugh and cheer. A woman whose beauty would be forever significant with speculation. (71)

To Ellen, Yaverland arrives almost as a character in a drama she has been struggling to create. As she watches him in her employer's law office, she thinks: "he could go on as he was doing, being much more than what one expected of an opera than a client, and she would follow him all the way." He has none of the "prudent despondency" she despises in Scots (14). On the contrary, he is "tall and royal" and a "natural commander of men" (58).

Ellen and Richard seem to have been dreaming of each other, and their tragedy in the second half of the novel, when Richard kills his half-brother and a pregnant, isolated Ellen faces a future alone with an illegitimate child, has disturbed readers, beginning with Wells, who deplored West's undisciplined baroque imagination. With its epigraph, the novel seems heavily deterministic: "Every mother is a judge who sentences the children for the sins of the father." Raymond Mortimer, West's friend and fellow critic, charged her with capitulating to an excessively Freudian rendition of family relationships.[17] Given the apparent grimness of the novel's ending, it is no wonder that West had trouble envisioning the conclusions of her earlier, fragmentary narratives.

Yet Ellen does not seem to despair--any more than West did when her liaison with Wells resulted in a child and in her isolation from the literary London she seemed about to conquer. Rather Ellen confronts a darker but

---

[17]RW to RM, n.d., PU.

also more challenging future, one that may stimulate her to reconceive her life--perhaps on more ambitious grounds, as West did when she regained her equilibrium with *The Return of the Soldier*. Indeed, the temper of that novel-- so different from her novice fiction--counsels a tragic sense of life's possibilities, an acceptance of reality--no matter how grim--as a heroic task. Better to be a human being dissatisfied than a pig satisfied, John Stuart Mill counseled in his essay on liberty, and West's advice is akin to that sad but also resolute attitude.

Ellen's optimism at the beginning of the novel--like Richard's--is romantic, even Wordsworthian in her craving for a French Revolution, just as Richard's enthusiasm is a little Wellsian, exciting but also naive for all his world traveling and affairs abroad. Richard and Ellen are twins or lover-shadows in that they share an ambivalence that goes unanalyzed in the novel but is referred to in the epigraph about mothers. For both lovers are inordinately attached to their mothers. What is said of Ellen is equally true of Richard: "the only person that belonged to her was her mother, who was very dear but very old and grieving" (132). Ellen's mother has never surmounted her Irish husband's abandonment of the family any more than Richard's mother has relinquished her obsession with the local lord who gave her the illegitimate Richard, her love child. Each mother has infected her child with a paradoxical desire to idealize and to vilify the opposite sex. Given West's beliefs in "sex-antagonism," that there is a natural tension between the sexes, and that she dedicated the novel "to the memory of my mother," it is not surprising that Richard's and Ellen's strengths and weaknesses arise out of their mutual attraction and distrust.

Although the novel's dedication might almost seem to be a hostile act-- and certainly West's letters reveal hostility toward her mother as well as guilt and loving admiration--it may also be an expression of gratitude to the mother for preparing the child for such an ambivalent world. Ellen's mother, at any rate, shares many of Isabella Fairfield's ethereal qualities, especially a bird-like gaiety and gift for music that makes her a spiritual guide in Ellen's life, as Isabella Fairfield is in *Family Memories* and in one of West's finest novels, *The Fountain Overflows*. What Ellen thinks of her mother is very close to what West said about hers: "a romantic, a poet, and a saint" (186, 195).

As Ellen falls in love with Richard, she also initiates an re-evaluation of her father, abandoning the "harsh Puritan moral vision of the young" which censures him for "deliberate ill-conduct" and adopting an organic sense of her parents "decaying" relationship, for which neither party is to blame (174, 193-94). This change is terrifying to Ellen because it deprives her of certitude, yet it is also surely a manifestation of her own maturing sense of complexity, though it is not a complexity that she can maintain with any consistency, any more than West could when she thought of her own father, who remained a sinner (*Family Memories*, 203).

Ellen surmises that Richard's lovemaking to her is probably very much like her father's courtship of her mother, and yet Ellen overcomes her feelings about male loathesomeness to love Richard, and she forsakes the righteous language of the suffragist to become his mate. Ellen struggles with this shift from seeing life in terms of political categories to seeing it in terms of temperament and desire. When she meets Richard's mother in a restaurant, Ellen remarks that it is terrible to see "these people being happy like this when there are millions in want." Mrs. Yaverland surveys the restaurant carefully and replies that they don't "strike me as being particularly happy." The restaurant is "on the map and so are they. . . . They's go anywhere else if one told them it was where they out to be. Good children, most people. Anxious to do the right thing. Don't you think?" she asks Ellen. A disconcerted Ellen is "unprepared for anything but agreement or reactionary argument from the old, and the was neither, but a subtlety that she felt matched in degree her own though it was probably unsound" (211). What makes *The Judge* a novel of continuing relevance is the way West manages to balance the personal and political in such scenes, a balance that she did not know how to handle heretofore.

It is natural for a discussion of *The Judge* to focus on Ellen, who makes such a charming appearance in the novel's first pages and to be disturbed by her envelopment in the tragedy at Yaverland's End, Richard's home in Essex. Angered at reviews that chastised her for producing a poorly shaped novel that swallowed up her attractive heroine, West observed to a friend that her work was not "ill constructed . . . it would be if my subject had been Ellen but it isn't - it's the eternal swatting of that fly youth and beauty by the accumulations of evil done by careless handling of beautiful things." That careless handling she attributed to Marion Yaverland's aristocratic lover, Harry, whose "pleasant vices . . . pile up into this tragedy which involved the innocent Ellen."[18] It is significant that West thought of Ellen as innocent and victimized by the past, for it was the view she would take of herself and the women in her family when she wrestled with the writing of her family memoirs. Of course, the emphasis on innocence is also what attracted her to *The Good Soldier*, and what made her model Chris Baldry after Edward Ashburnham. But that insistence on innocence, on making Ellen less culpable, also makes the novel more deterministic than it has to be. West humorously conceded the point when she told another friend that Thomas Hardy made his wife read to him the second part of *The Judge* "over and over again, it being the only book ever written as gloomy as his own."[19] When West fails as a novelist, she takes an almost perverse delight in absolving herself and her characters of responsibility.

At Yaverland's End, Richard seems not at all the independent figure Ellen took him for in Edinburgh. Mother and son are unnaturally close-- indeed, Marion has treated her illegitimate son almost like a lover, a

[18]RW to S. K. Ratcliffe, n.d., Yale.

[19]RW to Louis Golding, n.d., Texas.

substitute for the local squire who deserted her. Marion has indulged her passion for her love child in an appalling solitude. The village has shunned and even stoned her for conceiving a bastard. Her lover's butler, Peacy, marries and then rapes her, reneging on his promise not to have conjugal relations with her. His initial kindness and his avowal that he simply wants to make her respectable turns out to be a blind for his desire to propagate a child, Marion's second son, Roger, whom she cannot love. Richard, fiercely protective of his mother and contemptuous of the weak-willed Roger, will pay heavily--like Ellen--for becoming a projection of his mother's longings.

How to conclude the novel and to link the two stories--Richard's and Ellen's--baffled West and excited Wells's anxiety. Although she began writing the novel shortly after the publication of *The Return of the Soldier*, it would take her nearly three years to solve her structural problem. Both mothers must die; Richard must murder his brother Roger and be hanged. Only then, West thought, could the really exciting part of the novel begin. By then, however, she had a narrative almost three times the length of *The Return of the Soldier*. In her defense, West argued that her new novel was not "unrestrained and too exuberant. I could have written The Judge in 70,000 words (just as I could have written The Return of the Soldier in 200,000) but I didn't choose. I hate this undiscriminating pursuit of concentration. I believe it's been the desiccation of many a talent."[20]

West solved her structural problem in the novel's final pages by having Ellen's mother, Mrs. Melville, increasingly intrude into Ellen's mind, "especially in moments of loneliness or uncertainty." Similarly, Marion Yaverland dominates her son, and he clings to her in an almost infantile fashion. Richard murders his brother Roger, insanely angry because the feckless Roger has come home to spoil Richard's reunion with Marion, who has gone out to commit suicide, hoping that her final desperate act will

---

[20]RW to Sara Melville, n.d., Yale.

release her son to Ellen's love. Roger provokes Richard's wrath, alleging that his mother's suicide is the result of the as yet unmarried Richard's and Ellen's lovemaking, which Roger thought he had observed through a picture window at Yaverland's End.

Trained by her mother to seek a man who would be her king, Ellen takes Marion's place. Marion had imagined she was giving birth to a "king of life," and the novel concludes with Ellen's intention to consummate her love for Richard by bearing him a child before he is arrested for murder (271). In doing so, she is repeating Marion's "sin"of producing an illegitimate child. When Marion first meets Ellen, Marion conveys the consequences of giving birth to Richard: "I knew he would be illegitimate and that there would be much trouble for us both, but I wanted him so much that I couldn't bear them to kill him. So I risked it, and struggled through till he was born. So you see it's twice instead of once that I have willed him into the world. I must see to it that now he is here he is happy."

West had given birth to a son in similar circumstances and expressed similar sentiments. She knew that a mother's love, the most natural thing in the world, could become unnatural and tyrannical. Perhaps Ellen is strong enough to resist repeating the behavior of the mother who sentences her child for the sins of the father. The first half of the novel certainly conveys her inner strength. Yet it is difficult not to second critic Elaine Showalter's conclusion: "women are punished in this novel, punished for their innocence, for their self-betrayal, for their willingness to become victims."[21]

This reading of West's novel is as ambivalent as the novel itself, for like the epigraph, the story of *The Judge* can be taken two ways: as a deterministic statement, as a fact to be overcome. Ellen's future is in doubt,

---

[21]*A Literature of Their Own: British Women Novelist From Bronte to Lessing* (Princeton: Princeton University Press, 1977), 246. For a more hopeful reading of the novel's ending, see Bonnie Kime Scott, *Refiguring Modernism*, Volume Two (Bloomington: Indiana University Press, 1995), 138-39.

though she has clearly evolved to a state of consciousness that surpasses both her mother's and Marion Yaverland's obsessions.  Not surprisingly West herself was poised at a pivotal moment, preparing to make a decisive break with Wells, ending their ten-year affair and simultaneously beginning a new phase of her career, embarking for her first trip to America in the autumn of 1923.

# CHAPTER THREE

## 1923-1929

A lecture tour and opportunities to write for the best American newspapers and magazines rejuvenated West after her grueling work on *The Judge* and her traumatic separation from H. G. Wells, who would continue to send her letters proposing a reconciliation. Throughout the decade the former lovers argued about their diverging views of literature and about their son's education (he did poorly in school). She more than held her own, however, proving not only resilient but capable of winning a new American audience for her work as she took up residence in New York and traveled across the country in the mid-1920s.

West expressed her admiration for America in an introduction to Carl Sandburg's poetry, and in articles for *Harper's Magazine* that she hoped to organize into a book. Unlike many of her English contemporaries, she rarely took a snobbish or condescending attitude toward Americans. She was struck by the "go-getter" mentality of Americans who thought the pursuit of business brought them "nearest to salvation." She declared: "I have never been better entertained in my life than I was on a four hour journey from Chicago to a small town in Illinois by a business man of those parts who was able to tell me the history of every factory we passed. It was a story of triumphs and defeats that his commercial passion made as thrilling as a page of Froissart's Chronicles." America was a wide-open country, where a bold man thought nothing of giving up a safe job for the risk of pursuing profitable enterprise elsewhere. In England, where everything had been "defined to the last inch," such a man "running about our island like that . . . would fall over the edge."[1]

West tried her hand at commercial fiction with American settings. "The Magician of Pell Street," explores New York's Chinatown and reveals her liking for the tawdry but robust ethnic enclaves of the city. A newly married dancer is concerned that the curse she had a Chinese fortune teller put on her husband when she thought he had deserted her is now killing him. When she returns to have the curse lifted, she realizes that the magician is a fake, but she is moved by his own plight: he has been deserted by his Caucasian wife, who has gone to California with another man to get into the movies. The real magic, she discovers, has been worked by her husband, who has divined the fact that she wished him dead and has forgiven her. The sentimental ending hardly mars the story's effective exploration of what might be called the shabby occult--a subject much in vogue in the 1920s and appealing to West who attended her share of seances.[2]

West treasured her association with *The New York Herald Tribune*, not only because she was given twice the space of her *New Statesman* reviews, but because they offered her such "great publicity. It was like "working under a spotlight."[3] Certainly she used this forum as a star turn, writing some of her most diverting and provocative prose. Reviewing Thomas Hardy's collected poems she gave ample evidence that she revered him as a great artist, but she deplored his emphasis on the macabre and his apparent belief that such subjects constituted art by their very nature: "Really, the thing is prodigious.

---

[1]Introduction to *Selected Poems of Carl Sandburg* (New York: Harcourt Brace, 1926), 23; "These American Men," *Harper's Magazine*, September 1925, 448-456. See also "These American Women," *Harper's Magazine*, November 1925, 722-30.

[2]The story appeared in *Cosmopolitan* (February 1926) and is reprinted in *The Only Poet and Short Stories*, ed. Antonia Till (London: Virago Press, 1992), 61-96.

[3]RW to Letitia Fairfield, November 22, 1926, AM.

One of Mr. Hardy's ancestors must have married a weeping willow."[4]

The longer length allowed her comic digressions that she rarely found able to compact into her *New Statesman* reviews. For example, the locales and characters of a book on Mississippi steamboating amused her, especially the riddle of Mr. Thomas Cushing, who had been an opera singer in New York before becoming a pilot. How did that happen? she wondered:

> Was he by chance a man with a perfectly literal mind and a double character? Did a conductor he respected say to him one day in a pet: "You'd make a better Mississippi pilot, than an opera singer"? and did he, feeling a little hurt but anxious to be reasonable and not be silly about taking advice, immediately travel to the Mississippi and start finding out? And were his lost years deeply troubled because he never could meet anybody with sufficient technical knowledge in both arts to decide which he did best? And did he die tortured by the impossibility of settling the matter one way or the other? In my mind, he has done so. One sees his poor white face on his pillow, his blond whiskers neatly combed and trimmed, his bed linen got greatly disarranged, for he was a mild and self-controlled man to the last, bewilderment drawing a deep line between his brows. He would have liked to know.

The whimsy of this review followed one in which she attacks H.L. Mencken's *Notes on Democracy*. She calls his criticism of his country puerile. Of course, there were boobs and petty tyrants in modern day America, but they were pikers compared to what the aristocracy had done in England and in other parts of Europe, she points out. Democracy had developed, however imperfectly, to check the perfidy and corruption of the upper classes, which exhibited no restraint when power was concentrated in their hands. This is why the Whigs in England turned toward the people, not because of some misguided sentiment about the goodness of the poor and of the masses, as Mencken seemed to think. The murderous history of the Tsardom made his "horror at the American Legion's brushes with the Reds seem a fuss about a

---

[4]"Art: The Sitwells. Genius: Hardy," December 12, 1926, p. 6.

small matter." In this last point is early evidence of how she would react to another Red Scare, McCarthyism in the 1950s. Fears that it represented some fundamental flaw in the Republic seemed grossly exaggerated to her and proof of a defective sense of history.[5]

In one of her finest pieces, "The Long Chain of Criticism," West presented criticism as a continuous process, a dialogue that critics carried on about works of art, a dialogue that artists could not conduct on their own because they were so immersed in the creation of art they often lacked perspective. The critic brought the detachment of an outside observer who was not a party to the creation and could stand clear and look at it from a height. Of course, she conceded that the critic's view was not infallible, "his view will have its limitations, which, however, can be corrected by some other critic who will come along and read both the work and the criticism and in the light of both and his own state of mind can provide yet another interpretation."[6]

On her own, with modest child support from Wells, West turned to writing a serialized novel for *Cosmopolitan*, which would bring her $10,000, quite enough to live on for a year. West disowned *War Nurse* and got the publisher to remove her name from the title page when it was published as a book in 1930.[7] Not fully developed fiction, it has little dialogue and few dramatic scenes; the first person narration is sometimes monotonous. It is a rush job that reveals West's uncertain grasp of American slang and her occasional use of British expressions. Publicity for the novel stated it had been developed from a diary, though West said she took the story down as notes for a novel which proved useless.

---

[5]"Battlefield and Sky," November 28, 1962, 4; "In Defense of the Democratic Idea," November 14, 1926, 2-4.

[6]December 5, 1926, 1, 8-9.

[7]RW to Miss Stephens, February 2, 1948, Tulsa; RW to Letitia Fairfield, November 2, 1926, AM.

In spite of *War Nurse*'s limitations, it is a narrative of some power. The novel's heroine is Corinne Andrews (not the nurse's real name), who comes from a wealthy New York family and volunteers for service in World War I. She goes on an odyssey which--whatever its basis in fact--West cast as a quest for values, in which a young woman forsakes her family's Puritanism and materialism and forges her own identity. There are passages that step outside of Corinne's straightforward narrative, in which she speaks of the "sex antagonism" which makes women side with women and men side with men. Her curious combination of conventional and unconventional attitudes--her willingness to sleep with a married man, but her essentially monogamous nature--reflects similar divisions in West.

As one book reviewer guessed, the "transcriber has taken a good many liberties with the journal and has fictionalized it to a considerable extent."[8] Her family would have her make traditional choices: marrying a man with money and social position. She elects, on the contrary, to live in sin with a soldier, Waldron Hilder, and form a loving relationship that arises out of the intensity of their war experiences. Yet the war also separates the couple, and he eventually marries another woman, whom he finds he does not love. He returns to Corinne, who takes him again as a lover, even though to do so flouts the morality she had been taught to respect before the war. She eventually gives him up for the sake of his children, and she persuades him to return to his wife. If the war has released people like Corinne from the false values of their upbringings, it has not necessarily supplanted those values with something better: "If a lot of love-making that was done by boys and girls against time was beautiful, there was a lot more that was horrible, horrible," she concludes.[9] In an unusually grim ending for this kind of novel,

---

[8]"Nursing at the Front," *The New York Times*, April 20, 1930, 10.

[9]*War Nurse: the True Story of A Woman Who Lived, Loved, and Suffered on the Western Front* (New York: Cosmopolitan Book Corporation, 1930), 258.

48

she marries a rich man not because she loves him, but merely to find some resolution, no matter how forced, to her lonely existence. She finds herself wishing for another war, for another challenge to her spirit.

Even if the original model for Corinne expressed what West wrote, the shaping of that expression is unquestionably West's. As critic Tony Redd observes, several scenes from *War Nurse* anticipate her novel, *The Thinking Reed* (1935).[10] A friend wrote to West after reading *War Nurse*: "Anybody can see that it's straight reporting, with a flash of RW - as for instance the bit about the girl's feeling for her first love, as one would feel about a ring one used to wear on the third finger of a hand that had been amputated."[11]

The writing of *War Nurse* had interrupted a far more ambitious novel West had begun, dealing not only with her tormented decade with Wells but with her intermittent affair with British press baron, Lord Beaverbrook, which had ended abruptly and enigmatically. In *Sunflower*, Essington, a Liberal Party politician who has recently lost his high government office, follows Wells's program of acting as his young mistress's mentor and protector, while compartmentalizing her life, expecting her to cater to his whims and to baby him through his bad moods. Just turned thirty and having spent most of her twenties with him, Sunflower never wavers in her belief that Essington is a great man. But she has reached the point of wanting to leave him because he proves incapable of giving all of his heart to her and because he cannot force her to submit to his whims. Like the frustrated Wells, who never was able to convince his contemporaries about the necessity of the world state he wrote about with so much elan in his essays and novels, Essington grows increasingly fretful and aged as his views become outmoded.

Sunflower longs for a simpler, innocent existence--without the abstractions and institutions by which her friends and lovers are guided.

---

[10]"Rebecca West: Master of Reality" (Ph.D diss., University of South Carolina), 1972), 98.

[11]Emanie Sachs to RW, n.d., Yale.

Essington calls Sunflower stupid, but her sensitivity and great humanity is itself a form of intelligence that neither Essington nor Sunflower herself (cowed by his constant criticism) recognize. It is quite clear, for example, that she is maturing as an actress--a fact Essington begrudges her but which others repeatedly acknowledge. This merging of her talent and humanity is what makes her so attractive to Francis Pitt, who seems to her to be exactly the lover she has always wanted.

Pitt, an Australian millionaire, is a surrogate for Beaverbrook, who made his fortune in Canada and then became a power broker and confidant of Conservative politicians in Britain. Pitt represents precisely those qualities that Essington lacks. Sunflower craves Pitt's "rich and appetizing voice" like the "smell of good food cooking."[12] He has an ape's mouth, an over-large head, and over-broad shoulders that suggest an almost pre-human personality that is appealing because it is direct and unfiltered, somehow purer than the "tangle of transmuted sweetness kindliness and sensitiveness" that distinguishes the refined Essington, who is a "more recent, more edited kind of man" than Pitt (53). Pitt's lion color, earthy skin, and tawny hair, the deep lines in his face that remind Sunflower of the folds in an animal's hide, his broad paw-like hands and feet, his growling sounds of pleasure, convey an elemental quality that she luxuriates in after Essington's tortuous intellectuality. Sunflower is entranced by an extraordinary scene in which he crams his hands in a glass of port while his Borzois clamber over him licking the drops from his fingers. In short, Pitt has the animal magnetism that distinguishes males like Richard Yaverland.

Pitt's energy, his way of surrounding himself with all kinds of men and women, his behind-the-scenes politicking, his way of focusing on and practically burglarizing other people's personalities is a faithful rendering of

---

[12]*Sunflower* (New York: Penguin Books, 1986), 45. Page numbers for subsequent quotations will be cited in the text within parentheses.

what West found so fascinating about Beaverbrook. "Surely a man who loved one like that was God to one, for he made one. He gave one life," Sunflower concludes (241). In yet another telling phrase, he becomes a "king among men" (204). Of course, this idealization of Pitt collapses when he drops Sunflower. West outlined but did not develop scenes in which Sunflower tours America, entertains other suitors, and tries to recover her sense of humanity in a robust American climate.[13]

West abandoned the novel, apparently unable to resolve Sunflower's feelings or to come to terms with the role Pitt should play in the rest of the novel. She thought *Sunflower* "unbearably tragic," so much so that she was still waiting to imagine an ending that would do it justice. "Otherwise it is a terrible book - and I shrink from the moral responsibility of putting out anything so pessimistic," she wrote to Hugh Walpole. She also worried about how the powerful Beaverbrook might react to seeing himself portrayed by a former lover. Hearing that he had become "half mad, bitterly vindictive, and unscrupulous," she was "scared to death that people will identify the persons in 'Sunflower' and that he will wreak awful vengeance on me."[14]

When *Sunflower* was published in 1986, some feminists were shocked at the heroine's desire to submit to a man, although such a surrender is implicit in much of West's writing--in Margaret's cradling of Chris in *The Return of the Soldier*, in Evade's momentary capitulation to her husband in "Indissoluble Matrimony," in Ellen's search for a king in *The Judge*, and in West's deference to her husband Henry Andrews in *Black Lamb and Grey Falcon*. West's rebelliousness and her feminism grew out of her great anger

---

[13]The manuscript of *Sunflower* is at Tulsa.

[14]RW to HW, September 19, 1928, Texas. Walpole and West had recently made up their quarrel (see Hart-Davis, 284). For an excellent treatment of *Sunflower*, see Loretta Stec, "Writing Treason: Rebecca West's Contradictory Career," Ph.D. diss.: Rutgers University, 1993, 24-85. On West's abandonment of *Sunflower*, see RW to William Gerhardie, March 28, 1928 and WG to RW, March 30, 1928, Yale, and G. B Stern to RW, n.d., Tulsa; RW to Fanny Hurst, n.d., Texas.

that men often proved unworthy of her trust and of the great service a woman could render to a man, of the love given freely by a man's equal. For West, to love a man, to give herself wholly to him, was not to consider herself inferior per se, but to recognize that this was what love entailed: a surrender of the self in the act of love, a continual surrender of the self in a loving relationship.

To Sunflower and to West, there is only one route to happiness: "Everything was all right if only one had love"--a thought neither Essington nor Wells could endorse (36). Sunflower is taken with the story of a simple woman who lives for fifty years with a man who took her in after her husband threw her and her children out of his home. Knowing that her husband is still alive, she nevertheless commits bigamy, marrying her rescuer because it is his dying wish and because she has indeed loved him for so many years. Sunflower yearns for a love that is just that simple and that survives. She is fatigued by "a world where everything--politics, business, the arts, and scien- ces--were esteemed above life" (4).

Yet politics for West, if not for Sunflower, remained in the fabric of life. The dilemma, as always, was how to reconcile the personal with the political--a case in point: Emma Goldman's 1924 visit to England. "In so far as I wish to conserve the liberties won by the Liberals in the past, I am a Conservative; but in as much as I would gain new liberties worth the conservation, I am a Liberal, West wrote in an introduction to the English edition of Goldman's book, *My Disillusionment in Russia*. West vigorously defended Goldman in various forums--even writing a letter to Beaverbrook protesting an article written by one of his "rabbit-witted subordinates" she deemed unfair to Goldman. Goldman was worth "six of you (or three of me)," West lectured Beaverbrook, and the "most powerful Anti-Bolshi eye- witness I have yet encountered." She warned Beaverbrook not to queer Goldman's pitch by harping on her anarchism, which was sure to sidetrack her into defending herself. West wrote to her sister Winifred in evident satisfaction over the success of her letter's "unparalleled venom." He had not replied, but his paper the *Express* had treated the dinner for Goldman (on November 12, 1924) "a good show," West assured her sister. West thought Goldman a magnificent orator, and she complimented herself for a remark on the recent Conservative victory that had "travelled far and wide": "For the next four years we are going to be governed by our inferiors." Goldman said that after West's speech she was so filled with West's strength and beauty she wanted to embrace her, but doubted that the audience would understand her expression of affection. "It would not, by gum," West agreed.

West believed that Bolshevik tyranny represented an extension of, not a break with Russian history:

> The exact duplication under the Tsardom and under Bolshevism of a system that impedes the development of material prosperity, destroys individual liberty, and imposes general discomfort on the community, is a sign that, odd as it may seem to the Western mind, these are the ends towards which Russia likes its governments to work.

But no one on the British Left seemed to heed Goldman or West. On June 3, 1924, Rebecca wrote a note to George Bernard Shaw: "I wish you would do something to break up this cloud of cant about Russia that has settled round the brow of Labour." But Shaw would not even see Goldman, West reported to Wells and others on the Left were "rude to her before she begins to speak."[15]

West's twitting of both Conservative and Labor Party members recalls a comment *Time and Tide on her complicated*: "It is probable that if there is ever an English Revolution there will come a point when the Reds and Whites will sink their differences for ten minutes while they guillotine Miss

---

[15]RW introduction *My Disillusionment in Russia* (New York: Crowell, 1924), vi; RW to Max Beaverbrook, n.d., Lords; RW to Winifred Macleod, letter postmarked, November 17, 1924, AM; RW to Emma Goldman, February 7, 1925, Emma Goldman Papers, Tamiment Library, New York University; RW to George Bernard Shaw, George Bernard Shaw Collection, British Library.

West for making remarks that both sides have found intolerably unhelpful." As she said of Thackeray, she was "striped like the zebra with radicalism and conservatism."[16]

West's stripes were evident through her hectic journalistic and literary career in the 1920s. She had a lucrative contract with *T.P.'s Weekly* to write about whatever she wanted. She tossed off several articles for the *Daily Express* and *Evening News* on women's issues and social policy. She was in superb form as a public speaker, the *Yorkshire Post* calling her "by far the most interesting woman speaker of the day. . . . What is so striking about her now is the harmony between this quiet, reflective manner, and the thing that she wants to say. She has stopped being 'clever.'" She had a searching mind and did not rely on superficial ready-made remarks--like so many British writers who had toured America and had come home to pontificate. In *The Observer*, Cecil Lewis was dazzled by her range of topics--from the making of Hollywood movies, to the theater in Bath, to the distressing economic state of Great Britain. Mrs. C. A. Dawson Scott, a founder of the writer's organization, PEN, heard West speak at a Claridge tea on 9 December and then dined with her, "the most fascinating woman in London."[17]

In late July 1928, Jonathan Cape published *The Strange Necessity*, a collection of essays and reviews--West's bid to consolidate her literary position, to take the measure of the best literature of her time and simultaneously to display her own quality. The title piece is an autobiographical, intricate, informal, and meandering essay, allusive, oblique, and repetitive--a new form of writing for her that is not easy to follow. It had grown from six thousand to over thirty thousand words, she explained to Jonathan Cape, to

---

[16]"Miss Rebecca West," *Time and Tide*, July 16, 1920, 204-05; West's comment on Thackeray is from an undated *Sunday Telegraph* review in her clipping file at Yale.

[17]*Yorkshire Post*, December 9, 1927; *The Observer*, December 11, 1927, Yale clipping file; Mrs. C. A. Dawson Scott's comment is in her journal, courtesy of Mrs. Marjorie Lowenstein.

whom she provided a precis that cannot be bettered for its brevity:

> It begins with a discussion of James Joyce's Ulysses which is probably the first estimate to be done neither praying nor vomiting. In it I come to the conclusion that though it is ugly and incompetent it is a work of art. That is to say it is *necessary*. Then I go on to discuss what is this strange necessity, art which is so inclusive of opposites? - as for instance the paintings of Ingres and the books of James Joyce? This leads to an analysis of literature, and the discovery of a double and vital function it fulfils [sic] for men. Firstly it makes a collective external brain for man; secondly it presents certain formal relations to man which suggest a universe more easy in certain respects than the one he knows.

In a subsequent letter, she asked Cape if he could see to it that *The Strange Necessity* was "treated as a technical, high brow book? Reviewable really as a book on psychology."[18] She might have added that she had written a work of criticism and esthetics in the form of a novel, for in it she portrays the personality of the critic, herself, in scenes and in her version of stream of consciousness writing that is itself a tribute to Joyce and even more to Marcel Proust, whom she considered Joyce's superior.

The essay's first paragraph presents a scene. West has just closed the door of a bookshop and is walking down the street toward the Boulevard St. Germain in the "best of all cities." She is exhilarated not only because of where she is, but also because she has been sold a little volume "not exactly pretentiously, indeed with a matter-of-fact briskness, yet with a sense of there being something on hand different from an ordinary commercial transaction: as they sell pious whatnots in a cathedral porch." Suddenly she stops, exclaims "Ah!" and smiles "up into the clean French light." She spies a dove "bridging the tall houses by its flight," and she feels an "interior agreement

---

[18]RW to JC, Cape General Files, University of Reading.

with its grace," a "delighted participation in its experience."[19]  The city, the bookshop, the book, the bird, the day--all conspire to make her spirit soar, all make up her esthetic sense of life, the beauty that derives from the harmony human beings fashion out of their surroundings.  Art is the word for that harmony; criticism is the word for the consciousness of that art.

Her first paragraph constitutes, in miniature, her entire argument: art is what makes her whole and, gives her character its integrity.  What is more, art does the same for the world at large; it is a steady, cumulative fund of knowledge that is a kind of science, with each great book a type of experiment, in which the artist explores certain facets of human character--like a scientist tests hypotheses.

The first paragraph is also representative of the essay in that neither the bookshop nor the book is named, and why the book should be sold in a matter-of-fact but devout manner is not explained.  Often her points are withheld, and a reader not attuned to her reason for doing so will be irritated as she recycles her scenes.  Why doesn't she say it all at once?  Because she is implying she does not know it all at once.  She is writing, in other words, as she thinks, as she is formulating her ideas, which are based on her experience on this day in Paris.  To apprehend how she has arrived at her position on art she must be accompanied on her day, just as one follows the characters in *Ulysses* on their day in Dublin, just as one parses Proust's long sentences to understand the grammar, the structure of human consciousness.  Understanding art is not a matter of drawing a straight line between points.

In the second paragraph, West reveals she has been pleased by a poem she has just read in her purchased book.  It is titled "Alone," and she quotes it in full, stating that it may seem "inconceivable" that such an "exceedingly bad poem" should "bring pleasure to any living creature."  For it communi-

---

[19]*The Strange Necessity* (London: Virago Press, 1987), 13. Page numbers for subsequent quotations will be cited in the text within parentheses.

cates nothing. A single line will serve as a sample: "And all my soul is a delight,/ A swoon of shame." These are "words as blank as the back of a spoon," West remarks. Who is the author? she asks. Not, as you may imagine, some second-rate magazine poet but Mr. James Joyce. It gives her pleasure to know that this poem, a part of his collection called *Pomes Penyeach*, is awful--though "not noticeably the worst"--not because she revels in a great writer's inferior productions but because the poem confirms her judgment that he is a "great man who is entirely without taste," so that even his greatest work is marred by "gross sentimentality" (14-15).

West has now said enough to make that curious transaction in the bookshop comprehensible. She does not name the bookshop, but anyone likely to read *The Strange Necessity* in 1928, or any reasonably informed student of literature today, would know it is the establishment of Sylvia Beach, Joyce's champion. She stocked and promoted his work, which had become an object of virtually religious adoration by the avant garde. Joyce was the very type of the modern artist, complex and difficult. He was an icon, but he was also a fact, an indelible part of the esthetic landscape and therefore his work would be sold in precisely the energetic, business-like manner West describes.

West accuses Joyce of "gross sentimentality," and then stops to think why she should use the word sentimentality. Then, instead of providing the result of her thinking, she does what she says she did: she thinks. She recalls her summer in a Provencal village, where the men sit at tables with their necks crooked watching a game of

> *boules* that incredibly goes on, parting and reassembling as the automobiles fly past, in the puddle-pocked, wheel-harassed roads. It is not a likeable game. It brings two kinds of unpleasantness to the ear, for when the *boules* meet the spurting sound of their impact is like an exchange of rude remarks, and when they meet only with a little force, as must often happen in a game played on such a surface, that sound has the futile quality of feeble rudeness, of failure in an

enterprise where even success would have meant nothing
pleasant. And there comes from the onlookers never that tense
yet languid cry, only a little more than a deep breath, which
tells that a crowd is participating through attention in the deep
peace of a beautiful movement: instead came praising, blaming
"Oh's!" and "Ah's!" which show that they are not resting, that in
this pastime there has not been lifted from them the human
burden of discrimination and calculation, that load of pricking
needles. It is, therefore, better as one passes to raise one's eyes
to the great umbrella pine which is the steady roof to all the
squint-sitting people, making out of a hundred branches, a
million twigs, a form as single as a raindrop, casting a shadow
as of an undivided substance. It had seemed to me that the
men squatting at their *boules* were like the sentimental artist,
that the pine-tree was like the non-sentimental artist. (15-16)

For the reader in a hurry to get the point, exasperation has set in, for West
has only begun to introduce her metaphor; it will take her another four long
paragraphs to apply this metaphor to Joyce--the intervening paragraphs
elaborating on sentimental and nonsentimental artists, with allusions to Benjamin Constant, Stendahl, Arnold Bennett, Katherine Mansfield, Dickens,
Chekhov, and Ernst Toller. West took a day to think through her reactions
to Joyce; she is demanding no less from the reader.

The great artist, she goes on to reason, is like the undivided substance
of the great umbrella pine: he becomes what he makes, he fuses with his
theme, his consciousness absorbed in his story. He becomes his art as the
tree becomes a tree. He puts no more and no less force into his work than
is required to make it live. The adjustments he makes are automatic and
organic, which is a way of saying they do not call attention to themselves.
The great artist "knows the value of each character as one knows the weight
of an object one has held in one's hand; there is no part that rebels against
the whole; there is the peace of unity." The sentimental artist plays a game,
he is clever and wants to be seen as such; he scores points; he takes positions;
he moves an object so that it strikes and displaces another: *Shock* . . . one
hears that ugly sound." Sometimes it sounds even uglier when the impact is

weak. She supplies several examples of sentimentality in great artists, of instances when "we refuse to join in the game; we suspect . . . Charles Dickens when Little Nell is dying, and we feel that he relishes our tears as he would a kipper to his tea, and realize that if the logic of the book's being suddenly demanded an eleventh-hour recovery he would have hit the child on the head without the slightest compunction" (15-22).

This, then, is the bill of charges against Joyce: he is a "reactionary" sentimentalist, bent on shocking and manipulating his readers, as if art were a game of *boules*, with characters and scenes used as counters. His acolytes have been so bemused with his "heterodox technique," his modernism, that they have entirely overlooked his "enslavement to the sentimental." There is Gerty MacDowell, the "girl who sat on the beach to the detriment of Mr. Bloom's chastity. Her erotic revery is built up with as much noisy sense of meeting a special occasion as a grand-stand for a royal procession, in order that we may be confounded by the fact of her lameness." That this salient fact is withheld until the end of the scene is clearly a cheap, sentimental trick in West's book. She cites other examples, especially Stephen Dedalus's long monologues on esthetics. Why doesn't anyone ever interrupt this blowhard? West wonders. It is because he is the product of Joyce's "narcissism, a compulsion to make a self-image and to make it with an eye to the approval of others." Stephen "enjoys the unnatural immunity from interruption that one might encounter not in life but in a typical Freudian wish fulfillment dream." Such scenes do not live from within; their values have been "externally adjusted" (20-22).

Yet the very form of West's essay cum novel is a tribute to Joyce's method, especially in her effort to weave together emotions and ideas, the body and the mind. But she believes that human sensations naturally coagulate into sentences in the mind, and not into the fragmented strings of words Joyce favors. She dislikes his "verbal sneezes," and points out that babies, even before they can pronounce and understand words, speak in rhythms suspiciously similar to sentences (35). The conscious mind, she insists, has a grammar. It is perhaps why she likes Molly Bloom's soliloquy so much, proclaiming it "one of the most tremendous summations of life that have ever been caught in a net of words." Similarly, Leopold Bloom is "one of the greatest creations of all time," for in him "something true is said about man" (43).

Any two works of art, West asserts throughout her essay, resemble each other insofar as they promulgate a unity of effect that instills the same harmony in the reader, viewer, or listener--for she believes her argument applies to all the arts, which is why art is "inclusive of its opposites," of a painting by Ingres and a novel by Joyce, even though they are different from each other not only in form but in subject matter. Her view of art survives despite her long discussion of Pavlov and might actually be better without it, since her conclusion after several pages of pressing the subject seems reductive:

> And at the end of it [the novel] he [Trollope as an instance of a great artist] has established just how certain kinds of people act in certain circumstances that uncover the attitude to recurring and fundamental factors of life, just as Professor Pavlov has established how a certain kind of dog behaved when it was given meat powder under certain conditions. An experiment has been conducted, an observation has been made, bearing on a principle it has been faithfully reported. (56)

Was it worth the trouble of reading half the essay for this wrapup? Such passages and analogies harm the argument by proposing too great a symmetry between art and science. Thus the concluding sentence of this section rings too portentously: "We have strong grounds for suspecting that art is at least in part a way of collecting information about the universe" (88-89). The "in part" rescues the sentence, even if it does not redeem the whole argument. The Joycean/Proustian method that begins brilliantly in the first pages of *The Strange Necessity* is attenuated by repetitions and banalities.

The second half of the essay argues for the superiority of art, in certain respects, over science. Proust is her main exemplar of the artist who creates a "mind-consciousness which tells us fully about other people's minds" (101). Proust speaks to this "strange necessity," meaning the peculiar craving for an art that can put a finishing touch to life that life itself lacks. Art grows out of but transcends autobiography. Conceding that the roots of Benjamin Constant's novel, *Adolphe*, are in his life, West nevertheless demonstrates that his fiction's most striking effects are found precisely where he departed from fact. A writer's imagination, she posits, is like a mansion of many rooms, and Constant "simply opened the door of another suite of rooms and looked in and said: 'If I lived there, this and that would happen,' and his empathy forbade him to invent anything that was 'out of drawing'" (107). The rooms are like the different "phases of one's being," but the artist has extended the "human habit of watching other people and trying to deduce their inner lives from their behaviour. . . ." Just as an artist can draw another's body in proportion, so a writer can limn a life that is not his own. It is a feat of empathy that Proust performs repeatedly in *A la Recherche du Temps Perdu*, the very title of which suits West perfectly, since it implies he is conducting a kind of research into the human psyche that she contends art is best equipped to accomplish. "Recherche," with its connotation of looking again and again, also neatly applies to the repetitive, cyclical nature of her essay. Of Proust's masterpiece, she concludes: "There is not one character which utters one syllable or makes one gesture which is not uniquely appropriate and at once an inevitable growth of their destiny and a determinant of it, as syllables and gestures are in real life" (113-14). This comes close to claiming that Proust has invented an art which is almost literally the language of life. Without this language--or something like it--human beings can exist--like Pavlov's decorticated dogs--but they have lost the ability to make the connections between stimulus and response that Pavlov demonstrated, and can no longer analyze the world or perceive the unities upon which civilization is founded. Art is nothing less than the organ of pleasure that ties the world together for human beings. This is why, West reminds us in the last ten pages of the essay, she found so much pleasure on her day in Paris in what she finally names as Sylvia Beach's bookshop, closing one of the many circles in her argument. Whatever her quarrel with Joyce, his work has helped her to establish herself in the universe, to underhand why it is better to live than to die. This last point is a curious one, evolving out of her Freudian sense that human beings are caught between their conflicting impulses to live and to die, and out of an even more personal conviction that "life has treated me as all the children of man like a dog from the day I was born" (197).

*The Strange Necessity* ends on a note of brooding, yet transcending joy-- it could almost be scored for a symphony orchestra:

> And that I should feel this transcendent joy simply because I have been helped to go on living suggests that I know some- thing I have not yet told my mind, that within me I hold some assurance regarding the value of life, which makes my fate different from what it appears, different, not lamentable, grandiose. (197-98)

As she said of *Ulysses*, her own essay is a daring, extraordinary effort, for all its faults. That grandiose can be defined as both pompous and magnificent suggests the risk she knew she was taking in setting forth herself as an exemplar of her ideas.

The vehement critical reaction to *The Strange Necessity* angered West, for she felt personal animus behind many of the attacks: "most of the reviews are declarations of personal dislike against me by people I have never met, chiefly on the ground that I am a society butterfly who ought not to occupy myself with these serious questions," she wrote to a friend.[20] Even some of her closest confidants had reservations. One of her early mentors, the journalist S. K. Ratcliffe, concurred with West's sister, Winifred, who said "the public will never stand those dogs!' They won't. Even your special public

---

[20]RW to Alexander Woollcott, n.d., HH.

won't. If, illustratively, they must be there, I urge that they ought to be cut down." Ratcliffe thought the essay leaden and without her accustomed energy:

> You can make a demonstration about art and criticism run, not like a Matthew-Arnoldian brook or trickle, but like shall we say the Rhine at Basel! ... The swimmer has to use quite enough of muscle, but he will get on. And I don't think this example is right, or good enough for you. It ought to be triumphant.

Even critic Joseph Wood Krutch's praise of her Proustian prose echoed Ratcliffe's call for more Proust and less Pavlov.[21]

Conrad Aiken chastised West for writing

> very badly . . . If she could somehow manage to treat her audience a little less as if it were gathered for tea and her writers a little less as if they were dilapidated lions collected for the occasion to have their manes combed and their tails pulled--one might be surer of her future position. As it is, one feels that perhaps her future years are numbered.

William Carlos Williams admired her exposition, conceding that her argument had validity, but he objected to her "hieratical assurance," alleging that she had misread Joyce. His review convinced her that she now had become the target of Joyce's adherents. Edward Garnett seconded her view of Joyce, but continued his review with the devastating judgment: "Miss West struggles with Professor Pavlov and her materialistic confusions remind one of an enterprising baby with a bucket of tar. Everything round gets horribly smeared."[22]

Hugh Walpole praised Rebecca's method even as he took exception to many of her judgments, citing the "completeness of her investigatory power that is not to be found in many critics. The reader knows why and how she

---

[21]SKR to RW, April 30, 1928, Yale; *The New York Herald Tribune*, November 25, 1928, 3.

[22]*The Bookman*, August 1929, 212; *Transition* (1929), reprinted as "A Point for American Criticism," *Selected Essays of William Carlos Williams* (New York: Random House, 1954); "Channels and Sandbanks," *The Saturday Review of Literature*, November 10, 1928, 335.

achieves her particular positions, for there are no blurred edges to her processes." Wyndham Lewis, who had attacked Joyce in *Time and Western Man* on similar lines, sent her his compliments. She was gratified to receive a long letter (it has not survived) from Havelock Ellis, evincing a detailed understanding of her argument. George Bernard Shaw did not react to her treatment of him in her essay on her literary uncles (his mind was marvelous and shining but too thin), except to drop a sociable note, signing himself "your too affectionate uncle G. Bernard Shaw."[23]   West took Wells's initial response as a jab: "Dear Ex Panther/ The Strange Necessity is marvellous. It ought to have music by Stravinsky." He tried again: "Dear Pussy. I didn't dislike The Strange Necessity. I only said it ought to have music by Stravinsky. Can't I tickle you in the ribs when you dig into mine?" Nettled by her treatment of him as Uncle Wells, and her invention of a character, Queenie, to satirize the mawkish love affairs in his novels, he called her a "lazy Panther" repeating her "cherished delusions. There never was a Queenie but you've said it so often you've got to believe it." His next letter whined: "it sets people who havent read me against my books." Then he made a sweeping judgment:

> The Strange Necessity only does for your critical side what the Judge did for your pretensions as a novelist. You have a most elaborate, intricate & elusive style which is admirably adapted for a personal humorous novel. It can convey the finest shades of sympathy, ridicule & laughter. It is no good whatever for a philosophical discourse any more than it was for a great romance about the tragedy & injustice of life. You are ambitious & pretentious & you do not know the quality & measure of your powers. Some of the Return of the Soldier though the style is Conrad-haunted is admirable. Chunks of the Judge are magnificent. As a whole it is a sham. So is this book a sham. It is a beautiful voice & a keen & sensitive mind doing "Big thinks" to the utmost of its ability -- which is nil.

---

[23]*The New York Times* (2 December 1928), 12; West reports the reactions of Lewis and Ellis to her sister, Letitia Fairfield, in a letter postmarked July 27, 1928, AM: GBS to RW, July 13, 1928, Tulsa.

> God gave you all the gifts needed for a fine & precious artist
> & he left out humility. And humility in the artist is what
> charity is in the saint.
> There my dear Pussy is some more stuff for your little
> behind. You sit down on it & think.

Wells did not mention it, but part of his anger was surely aroused by the personal images of him in *The Strange Necessity* shut up in a drawing room, putting out all the lights except a single lamp with a "pink silk shade," and sitting at the piano having a "lovely time warbling in too fruity a tenor." She continued this demasculinization in her comment on the "passages where his prose suddenly loses its firmness and begins to shake like blanc-mange" (199-200).

West may have been miffed that in *The World of William Clissold* (1926) she appears as the fearless Helen, who is disposed of with smug superiority. Helen is not a malign portrait--indeed she embodies many of West finest qualities--but West resented his characterization of their "selfish fellowship" and her fictional transformation into a successful actress devoted to the business of exploiting her personality. And of course the artist's personality is one of the major concerns of *The Strange Necessity*.

Arnold Bennett lauded West's acuity and facility but deplored her need to perform: "She must be odd," and it led her into "irresponsible silliness." In effect, he accused her of being arbitrary in words that were perhaps meant as a tit-for-tat, since she had remarked in her essay "Uncle Bennett" that "there are innumerable occasions when one suspects that he writes, not because he has something to say, but because of that abstract desire to write, which is hardly ever the progenitor of good writing" (204).[24]

An *Evening Standard* reporter, who had come to interview West about her book, published on August 24, 1928 (under the title "Rebecca West Hits

---

[24]"My Brilliant But Bewildering 'Niece,'"*Evening Standard*, August 9, 1928, Yale clipping file.

Back") what she named to novelist Fannie Hurst a "tissue of lies" concerning what she had said about Bennett and his review. She was quoted as saying, "Mr. Bennett suffers very unhappily from the defect of his virtues, which are, of course, those of a very good solicitor's clerk." Letters were printed in the newspaper taking exception to Rebecca's remarks, and the *Evening Standard* even ran a contest, requesting from readers the best imaginary conversation between the two literary adversaries. An outraged West sued the paper for libel. She had never liked Bennett--that "old ass" she called him in a letter to her publisher, Jonathan Cape--but she had treated him as a major writer, and she would not brook a misrepresentation of her position.[25]

One of West's friends, Stacy Aumonier, tried to soothe her over the Bennett interview: "It sounded a bit cheeky," he admitted, "but this is expected of you." (The interview had her referring to "old Bennett" and expressing skepticism that he had even read *The Strange Necessity*). The worst thing she could do was to make a legal case out of it. Reminding her of her big reputation, which should rest on her work alone, Aumonier concluded: "There is a disposition in certain quarters to make you notorious, & this you want to avoid like the plague. You can afford to do so. You do not want to reach that point where people say: 'Oh, that woman again!' You know what I mean?" She wrote to Bennett in September assuring him that she was aghast and humiliated by the interview, especially by a sentence referring to him as one of her "implacable enemies." Bennett replied graciously, saying the phrasing of the interview did not seem hers and that one had to be wary of interviewers who could get things "wildly wrong" even with the best of intentions. In an out of court settlement she secured an apology from the newspaper and recouped her legal costs.[26]

---

[25]RW to FH, n.d., Texas; RW to JC, Cape General Files, University of Reading.

[26]SA to RW, August 23, 1928, RW to AB, September 14, 1928, Yale; RW to AB, n.d., Arnold Bennett Collection, University College (London); AB to RW, September 20, 1928, Yale.

No legal victories, however, could soothe West, who believed that her personality and her sex had contributed to her critical drubbing. Hugh Walpole pointed out to her: "You *have* in your literary life laid about you lustily and you have in your published works at present a small showing numerically. So think the cry goes up from all the hurt ones: 'What the hell is she bashing us for when she does so little herself?'" But she had a prominent place no one could deny. He admitted he did find her difficult to understand, but most people had only a handful of friends who really grasped their nature. She should write for herself and for them. Nothing else mattered, he advised her.[27]

West had tried to show in *Sunflower* how a sensitive woman could become the target of even the men who loved her. She had felt that kind of hostility emanating from her lovers, chiefly Wells and Beaverbrook. She had undergone psychoanalysis in Italy to explore the sources of her ambivalent relationships with men, tracing her troubles right back to early childhood scenes with her father--a lover-like but also a looming threatening figure. His patriarchal politics had grounded and structured her earliest education; they had also stifled her, she believed. *The Strange Necessity*, meant to show her critical mastery, had only provoked the animus of her critics. Wells had tried to put her in her place. What was it about women artists that so unnerved and riled men?

Worried that Walpole might be right--that her career would be viewed as "sterile and erratic,"[28] West wrote a novel, *Harriet Hume*, that tries in a lighter, whimsical vein, to explore the roots of sex-antagonism. Through fantasy and comedy, she essays the issues of *Sunflower* and *The Strange*

---

[27]HW to RW, September 26, 1928, Yale.

[28]RW to Hugh Walpole, September 19, 1928, Yale.

*Necessity* in a way that recalls Wells's quest for the "lover-shadow," the twin that would complete male and female halves, the reconciliation of opposites, that every artist, West argues, must achieve.

As she worked on *Harriet Hume*, West realized that Virginia Woolf in *Orlando* was grappling with the same set of issues. Orlando, born in the Elizabethan period and still alive, exemplified the development of civilization and of both sexes. Especially intrigued by the passages in which Orlando undergoes a sex change from male to female, West maintained that they were the heart of the book because Woolf was "debating . . . how far one's sex is like a pair of faulty glasses on one's nose; where one looks at the universe, how true it is that to be a woman is to have a blind spot on the North Northwest, to be a man is to see light as darkness East by South." Woolf wrote to West in appreciation: "I can't tell you how it exhilarates me to feel your mind running along where mine tried to go (what a lot more you have guessed of my meaning than anybody else!) and expanding and understanding and making everything ten times more important than it seemed before."[29]

Harriet Hume, a pianist, is the artist who by reading her lover's mind strips him of his self-deceptions. She is a "white witch" who, in the words of the novel's epigraph, is "mischievously good." Arnold Condorex, a politician whose name suggests both his scheming, predatory side and his kingly, even noble qualities, is confronted by Harriet on the eve of his ruin. She is his better half, his conscience, whom he rejects but continues to confront on every occasion he sees her. Angered by her exposure of his plotting (he has become a government minister through various intrigues), he ends up trying to murder her for standing against his ambition to dominate and to move up in the world.

Condorex has no personal characteristics linking him to Beaverbrook,

---

[29]"High Fountain of Genius," *The New York Herald Tribune*, October 21, 1928, 1, 6; VW to RW, n.d., Yale.

but he is a self-made man who finds his position always precarious because he has not been born to wealth, class, or position. He has had to scramble for everything and thinks of his entire life in terms of the power he is gaining or losing in every turn of the political wheel. Clearly in love with Harriet, he nevertheless rejects her as abruptly as Beaverbrook rejected West, because Arnold sees that Harriet's love is all-enveloping; it penetrates deep within him, and it is not something he can control. To invite her into his life as an equal is to lay bare thoughts to which even his closest confederates have not been privy. Arnold's fitful courtship of Harriet, in other words, mimics what had been Beaverbrook's on-again, off-again approach to West. Every time Arnold meets Harriet, he falls under the spell of her exquisite art; every time she provides evidence of her prescience he flees.

Harriet is like a work of art looking for a body in which to incarnate herself. She is attracted to Arnold because of his immersion in the social and political life of Westminster, the seat of government. She is a creature of her South Kensington flat, which conforms in basic details to West's at 80 Onslow Gardens in South Kensington, and Harriet is pictured as a goddess in her garden awakened to life by Arnold as Adam, whom she is quite willing to make the first man in her life, just as he is in her thoughts. Her power to invade his mind, exposing the conniving world he actually lives in, enrages him because he has to examine himself and consider the implications of his actions. He knows that what he is thinking appears only a second later in Harriet's mind. But that it is a second later is what makes it art, not life. As Harriet laments, "I know it, yet I know it a second too late! 'Tis the artist's special quality and defect!"[30] Art can only master itself--not compete with the world in which Arnold wants to be king.

Harriet's yearning for Arnold, the need to complete herself in the man

---

[30]*Harriet Hume* (New York: Doubleday Doran, 1929), 104-05. Page numbers for subsequent quotations will be cited in the text within parentheses.

she loves, is, of course, what motivates many of West's heroines. But what allowed West to complete *Harriet Hume*, after the false start of *Sunflower*, is the fact that her experience with men had become emblematic of more than her life; what happened to her had also happened to her friend, the pianist Harriet Cohen, who served as a model for Harriet Hume. Something about Harriet Cohen's waving to West from the balcony of a house in Regent Park's Terrace had summed up life in the city, fleeting but self-contained. Harriet Cohen also had the gift for making time seem as though it "spun about round her," and West aimed to capture something of that "amiability, which wanted everything to be smooth and kind," in her novel. Her friend had a "chirping, Londonish voice . . . It sounded as if we were all new children on our first day at school, holding together and laughing among ourselves to keep up our hearts."[31]   West also gave Harriet Hume her friend's bad eyesight, and Cohen's penchant for disastrous love affairs may have suggested the scene in which Arnold aims his pistol at Harriet in her flat.

One of Harriet Cohen's affairs had been with Max Beaverbrook. "Dark, spirited, emotional"--these words for Harriet Cohen obviously apply to West as well--Harriet had become entranced one evening as she watched Beaverbrook in his home declaim from a book in the Old Testament. A minister's son, he was able to recite the entire book in an awesome and moving fashion. Afterwards he turned to Harriet, stared into her eyes, and said "You are Esther - Esther from the Bible." Then at one of Beaverbrook's dinners in the Savoy, she met Winston Churchill, who greeted her with, "So you are Esther."[32]

The anecdote is a measure of how Beaverbrook could dominate a person's life, making Harriet into a character of his own devising, and making

---

[31]RW, untitled typescript, Tulsa.

[32]Anne Chisholm and Michael Davie, *Lord Beaverbrook: A Life* (New York: Knopf, 1993), 246-49.

her think she had somehow been put at the center of his world. Arnold Condorex elevates Harriet Hume in a similar manner with grandiose tributes: She is "like a porcelain in its shining quietude." She has a "classically perfect form." She is the most "aethereal" woman he has ever known. "Loving her was like swathing oneself with a long scarf of spirit" (5).

The sudden shift in Arnold from ebullience to evasiveness is exactly what Harriet Cohen experienced with Max Beaverbrook. She wrote him imploring letters: "I always feel when I am with you, that we just adore each other." Yet he was the one man who didn't want to see her and perhaps didn't even like her. It mystified her--as it did West--how this man could turn the language of love on and off.[33]

Arnold, like Max, has it in him to think like an artist and to appreciate art. "How like you are to me," Harriet tells Arnold (23). She assures him that had he wanted to, he could also read her mind. But he chants, almost like a mantra, "a man must rise in the world" (49). The last thing Arnold and his prototype Beaverbrook wanted to do was to enclose themselves in a woman's private world--as enticing as Cohen's flat and West's 80 Onslow Gardens had been for their lovers. If West felt rejected as a woman, Harriet is the principle of femininity itself which Arnold rejects, for he declares that he has "never known a woman with more exquisite understanding of the female person" (77). Because he so wants to feel superior he spurns even Harriet's compassion.

As an embodiment of art, as still as a tree in her immovable grace (remember West's image of the tree in *The Strange Necessity*), Harriet represents everything that Arnold cannot manipulate; she becomes for him a strange necessity which he confronts at the end of the novel. He regards her as his "malign opposite" and he tries to treat her like a political opponent who must be gotten out of the way (237). But as she says earlier in the novel,

---

[33]Ibid.

she refuses to die, and she invokes the aid of two policeman who (it is gradually revealed by their use of the past tense) are dead. There is a hint that Arnold has shot himself and that this last scene of stalking Harriet occurs in a spectral realm on the edge of eternity, the point at which the couple can be reconciled, since both are beyond the contest of individual wills.

The style of *Harriet Hume* is arch. The prim and formal quality critic Joseph Warren Beach admires, has put off some readers. Virginia Woolf thought it "tight and affected and occasionally foppish beyond endurance, but then it is a convention and she does it deliberately, and it helps her to manufacture some pretty little China ornaments for the mantelpiece."[34] The style helped distance West from the anguish of *Sunflower*, while remaining faithful to the earlier work's themes. *Harriet Hume* does somehow have the quality of Mozart--as Beach suggests--the music West often played to calm herself. It also reflects her versatility, for it is as different from *The Judge* as that novel is from *The Return of the Soldier*. *Harriet Hume* has some of the poetry, founded on sharp observation, that West lauded in *Orlando*: Harriet observes the chaperons at a party dozing in their "corsets like jellies left overnight in their moulds" (177).

The novel's best sentences carry the rhythm of a fantasy, a self-enclosed world. At its finest moments *Harriet Hume* demonstrates how politics can become a fantasy, a matter of words in a game agreed upon by its participants that bears little connection to reality. The joke in *Harriet Hume* is that Arnold has received his title of Lord Mondh by writing about and championing an obscure Far Eastern country, Mondh, that does not exist. His title--indeed his whole reputation--is built upon nothing. But he speaks so learnedly of Mondh that his words are treated as facts. Of an old, decrepit politician Harriet remarks: "Though he himself is not quite a living man, his

---

[34]*The Twentieth-Century Novel: Studies in Technique* (New York: D. Appleton-Century, 1932), 493-95; Nigel Nicolson and Joanne Trautmann, *The Letters of Virginia Woolf, 1929-1931, Vol. IV* (New York: Harcourt, Brace, Jovanovich, 1979), 88.

faltered words and shaken gestures reflected, like an old and clouded mirror, the speech and carriage of a living man" (177). The circularity of the sentence apes the circularity of the political world, palsied and corrupt, and a mere shadow play of the real world it purports to reflect. *Harriet Hume* is a satire, a biting account of the futility of political factions, of the way every seemingly sly grab at power rebounds viciously on itself. Yet the mood at the end of the novel is one of conciliation--not that the conflict between men and women has been resolved--but rather that the warring sides of an argument have conceded each other's good points without relinquishing their dispute. For Harriet does not know what eternity has in store for them as a couple; what she does know is that there is such a thing as an amity of opposites.

Wells concurred. He wrote to West calling *Harriet Hume* "charming. It's more your stuff than anything you have ever written hitherto. You've got your distinctive fantasy & humour into it and it gives play for just the peculiar intricate wittiness which is one of your most delightful & inimitable characteristics." He saluted her as a writer who had wakened from her "intellectual trances. It's a joy to praise you unreservedly. Homage & admiration." He recommended that she read Jung, because she was "driving at the same thing in the love-antagonism of Harriet & Arnold. To use Jung's slang she is Arnold's *anima*." Wells's praise did not mollify her: "I got a letter from H.G. praising Harriet Hume but expressing wonder that I should have been capable of writing it in my state of deplorable abandonment to sloth and bad habits," she wrote to her female friend and fellow novelist, G.B. Stern.[35]

---

[35]HGW to RW, September 13, 1929; RW to GBS, n.d., Yale.

# CHAPTER FOUR

## 1928-1933

In June 1928, West began writing a monthly column for an American magazine, *The Bookman*. She ranged among discussions of friends, books, politics, plays, her summers in France--virtually anything on her mind. Always gravitating toward attractive but misunderstood outsiders, West devoted a part of a *Bookman* essay to the exquisite Elinor Wylie, a fragile and beautiful poet, who had died at forty. West defended her maligned friend, rumored earlier to have made a suicide attempt by throwing herself down the stairs. Much of Wylie's febrile, erratic behavior West attributed to high blood pressure, and to a sensitivity easily violated by the crass milieu of the 1920s. West also lauded Wylie in *Time and Tide*, calling the poet's so-called egotism actually "an unbridled passion for perfection." West valedictory echoes her elegy for D. H. Lawrence as one of the ethereal but tormented geniuses of modern art: "I do not believe we have left to us ten percent of the beauty Elinor Wylie might have created had she been permitted by her own constitution to know peace."[1]

Much of West's *Bookman* commentary culls through her fund of social and literary observations. She retails a few jokes--like the one about the French writer suffering from a bad case of the flu, "la grippe," whose shaky command of English caused her to cable her English colleagues: "Cannot

---

[1] "A Commentary," *The Bookman*, March 1929, 54-59; "Miss Rebecca West," *Tide and Tide*, January 18, 1929, Yale clipping file. West's elegy for Lawrence is reprinted in *Rebecca West: A Celebration* (New York: Viking, 1977), 383-95.

come; am being gripped in bed." West provides this memorable sighting of a formidable French figure: "She had something of the stance of a Spanish fighting bull, and I felt a nervous impulse, as I retreated before her, to make it quite clear that I had never been a matador and had, indeed, always felt a peculiar affection and regard for bulls." She had a "personality so strong that for her parallel one has to go outside life to great literature and cite the Wife of Bath. For thirty years she has been putting into infallible artistic form her gross, wise, limited, eternal views about life." It was Colette.[2]

West rebutted William Carlos Williams's allegation that her reservations about Joyce in *The Strange Necessity* constituted a defense of the English critical tradition. Evidently he did not know that she was half Scotch and half Irish, and that her progenitors had always regarded the English as "incomprehensible foreigners." West avowed that her mother thought no Englishwoman was "fit to have a child," and that her father asserted that no Englishman knew how to ride a horse properly. Her father's English was a pedantic eighteenth-century variety, and her mother's came out in a "Gaelic sing-song." She herself had been taunted for speaking her own amalgam of the two in a London kindergarten and jeered in Edinburgh for not speaking like a Scot. Clearly Dr. Williams had been misinformed, said West, burnishing her cherished outsider's pedigree.[3]

She also parted company with Joyce's fellow modernist, T.S. Eliot, whom she names in an essay, "Tradition in Criticism" as opposing her advocacy of a kind of criticism that "takes almost the likeness and habits of imaginative work." She championed Addison, Charles Lamb, Leigh Hunt, De Quincey (the "Liszt of essayists"), and Leslie Stephen, who treated a "book or poem as if it were an experience like any other and wrote a subjective account of it." Conversely, some of the best criticism had been practiced in novels,

---

[2]"A Commentary," July 1929, 279-84; "A London Letter," November 1929, 518-23.

[3]"A Letter From Abroad," February 1930, 664-68.

such as Proust's handling of Anatole France as Bergotte in *A La Recherche du Temps Perdu.*

In *The New York Herald Tribune,* West recognized Eliot as a "great genius, a great poet," but she challenged his immense prestige as a critic. Undoubtedly one of the age's "fertilising forces," the purveyor of a "thousand illuminating hints" in the area of "specific criticisms," he did with difficulty what Edmund Wilson did with ease. Eliot's stiffness sometimes prevented him from understanding other writers' work. She deplored Eliot's praise of the French critic, Julian Benda, who was as "fond of quotation as a schoolgirl with a nice new album to fill." Benda's argument flowed as "wildly as the hair over her shoulders." Yet Eliot had praised the "formal beauty" of Benda's writing. "At that rate he must find a haystack as beautiful as the Parthenon," West concluded. She saw his praise of antithetical writers, Charles Maurras and Benda, as an example of the "intellectual confusion which is Mr. Eliot's bugbear." Eliot's espousal of writers who took such different views of religion and of the past suggested to her "an emotional reaction, proceeding from the workings of some dominant fantasy which never rises to the level of consciousness where it can be checked by the intellect." Thus he rejected not so much the present as reality itself. In his essay on Dante, for example, he omitted everything about Dante that made him human: "the haughtiness, the vindictiveness, the obsession with temporal matters co-existent with a perfect recognition of their real unimportance compared with eternal matters; all that is washed away, and a blankly ideal figure is left." She agreed with Eliot that human beings often gave a false picture of reality, but investigation of what made them falsify the picture should be the critic's task. Whereas Eliot claimed that the personality of the artist was irrelevant, and that biography had no function in literary criticism, West urged the opposite: "just now, and for some time to come, literary criticism must be largely a matter of psychological research."[4]

West took on Eliot as the most distinguished representative of a school of self-proclaimed classicists she condemned in the last chapter of her collection of reworked *Bookman* articles, *Ending in Earnest*.[5] She was breaking off her connection with *The Bookman* "in earnest" because it had taken to adopting a false view of literature personified by critics who deemed themselves "in possession of the full tradition of mankind, and cry out on the romanticists who have repudiated it." In America, Eliot's allies were Professors Irving Babbitt and Paul Elmer More. In France, Maurras, Gide, and Maritain were among those whose puffed-up erudition she scorned. The greatest works of art, West maintained, were both classical and romantic, and the greatest artists produced oeuvres that contained both. Such artists discovered new material, thereby breaking the "mould of the universe." In this respect, they were romantics. But in remaking the mould into works of art, they re-established order and restored classicism. Far from being opposed to each other, romanticism and classicism were vitally necessary to each other--as Paul Valery, a great poet expressed it: "All classicism assumes an anterior romanticism." These pseudo classicists, she noted, were not creators. Even Eliot had ceased to create significant works of art after *The Wasteland*, and Gide--a writer of undeniable force--had not fulfilled his promise. Far better to rely on Proust, Joyce, Lawrence, Aldous Huxley, and Virginia Woolf--all of whom embodied the creative and critical spirit required to understand the nexus between romanticism and classicism.

The term "in earnest" can also be defined as a kind of downpayment, a token of something to come. In West's case, it signified her determination to practice a critical method at once personal and professional, a heartier,

---

[4]"The Benda Mask," December 29, 1929, 1,4; "The Weaker Image," January 5, 1930, 1,8.

[5](Garden City, New York: Doubleday Doran), 1931.

more flavorful, more human approach than the wizened strictures of Eliot and his school. Practicing her own brand of biographical literary criticism on the story of Lord Byron and Lady Caroline Lamb, West resumed her study of male hostility toward women and the need to punish the sexual woman. In rehabilitating Lady Caroline and defending her from the attacks that had the effect of justifying Lord Byron's abuse of her, West speculated:

> Is it that our first fantasies about life make us long to lay hold of the woman, the mother, and keep her immobile so that we can cling to her, while the man, the father, can wander if he wants, and that in consequence a woman whose spirit flies about the universe, beating herself against the bars, shocks us and we will have none of her? It may be so.

It is not hard to see the figure of Rebecca West showing through her tribute to the "tragic and splendid" Caroline Lamb, or to sense the foreboding in her mother's mind as her difficult son Anthony came of age. Apologizing to *Tribune* editor Irita Van Doren for turning in copy that far exceeded her usual word limit, West pleaded forgiveness for "overwriting. . . . Caroline Lamb sweeps me off my feet. I almost cry as I write it and I can't bear to cut it I suppose for that reason."[6]

West's use of psychological criticism and her renewed exploration of sex antagonism are evident in her dissection of Andre Gide as an exemplar of the male mind. Gide's power resides in his capacity to "honestly describe" male fantasies, the ones that lurk at the bottom of the male child's mind, which have "determined the whole course of his life." In Gide, the hatred of women turns into promoting homosexuality, and to West this homosexuality is subversive, constituting a rejection of women. She explores Gide's powerful early novel, *Isabelle*, as a peculiar kind of male fantasy. She had come to it after re-reading most of his other work, searching for the reason why she had found him compelling and yet ultimately dissatisfying. She contends that the

---

[6]"Byron and Lady Caroline Lamb," *The New York Herald Tribune*, December 22, 1929, 1,4,10; RW to IVD, n.d., Irita Van Doren Papers, Library of Congress.

novel's outward events are actually an autobiographical allegory, and an extension of several myths locating the source of evil in the woman as mother and wife. Isabelle is the sexual woman and a projection of Gide's infantile fantasy. The novel has her cripple her child: "that is, she has inflicted on him the pain and humiliation of birth. She does it as a result of her efforts to appear the virgin she is not; an incident which expresses the resentment the child feels when it realizes that its mother, whom it has always revered, must have had sexual relations with its father." This shifting of blame to the "non-virgin woman" is, West submits, "a soothing repetition of a fantasy with which we are already acquainted, it recalls us to an earlier, and less exacting, stage of our existence, just as a nursery lullaby takes us back to the time when we slept in a cot." It was to a cot that West reverted in her "Father Violation Memory," a private account she wrote of her psychoanalysis, which evoked her dawning consciousness of the power of sex when her father loomed over her offering the tip of his penis to her mouth.[7]

In 1929, a legal battle with Wells over Anthony's education touched off a resurgent feminism in West at precisely the time she detected that "anti-feminism is so strikingly the correct fashion of the day among the intellectuals." It was not so before the war, when the best writers were pro-Suffrage, a rueful West remarked. She was heartened to hail Virginia Woolf's *A Room of One's Own* as an "uncompromising piece of feminist propaganda; I think the ablest yet written." The passage on Shakespeare's imagined sister, also a genius, but checked by the physical and mental restrictions put upon her sex, so that she died with her "plays still in the unopened packet of her brain," seemed absolutely right to West, who always saw the world as a conspiracy designed to thwart her.[8]

---

[7] "A Letter from Abroad," *The Bookman*, December 1929, 433-49. On West's memory of her own sexual abuse, see Carl Rollyson, *Rebecca West: A Life* (New York: Scribner, 1996), 114-116.

[8] "A Letter from Abroad," *The Bookman*, January 1930, 551-57.

In "It Used to be Unladylike," West reminisced about her birth at the "tail-end of the lady period in the last decade of Queen Victoria's reign" in order to rebut anti-feminism. She sought to remind women that if they felt "buffeted by the conditions of to-day," they should have no illusions about the past. "For it was the rebellious ladies themselves who brought it to an end; and they knew where the shoe pinched." West recalled what it was like to wear petticoats, "secured by strings which invariably slipped inside the band at the laundry." Discovering the problem while dressing for school, she had to resort to a bodkin, usually already in the hands of her sisters, who also employed the instrument to

> thread in and out of our underclothing the baby-ribbon which it was unladylike not to have, and even more unladylike not to have of certain defined colours--white, pale pink, or pale blue. A girl at school was, I remember, utterly condemned and cast down because she revealed that she had mauve ribbon threaded through her camisole.

Corsets were compulsory, although by running about as they liked West and her sisters broke the side whalebones above the hips. Then the trick was to steal away to the bedroom and with nail-scissors cut into the corset, extracting the broken bone and discretely disposing of it behind the fireplace. West escaped the torture of being fitted for an old-fashioned dress, which had a skirt and bodice full of an "infinite number of gores, and had a boned under-bodice, and sleeves containing yards of material arranged in ways that one could not credit had been devised to cope with the simple task of covering an arm." She saw her mother grow faint during the ordeal of a dress fitting. "How completely dedicated to beauty and uselessness was my mother's form!" West exclaimed. Women were shackled to their garments in a world of "hobbled elegancies." Not only couldn't women move freely, they could barely breathe or speak with any liberty. The slightest change in style might have life-altering consequences: "I have a childish memory of seeing a girl wearing a portentous hat covered with lace and feathers, and hearing her mother complain bitterly after she had left the room that she had ruined her chances with some young man by appearing before him in this erection worn at the wrong angle."[9]

The formality of this period bewildered West. Calling cards symbolized it: "You had to call on people on certain occasions, dictated merely by formality, not in the least by any desire on your part to see them, or on their part to see you; brief calls, such as rabbits might pay on other rabbits in their burrows, with much scattering of white tails." The card competition baffled her: "It was a game as complicated as auction bridge, with no chance of winning anything." Some visits demanded one card, others two--or a husband's card, and sons' and daughters' cards. "Sometimes in a perfect frenzy of mysteriousness, one turned down the corners of the cards. I know that people still do this to-day, but only in places and circles where they are not very busy. But in the old days everybody did it. London was one vast paper chase."

West's sister Letitia caused a scandal because she consented to speak with another woman in a debate at a Men Student's University Union. It was considered indelicate--a woman among so many men for intellectual purposes, yet Letitia had often danced with the same men in the same hall. It was unladylike to walk on certain streets, to go to the theater or to a restaurant in each other's company rather than with a man. A friend had recently produced a note West had written to her before the war, inviting her to the theater, and adding apologetically: "I don't mind going without a man if you don't."

In "Phases of Modern Womanhood," a series of articles for *Royal* magazine, West argued that The Flapper and the other excesses of youth deplored in the press by opinion makers reflected their opposition to social

---

[9]Woman's Journal, May 1929, 30-31; "A London Letter," *The Bookman*, June 1929, 417-22.

change. Newly educated and sensibly dressed women still confronted many difficulties with men, especially the sporting and hunting type, who looked as if he would be "more at ease if he could neigh instead of talk." Calling herself a "Patient Griseldaish type of woman," West wondered if she should obtain a lump of sugar and offer it to him in the flat of her hand. "Or ought one to make him feel at home by letting out a long girlish whinny?" The comedy that marked her contributions to *The Freewoman* returned: "And how often, when in the company of men who play tennis and cricket not only with their bodies but with their souls, have I thought out a new function for the gasmask." Now such men could serve a purpose: "Many of them dance well." If only they had gasmasks, thick quilted ones, which "might be lifted only for eating," thus rendering their words "as little compulsive on the attention by sound as they are by sense." She conceded, of course, that these men had their childish female counterparts.

There was much to be worked out in modern marriage. Not surprisingly, West's treatment of the young mother had a special vehemence: "How easy is housekeeping for a childless couple compared with housekeeping for a couple with only one child! How tiresome cooks become! How evanescent parlour maids, who seem to pirouette through the door and out again with the agility of something in the Russian Ballet." Housemaids reminded her of the turbulence and indiscipline of the French Revolution. "Has anyone ever told the truth about children's nurses?" Their demands were insatiable; they were moody and jealous of their charge's affections. And how tempting it was for the male to score a point: "You don't seem very good at managing servants, my dear!" West counseled patience and empathy for the help (an attitude she rarely adopted herself), pointing out that they no doubt wished they could lavish attention on their own families, and their frustrations accounted for the "abnormal amount of breakages" in households with servants. With separate sections on the Flapper, the young woman, the young wife, the young mother, and women's work outside the home, "Phases of Modern Womanhood" constituted an ambitious attempt to couple anecdotal autobiography with the social history of women for a popular audience.[10]

"Woman as Artist and Thinker" (1931) recast the argument of *The Strange Necessity* to demonstrate that the paucity of great women artists had nothing to do with their innate qualities, but was rather a product of cultural conditions and an inherent sadism in men who could not abide the notion of the equality of the sexes. Women had the same cerebral cortex as men, they produced art in the same way as men, but they were held to different standards. Because the community demanded monogamy of women, a polyandrous woman like George Sand was considered a slut: "Her books are spoken of as if they were the equivalent of a too opulent bosom heaving behind a soiled kerchief above shamelessly constricting corsets." The creative woman was deemed a vampire "who must owe her creativeness (since that cannot be conceded as natural in her sex) to her theft of some man's virility." Hence Sand was supposed to have sucked the life out of Chopin. "Had a Scotch farmer's daughter had the finest lyrical gift in the world and had bred by all comers as Robert Burns did, she would hardly have been encouraged by the fashionables of Edinburgh as he was." West concluded that no matter what progress feminists might make men would have an "instinctive repulsion to women's work, that would lead to them launching unjust accusations against them." The image for men was the knife--good not only for cutting flesh, she admitted, but also for shaping works of art. The image for women was the box, for women like to "shut up things and preserve them," showing conflict but expressing their "preference for harmony rather than revolt." A female Shakespeare would not have rendered Desdemona as a "weeping nullity," Cordelia as a "shadowy young girl." Still, "women have nothing whatsoever to preen themselves over in their differences from men." Like

---

[10]"Phases of Modern Womanhood," undated article in Yale clipping file.

men, women saw only by halves; a woman Shakespeare would probably have presented Othello as a "brutal nullity" and Lear as a "shadowy old man." She detected in women "an equal disposition to castrate men."[11]

Two stories from the late 1920s, "Life Sentence" and "There is No Conversation," renewed West's sense of "sex antagonism." "Life Sentence" centers on a woman with a double self expressed by her name and its diminutive: Josephine, ambitious and business-like; Josie, vulnerable and naive. As the virginal Josie she attracts Corrie Dickson, who proposes to her and then tries to withdraw, confessing to her his fear that he does not love her as much as she deserves. But when he offers to honor his pledge, he is surprised that she accepts him, as though it is a business contract that is at stake. Their marriage gradually sours, for Josie has never really forgiven him for trying to jilt her at the last minute. Also, she inherits a sizeable sum from her father and begins to invest in property and real estate projects, becoming Josephine, a kind of empress of finance, while Corrie remains modestly successful and daunted by his wife's ravenous appetite for investments. She eventually rejects him for another man, who is willing to absorb himself completely in her commercial schemes. Corrie and Josie meet only one more time, when each thinks the other has been ruined by the 1929 stock market crash. In fact, both have protected their capital and have come to the meeting expecting to help the other. Their generous impulses stymied, they resort to rancorous attacks on each other, until they are interrupted by a bell-boy who has come to collect Corrie's bags for a train he has to catch in ten minutes. The couple is aghast--they thought they had at least another hour to thrash out their conflicting feelings. The ambiguous ending is one of West's best, because the couple's despair is the result of their "life sentence" of love and hate. Corrie had originally used the phrase as a way of charac-

---

[11]"Woman as Artist and Thinker," *Woman's Coming of Age: A Symposium*, ed. Samuel D. Schmalhausen and V. F. Calverton (New York: Liveright, 1931), 369-82.

terizing his marriage, which he thought he had escaped in divorcing Josie and remarrying, but the phrase expresses the irony of their fate: they can neither reject nor accept each other. Their relationship hinges on the back-and-forth of their marital history, on the Josie/Josephine dichotomy that neither of them can resolve. Josephine has usurped Josie in Corrie's mind--as is evident in his remark about his second wife: "she's a real woman, the kind that can't look after herself." The implication, of course, is that by adopting a man's occupation Josephine has made Corrie impotent--almost a woman himself, as his name suggests.

The story's dynamic is deeply autobiographical. Isn't this what men were always doing to West? Pulling out at the last second, after they had gotten her pregnant with the idea of loving them, or saying she had made them impotent?[12] She was angry, she could not forgive them, and she was hurt--as crushed as a little child would be by such sudden rejection. She could not let go. West's secretary, June Head, remembers that on the way to a summer villa in France they stayed in adjoining rooms in a Paris hotel, where at night she could hear a restless West crying out Beaverbrook's name, arguing and pleading with him, and recapitulating their tortuous affair. "I could hear her all night. . . . She wanted to go back."[13] Josie's attacks on Corrie are so poisonous that he exclaims: "one couldn't tell the difference between you and a rattler if one went by the tongue." Yet when Josie feels herself under attack she behaves like a "little girl who had put on her mother's dress, and had been caught."[14] In *Confessions and Impressions*, Ethel Mannin observes the same dichotomy in West, who used her "tongue like a whip" and yet was "small and provocative, rather like a lovely naughty

---

[12]Beaverbrook and other men had said as much to West. See Rollyson, 104-05, 115-16.

[13]Interview with June Head.

[14]"Life Sentence," first published in *The Saturday Evening Post*, October 25 and November 1, 1930, and reprinted in *The Harsh Voice* (London: Virago, 1982), 41.

child."[15] In *Heritage*, Anthony West's novel about his mother and father, Richard likes his mother best when she breaks out into her "irresistible gamine smile." She became the "naughty child . . . and stopped being the wronged mother."[16]

"There is No Conversation" is composed of contrasting monologues, exemplifying the narrator's contention that, "There is no such thing as conversation. It is an illusion. There are intersecting monologues, that is all." The first monologue is conveyed to the narrator in Paris by Marquis Etienne de Sevenac. She is surprised to learn that he has lost his fortune and is selling his beloved paintings. He then explains that his ruin has been accomplished by an American woman. The Marquis is fifty, prides himself on his youthfulness, and dreads growing old. He seeks the company of younger women, but during a dry spell in his social season he romances Nancy Sarle--more out of pity and boredom than any real interest in her. Because she is in her mid-forties, plain, and a stranger to Paris, Etienne presumes that she has never had a man show her a good time. She welcomes his advances, and he assumes she has become entirely dependent on him. He is so smug about his attractiveness that he fails to gauge this woman accurately. He notices, for example, what he thinks is a toy train engine on her writing desk. "That's not a toy!" she barks in a man's "grim, rough voice." Her eyes bore into him like "two steel drills." Although Etienne is discomfited, his comment reveals why there can be no dialogue between him and Nancy: "I do not think women understand how repelled a man feels when he sees a woman wholly absorbed in what she is thinking, unless it is about her child, or her husband, or her lover."[17] In fact, Nancy is a railroad executive

---

[15]*Confessions and Impressions* (London: Jarrolds, 1930), 118-19.

[16](New York: Random House, 1955), 62.

[17]"There is No Conversation," *The Harsh Voice*, 63, 79. Page numbers for subsequent quotations will be cited in the text within parentheses.

and owner. When she discovers that he does not love her, she takes her revenge in financial machinations that destroy the value of his American railroad stock. At least, this is how Etienne interprets her actions.

The narrator is so fascinated by Etienne's portrait of Nancy that on her return to New York she finagles a friendship with Nancy, eager to hear the other side of the story. Nancy admits she has made a fool of herself over Etienne, although she was never quite the love-lorn creature Etienne fancied. Rather, it was his seeming faithfulness and willingness to serve her that recommended him to Nancy. If Etienne has a crude sense of women--seeing in them only what is to be got out of them as lovers, Nancy is equally coarse: "He always came round just like a dawg, when you said" (117). The truth is that Nancy had been planning to drive down Etienne's stock even before she met him, and she would have refrained from doing so only if Etienne had explicitly declared his love and devotion to her.

The narrator is desolated. She had been expecting to find in Nancy an inconsolable lover. Quite the contrary, Nancy dismisses the episode--just one of many in the ambitious life of a woman who has married three times and earned enormous wealth. The narrator knows Etienne is a cad--indeed she suddenly reveals that she had been married to Etienne for ten years! In Nancy Sarle, she hoped to find a justification for her obsession with a man whom she knew was unworthy of her love. The story ends with the narrator protesting too much: "Yet Etienne means nothing to me. He means nothing at all to me" (130). The reverse seems to be the case. Even though the narrator has remarried and has children, she has not been able to let go of Etienne, and her fixation on him seems all the more perverse, given Nancy's dismissal of him from her life.

It is a clever story, enhanced by West's sure grasp of both European and American idioms, and by the astutely shaped monologues in which Etienne and Nancy are allowed to reveal themselves gradually. That it is also the narrator's story is deftly concealed until the end. Nancy is like no woman

Etienne has ever encountered, for she is the new type of American commercial temperament that astounded West because of its single-minded pursuit of profits. Like West, the narrator is drawn to the energy such figures put out, but also like West, she is appalled by their emptiness. Nancy's sensibility is as much of a desert as Etienne's, and the narrator is herself obliterated by her absorption in their alternative but equally barren worlds. The characters and the story are far removed from what West experienced with Wells and Beaverbrook, and yet the narrator's agony over having spent ten years with a cad certainly evokes the trauma West still could not overcome.

West's marriage on November 1, 1930 to Henry Andrews, a banker working for the German firm, Schroders, seemed surprising to many observers. A PEN intimate of West's attending the wedding observed that "she had chosen to be married in the *depths* of the country because her cousin was the parson there. As she isn't a Christian or he either I wondered over this church ceremony. I think the parson must also have wondered for he cut it as short as possible." Another friend said: "It was startling to hear her confident voice intone the solemnities of the Anglican marriage service. She looked very well and seemed very happy, and her husband appears to be a good sort, a man of substance and humility, the proper backdrop for a novelist's stage." Still, it was hard to picture West "walking up a church aisle and being given away by your sister [Letitia]. It would have been easier to think of you dashing off to Gretna Green or strolling into a Registrar's office one foggy day on the impulse of the moment or being abducted by some one who insisted on marrying you willy-nilly!" A newspaper report expressed what seemed like a momentous change:

> So the advanced radical, the labor sympathiser, the woman who in 1922 spoke to me so scornfully about bankers, reorients her life as the wife of a rich and active capitalist, a man so astute that last year, over the deep of the depression, he added around a quarter of a million dollars to an already large

fortune. You can see something of the influence of this money-making man in her later work--the new technical knowledge of finance, the concentration on an angle of life hitherto strange to her.

But if West was not an orthodox believer in Christianity, Wells had detected early on how much she craved respectability and the comforts of tradition. The "rites and ceremonies of the Church of England"--as the marriage certificate put it--were observed with two modifications: the word obey was omitted from the bride's vows, and the bridegroom promised not to endow but to share with his bride his worldly goods. If West had been an advanced radical, she had parted company early with her kind in rejecting the model of Soviet socialism. If she had spoken scornfully of bankers, well, she had also enjoyed their company in her American travels long before she met Henry Andrews-- and he was hardly the conventional type of banker, a deeply learned man with literary passions. As she later wrote in a manuscript notebook, she was distressed by the press reports of Henry's wealth, which were not true, but which she and he abetted by living in high style--largely on her earnings and his bank salary until he inherited a substantial sum from his Uncle Ernest. From the mid-twenties--a good four years before she met Andrews--West was writing sympathetic short stories about American businessmen and women, so that Henry's appearance in her life did not so much redirect as confirm the trajectory of her development.[18]

West's new life with Henry Andrews included a handsome flat in London's Portman Square, complete with butler and sumptuous furnishings. She worked hard to support the couple's rich tastes. She sold herself into bondage--as she termed it to Alexander Woollcott--to the *New York American*,

---

[18]I have drawn on accounts of West's wedding in a journal of Mrs. C. A. Dawson Scott, courtesy of Marjorie Lowenstein; Raymond Swing to John Gunther, December 9, 1930; Marion Fletcher to RW, November 10, 1930; unidentified newspaper clipping, Yale; RW's manuscript notebook, Tulsa. On West's craving for respectability, see *H. G. Wells in Love*, ed. G. P. Wells (London: Faber and Faber, 1984), 98.

writing "I Said to Me," two six hundred word columns each week for twenty pounds. This on top of an agreement with the *Daily Telegraph* for a weekly review of books at fifteen guineas a week. To her friend, Winifred Holtby, a fellow board member on *Time and Tide*, West reported that she was "hideously overworked," having found writing two articles of six hundred words a week "far more difficult than writing two articles of 6000 words a week."[19]

The tone of the *New York American* columns (1931-1933) is chatty, with almost none of the literary analysis that distinguishes her *Bookman* work. She covers a range of subjects--commenting on travel, spiritualism, poltergeists, telepathy, her fondness for America, the current state of the theater, politics, and the economy (several columns reflect the Depression-era suspicion that capitalism had entirely broken down). She defends the dole (arguing that workers have to be supported while out of jobs to preserve public peace). She excoriates the Conservative government's plan to cut teachers' salaries by fifteen percent. She laments the plight of miners whose dangerous and dirty work is the shameful price for lighting and heating capitalist England. Yet she has little faith in the socialism she espoused in her youth, calling it a "formula worked out in the vanished Age of Abundance" that could not be applied to the present "Age of Deficiency."[20]

West attacked Soviet Russia for having "misled the progressive world and wasted its moral and intellectual forces at a time when they were most needed for constructive purposes." It has "refused liberty to its citizens" and promulgated a Five Year Plan which "makes people believe that if one uses machinery very fast instead of thinking, everything will come out all right, just as Victorian England and twentieth century America believed." She has little patience with those who champion Communist Russia because it has

---

[19]RW to WH, n.d., Winifred Holtby Collection, Central Library, Hull.

[20]"I Said to Me," September 29, 1931, 13.

destroyed the class system and given hope. It has been put to her that the British do not have the courage to revamp their own system and that her anti-Soviet position represents the attitude of a "finicky intellectual who makes no allowances for the difficulties under which Russia is working." She retorts that because the Russians call themselves Communists they are exonerated; if their methods were employed by a British government they would be denounced as "crimes against liberty." Instead of frankly admitting that a "new attitude to reality" has to be worked out, progressives pursue the pretense that the political and economic problems of modern life are being solved in Soviet Russia.[21]

West alerted her readers to the disaster that had been avoided in the recent German elections. Hindenburg had been re-elected, and Hitler's "crazy aggressiveness" had been rejected--at least for the moment. "But if anyone wants to know what that election meant, what unwholesomeness it repudiated, let them read Dorothy Thompson's 'I Saw Hitler,' which is a superb piece of journalism." She had spent a week in Germany in the autumn of 1931. "I never loathed any place so much as Berlin," she wrote to her sister Winifred Macleod. She found Germans "perpetually in a state of inflamed exaltation over their own commonsense and other people's lack of it." Many of them seemed to be "happily look[ing] forward to a Hitlerite government, which will shoot all the Jews." They rejoiced over the failure of a bank because its president was a Jew. She and her husband had been invited to dinner by one of the most important bankers in Germany. West wore an afternoon dress of wine-colored chiffon and found herself out of place among women dressed in "very ugly tweeds." They gazed at her dress with "deep hatred," and she could hear them grousing quietly about the extravagant habits of the English and the "bad taste of those in flaunting their riches before the martyred Germans," although she was certain her dress cost

---

[21]"I Said to Me," January 26, 1932, 13; February 26, 1932, 15.

no more than six pounds and their tweeds closer to sixteen. The food was poorly cooked and pretentious. Germans who spoke English refused to do so. It was mainly people under fifty who behaved so badly, West reported to Winifred. She saw them as "personifications of ruined Europe."[22]

West would be given the opportunity to write a more extended meditation on a ruined Europe when Virginia Woolf wrote to her on September 18, 1931, asking her to contribute a piece for the Hogarth Letter series. She had complete freedom to write on whatever she chose, the length also to be determined by her. She would get a twenty-five pound advance and a ten percent royalty. Then Woolf added: "I urge this on you not only in my capacity as publisher but as an admirer who actually drove 8 miles the other day to buy a copy of the Daily Telegraph in order not to miss your article. This is not an effort I am in the habit of making, but a proof of the great admiration with which I hold your work."[23]

Flattered by the invitation, West proposed to write *A Letter to a Grandfather* "from a woman whose family has the power of seeing visions and who has just seen what is this age's form of what would have in other ages been a vision of the Madonna or Christ." It would be a difficult, densely intellectual piece, which complemented her recently published story, "They that Sit in Darkness," about a family of mediums, who in spite of their own fakery, continue to yearn for a sight of things beyond this world, for a seance in which spirits did move things and people, a "magical transfusion of matter, a sieve-like quality of this world that let in siftings from eternity."[24]

---

[22]"I Said to Me," April 21, 1932, 13; RW to WM, n.d., AM.

[23]Tulsa.

[24]RW to VW, Hogarth Press Collection, University of Reading. "They That Sit in Darkness," *The Only Poet and Short Stories*, ed. Antonia Till (London: Virago Press, 1992), 161.

West persistently doubted the spirit realm, but she could not leave it alone--because the reality she knew robbed her of so much. She was grieving over the death of her childhood friend, Flora Duncan, to whom she would dedicate her biography of *Saint Augustine* (1933). A West intimate, had written to her: "I know why it bothered you when Flora's mother said that about her leaving a blank; it's because it was an acceptance of her death as a commonplace event; which is horrifying when you love someone." West abhorred blanks and wrote to another friend asking her to arrange a meeting with a medium who might offer an insight into Duncan's unhappy last days.[25]

*A Letter to a Grandfather* is signed by "C. B.," the most recent female descendent of the Beauchamp family, who has just experienced "my share of the vision that comes to each generation of our family." Exactly what she has seen and what it means is difficult to puzzle out, because it is not really comprehensible in human terms. It is a vision of God; it is "one moment when life was presented to you as a unity," she says to her grandfather, who has experienced his own version of the vision.[26] Like *The Strange Necessity*, *A Letter to a Grandfather* is rough going because it attempts to recreate process--in this case not the esthetic process but a religious experience that overwhelms the self. What the two works have in common is a quest to meld this disparate world into one, into an apprehensible image.

C. B. experiences something exactly opposite to the modern notion of self. She contrasts it to buying clothes, which is "so Berkleyan. One wraps the self in gorgeousness as if to say, 'There's nothing but you really, the universe is just a figment you keep on creating, if I give you all these lovely presents will you make me a lovelier universe?'" (6) The religious experience,

[25]Emanie Sachs to RW, n.d., Yale; Marjorie Watts, *Mrs. Sappho: The Life of C. A. Dawson Scott, Mother of International P.E.N.* (London: Duckworth, 1987), 133.

[26]*A Letter to a Grandfather* (London: The Hogarth Press, 1933), 33. Page numbers for subsequent quotations will be cited in the text within parentheses.

the abbey that C. B.'s original ancestor built to commemorate his vision, reminds her of the limitations of the self, of its inability to measure the world, to grasp the unity behind appearances: "But a man cannot stretch more than a certain distance from his head and his belly; and that makes him a tense and interesting pattern worked on the surface of infinity" (11). Christ on the cross is an image of that imprisonment in time and place and of a yearning for an experience that transcends the suffering of such limitations. In the abbey, C. B. has seen the dove:

> the thing that flies forth, the *logos*, the symbol of the spirit . . . the full life of which is lived only by certain human beings, and by certain parts of human beings, which flies forth and pillages the material life with its sharp, greedy beak of criticism, while the natural man stands by and curses, seeing his relationship with his environment ruptured, yet knowing himself under an ineluctable obligation to support the life of the spirit. (12)

In her own family, most of the men have been materialists, men of action, "interrupted only every two hundred years or so by a man of the analytic type who employs artists or is himself an artist." It makes her think of the "Italian philosopher's theory of the human spiral, which implies that man passes through alternate phases of determinism and free will" (15). She is referring to Vico, who has profoundly influenced many modernist writers. As in her family, so in the history of humankind, individuals have been surfeited with experience and have acted almost like automatons, victims of an "obvious determinism." Eventually, however, the overload of experience is inventoried and digested; human beings impose patterns on their behavior, exert, in effect, free will. History, then, is the spiral of these centrifugal and centripetal forces, intersected by the efforts of individuals who at any moment may succumb to or conquer their experiences (15)

This is a philosophy of history not easily or neatly proven, C.B. concedes, but it has made enormous imaginative sense to artists, and it helps her to account for her family's generation-by-generation visions of the whole, of the unity of experience. Each age, she realizes, has adapted the vision to its temperament, so that, for example, it appears in a rational, ordered form in the eighteenth-century, as a God approximating the guise of a Romantic poet in the nineteenth-century. The varieties of religious experience change but not the "persistence of the life of the spirit" (25). Human beings can kill doves, but not the dove, the Holy Ghost.

Although it is a religious statement, *A Letter to a Grandfather* is also a political manifesto, an answer to what was happening in Germany and elsewhere in Europe. As early as 1925, West had traveled through Central Europe, reporting for *The New Republic* on the uneasy peace, in which Austrians brooded over territories lost to Italy in the war and Hungarians expressed an incorrigible hatred of neighboring countries. It was "sad rankling stuff," rotting away life and turning "all spiritual forces to daydreaming."[27]

*A Letter to a Grandfather* is an effort to reawaken a sense of the spirit, which has attenuated over the past two centuries. Romanticism emphasized the sensating individual, a necessary phase for humanity to go through in order to have experience to interpret, but by itself romanticism was destructive. West had already argued that romanticism needed classicism, a sense of objective form, to critique it; otherwise all one had was that Berkleyan revelry in solipsism, that clothing of the self. She saw a corrective in the nineteenth century scientist's emphasis on the idea of coherence and on ascertainable fact, for it rooted humanity once more in a quest for the unity of experience.

West had written to Hugh Walpole that in another age she would have looked on herself as one who had sinned against the Holy Ghost. She had in mind her complicity in the human tendency to destroy the unity of experience. She has C. B. say, "I loathe the way the two cancers of sadism

---

[27]"So This is Peace!," March 4; "Post-War," March 11, 62-64.

and masochism eat into the sexual life of humanity." In West's letters, it was usually Wells or Beaverbrook--and later her son Anthony--who perpetrated these sins, but what made her so ashamed, especially about Beaverbrook, is that she had played his game and could be accused of being something of a sadist and masochist herself. That she had sinned against herself and against the life of the spirit was almost more than she could ever bear to admit, but her confessions sometimes came out in her hasty late night scribbling of memoirs that never saw the published light of day: "My twenties were joyless and overworked and lonely, but this was entirely my own fault. I lost patience with my home life too soon and tried to arrange my life for myself and did it badly." Such a naked declaration of error is rarely made in West's correspondence or her published work.[28]

C. B., like West, does not have the consolations that others in the 1930s used to impose a unity of experience on themselves. West believed in tradition--as she demonstrates in her biography of *Saint Augustine*--but in her time "tradition has been thrown out of the window by all parties, even by those who pretend to be traditionalists," C. B. concludes. The Roman Catholic Church had gained converts who did not believe in revelation, but who disliked the disorder of life without authority. What authority could the Church have, however, if its basis of authority--revelation--was denied? Such conversions were void but no more fatuous than those of the "Left Wing, who have thrown the whole tradition of economic idealism out of the window, and babble of nothing but Russia" (35). The "harsh effort" in Russia entranced the Left:

> They are in love with cancer, they want the love of man for his kind to be eaten away like the love of man and woman by sadism and masochism. That justice should be done without passion and stripes would disappoint them, they have not got

---

[28]RW to HW, September 19, 1928, Yale ; manuscript notebook, Tulsa.

> out of the fateful ring-fence of primitive ideas where every good
> must be paid for by pain and sacrifice. (35-36)

This is as much to say that Stalin was supported--indeed embraced--*because* he was a monster, that the gauge of positive historical change was the millions of deaths consecrated to a cause. Such passages reflect West own quest for the unity of experience, for a way of allying the personal and political as symptoms of the same sin.

*A Letter to a Grandfather* ends in a dramatic scene--the vision C. B. has had of a tall, gaunt Negro carnival barker on the platform of a merry-go-round composed of miniature automobiles. It is an image of a whirling world--never quite the same at any moment, but all of a piece nevertheless. The Negro calls people to the cars and is immediately aware of the traffic problems they create. As he drives them on with his cane, making sure that the merry-go-round is full, they seem to lose their volition. He uses his cane, in other words, as a shepherd's staff, and he takes the same degree of pleasure and irritation in herding his flock as a shepherd might. Then he holds his cane rigidly on the level, so that it looks like an iron bar, suggesting both discipline and judgment. The merry-go-round revolves, and the barker mesmerizes his audience with a hand trick, thrusting the first finger and thumb of his right hand into a circle he has made out of the first finger and thumb of his left hand. "His teeth shone, his rolling eyeballs exhibited the whites of his eyes; it was as if a gleaming bird, a dove shot forth from his face and in its flight became his finger" (41). It is a cheap trick, a tawdry show. But it delights the crowd as though it were a firework; it is a revelation, an emanation of the spirit. C. B. says she is ashamed of her revelation. Why? Because it is not the traditional one of literature, in which she would appear

> sweet, full of acknowledgment of guilt, infantilely ready to
> admit our corrigibility, free from exaltation in dark things. I
> feel that in my spiritual apotheosis the nice thing would have
> been for me to be like the clergyman's mournful widow,
> muttering about my Waste Lands, moaning because it is Ash

> Wednesday, or to be a Romantic, melting and guttering with my own heat like a candle, or to be a simmering pot of ethical activity. (43)

This direct strike on the literary tradition, especially on T.S. Eliot, is meant as a way of suggesting how little "comfort or benignity" C. B. takes from her vision, and to remind herself that for the human being the true religious experience is likely to be grim, not grand. If the first in her family to have a vision saw a gaunt figure extended on a cross, she has also seen the same thing in the Negro's form; she experiences the same "attempt to cover all, to know all, to feel all, although fixed to one point in the universe, and thereby pinned to ignorance" (43-44). Advancing a sense of predestination that will be worked out in Rebecca's biography of St. Augustine, C. B. announces: "I also know that some are born to be saved and some to be damned, that the pulse which is heard through time and space beats to some other rhythm than human justice." The spirit that she sees is not "holy or independent." It is rather the "white product of dark gestures, the refined descendant of man's primitive play." In the Negro's dark gestures and primitive play is found the unity of experience, of Christ on the Cross stretching toward eternity. It is not a pretty or an ennobling vision, but it is a revelation of tragedy that has come back into her life. It is a vision that kindles "the will to belief" (44). C. B. is careful not to say that in fact she believes, merely that the idea of the spirit has been resurrected, and that it brings, she sees, "an inevitable happiness" (45). West herself would get no nearer to revelation, but would pursue the will to do so in her biography of Augustine.

In his review of West's biography, S. K. Ratcliffe observed that it might surprise readers that she had chosen Saint Augustine,[29] a subject commissioned by Peter Davies in England as part of a series of biographies and

---

[29]*The Nation*, June 21, 1933, 703-04.

published by Appleton in America. But she had been reading this great father of the church since her teens, having been introduced to him by a Jesuit friend of her mother's shortly after her father's death. Both Augustine's gloom and his energy suited her; he wrote a prose deeply pessimistic about humanity, but he lived an energetic life, saving souls and spreading a sense of the spirit to which human beings could aspire. He had been a Manichean; that is, a believer in two separate realms of good and evil. When he embraced Christianity, he came around to the view that good and evil are part of one realm and inhere simultaneously in the soul. Man's fall from paradise, his fatal will, had ensured that he would have to struggle with the warring elements in himself. Man had become, in other words, "a problem to himself"--to vary slightly the wording of Augustine's spiritual autobiography, the *Confessions*, in which he says, more than once, that he became a "problem to myself."[30] Augustine was so good at dramatizing this problem, the nature of evil, that he has been accused of remaining a Manichean, for evil in his writing seems to take on a life of its own, like an invasive cancer. West's temperament made her a natural Augustinian--a problem to herself, and possessed of a powerful sense of evil outside herself that made her seem a victim more than a violator, a feminist Manichean, as critic Moira Ferguson puts it.[31]

At precisely those moments in the *Confessions* when the ambitious Augustine might have taken responsibility for his own sins--for example, when he abandons his concubine--he resorts to the passive voice: "The woman with whom I had been living was torn from my side as an obstacle to my marriage and this was a blow which crushed my heart to bleeding, because I loved her dearly" (131). West notes such instances of his evasiveness in her biography,

---

[30]*Confessions* (New York: Penguin, 1961), 223, 239. Page numbers for subsequent quotations will be cited in the text within parentheses.

[31]"Feminist Manicheanism: Rebecca West's Unique Fusion," *The Minnesota Review* 15 (1980):53-60.

but did she see how profoundly they applied to herself? For all of his soul searching, there is a curious lack of introspection in Augustine, as there is in West. Both were easily hurt by criticism and supported by strong mothers, which led Augustine to admit that his malice issued from his "pampered heart" (47). Spoiled children easily take offense and are merciless with their adversaries. When West's version of Augustine was attacked by a rather petulant young scholar, Randolph Hughes, she retaliated in kind, engaging in the sort of invective and posturing prevalent on the playground, and provoking Randolph's sister, Margaret Shaw, to write to West: "If you and Randolph were my children, I would slipper you both very soundly and send you to bed to think it over."[32]

Like Augustine, West wanted to annihilate her critics because they aggravated her sense of vulnerability. As one reviewer said of her subject, Augustine suffered from "a feeling of uneasiness about his status."[33] She traced this anxiety to the difference in social levels between his mother and father, thus re-enacting her own family drama by endowing Augustine's father, Patricius, with an aristocratic reluctance to abandon a well entrenched and comfortable paganism for his wife's lowly Christianity. Moreover, Augustine was a provincial, as far removed from the center of power in Rome as West had been in Edinburgh.

West lavished so much attention on the relationship between Augustine and his loving mother, Monnica, that reviewers and later commentators have both praised and blamed her for her pioneering Freudian approach. The label infuriated her, and she reproached her critics for not noticing that Augustine himself placed extraordinary emphasis on his mother's role in his life.[34] This is so, but it becomes more emphatic in West's

---

[32]MS to RW, June 19, 1933, Yale.

[33]*The Times*, February 2, 1933, Yale clipping file.

[34]"I Said to Me," *The New York American*, March 28, 1933, 13.

narrative because she strips away his pietistic language and psychologizes every aspect of his life and theology, assigning scant room for how his own epoch may have shaped his behavior. He resembles nothing so much as a character in one of her novels. As critic Peter Wolfe points out, Augustine's "penchant for travel, his obsession with sex, his stern self-criticism, strong mother, and his hatred for a father he hideously comes to resemble" is reminiscent of Richard Yaverland in *The Judge*.[35]

Not surprisingly, another critic, Harold Orel, finds in Augustine's attitude toward his parents a parallel to West's ambivalence about her father and worship of her mother. Augustine's indebtedness to his mother in West's biography, "goes well beyond what Augustine tells us." Orel notes that in *The Fountain Overflows* she attempts to exculpate her father and find reasons for his fecklessness, just as she tries to rescue Augustine's father, Patricius, from his son's hatred by suggesting Augustine's standards may have been unreasonable and Patricius had led a troubled life. Orel's insight, by the way, did not endear him to West, who saw and rejected the import of his manuscript, especially those parts that dealt with her family background.[36]

West also treats Augustine as a powerful father figure, as the authority for her own attitude. He is the first modern man, she claims--a precursor of great artists such as D. H. Lawrence and Proust. Her reading of Augustine is sustainable because in taking the development of his personality as his subject he exhibited modernist tendencies. He also has the twentieth-century artist's preoccupation with time and with how human beings perceive it. The emphasis he places on subjectivity is extraordinary: "It seems to me, then, that time is an extension, though of what it is an extension I do not know. I begin to wonder whether it is an extension of the mind itself" (274). This

---

[35]*Rebecca West: Artist and Thinker* (Carbondale: Southern Illinois University Press, 1971, 37.

[36]*The Literary Achievement of Rebecca West* (New York: St. Martin's Press, 1986), 80.

sounds like a theory of relativity, couched in a musing, even playful language, full of doubt, such as a modern artist might use. It is unlikely that the intervening centuries between Augustine and us can be canceled so easily-- although West wanted to do just that: "I have meant again and again to . . . thank you for your review of what is known in this household as Gus," she wrote to Winifred Holtby.[37]

In his acclaimed biography, *Augustine of Hippo*, Peter Brown sees the episode of Augustine and his concubine quite differently from West, who believes he suffered horribly over abandoning her. Brown treats the concubine as a "traditional feature of Roman life" that Augustine--given his views of all women as Eve, "the temptress"--would not find so hard to aban- don. Brown, a biographer who puts more distance between himself and his subject than Rebecca West does, quotes another part of the *Confessions*, in which Augustine calls his life with the concubine "the mere bargain of a lustful love."[38]

Yet it was West's political purpose to write a book that might have been titled, *Saint Augustine, Our Contemporary*. She begins her biography by demonstrating that he was born at a time when the world seemed to be deteriorating, when the Roman Empire was crumbling, when nature itself--as one Church father wrote--was apparently exhausted. The earth seemed to lose its fruitfulness and sense of possibility. Moreover, various heresies beset the one true Church: not only Manicheism, but Arianism (that Christ was not divine), Pelagianism (original sin does not obtain and man's will is free to achieve righteousness), and Donatism (only a righteous priest can administer the sacraments). Each heresy struck at the idea that the spirit, the divine principle, was whole and indivisible, above and beyond the limitations of time and place. Augustine fought fanatically against heresy, maintaining that the

---

[37]RW to WH, n.d., Winifred Holtby Collection, Central Library, Hull.

[38]*Augustine of Hippo: A Biography* (Berkeley: University of California Press, 1967), 63.

spiritual life had to be a unity of experience; it should not be fragmented by any belief, no matter how consoling or humanly appealing.

As an Augustinian, West had lashed out in *A Letter to a Grandfather* against false converts to the Church and the Communists. As Peter Brown observes, the Manicheism of Africa in the 370s and early 380s, was rather like Communism in England in the 1930s; "it had spread rapidly and, despite an exotic and highly doctrinaire core, it could still mean many things to many people."[39] In *The New York American*, West described fourth century Rome and its African province in terms that linked it inescapably to the present: "A civilization which rivaled our own," which included a sumptuous city, Carthage, with a million people, great buildings and shops and theaters reminiscent of New York, and a countryside "fat as butter with prosperous farms" and "sizable and orderly cultured towns," it all ended with a crash and "went down the sink." The empire had become bloated with bureaucrats and soldiers, the citizenry overtaxed, the "upper classes were harried and the lower classes starved." The system refused to correct itself by permitting dissent and free discussion that would have acknowledged its severe failings. "It is the easiest sophomore trick to decry democracy and lots of people are doing it. But the past is full of tragedies that tell us how much worse it might go with us today if our form of government were less democratic."[40]

Later, in *Black Lamb and Grey Falcon*, West makes explicit the parallel embedded in though not expressed at the beginning of her biography: "I had written . . . a life of St. Augustine to find out why every phrase I read of his sounds in my ears like the sentence of my doom and the doom of my age."[41] Her contemporaries were following false gods, thus splitting themselves from a recognition of the spirit, of humanity in its wholeness. Drawn perversely to

---

[39]Ibid., 54.

[40]"I Said to Me," October 11, 1932, 15.

[41](New York: Viking, 1986), 1084.

death-inflicting ideas, she meant to jolt people out of them. As Dale Marie
Urie suggests, West "discusses Augustine's theology with the knowledge that
those ideas have had a jarring impact on the civilization of not only his day
but of hers as well."[42] She coveted the same disruptive role for herself. She
had begun her career in *The Freewoman* (June 6, 1912) dismissing the
Calvinism of her native Scotland, deciding that it was "impossible to argue
with a person who holds the doctrine of original sin." Her own experience
and her reading of history had caused her to recant:

> If we examine ourselves carefully we cannot claim to have free
> will. We exercise what looks like a free faculty of choice, but
> the way we exercise that faculty depends on our innate qualities
> and our environment, and these always bind us in some way or
> another to the neuroses which compel us to choose death
> rather than life. We cannot break this compulsion by the
> independent efforts of our minds, for they cannot function
> effectively unless they learn to depend on tradition. Augus-
> tine's view that we are full of original sin, that we do not enjoy
> the free use of our wills, and must link ourselves to the eternal
> if we are to be saved, is at least a symbolic interpretation of
> something that the most secular-minded must allow to be
> true.[43]

Implicit in West's rejection of romanticism--at least of romanticism as a self-
sufficient guide--and her extolling of classicism and of the artist as a kind of
vessel of tradition, is a religious conviction that human beings can only
complete themselves by appealing to the spirit. Unlike Augustine, of course,
she has not worked out a theology; even as she embraces his determinism she
shies away from his doctrine, calling it only a "symbolic interpretation,"
making him once again not a law-giver but an artist and psychologist.

By 1933, Rebecca West had brought together her esthetics, politics,
and religious convictions. Using herself as subject in *The Strange Necessity*,

[42]"Rebecca West: A Worthy Legacy" (Ph.D. diss.: University of North Texas, 1989), 123.

[43]*Saint Augustine*, in *Rebecca West: A Celebration* (New York: Viking, 1977), 215.

and surrogates of herself in *A Letter to a Grandfather*, *Saint Augustine*, and *The Thinking Reed* (the novel she would soon begin to write), she was evolving an autobiographical, historical, and fictive vision, a kind of historiography of self and soul that she would stretch across the canvas of Central Europe she presents in *Black Lamb and Grey Falcon*, one of the masterworks of the twentieth century.

# CHAPTER FIVE

## 1933-1936

The impression persisted that West's marriage to Henry Andrews, her writing on Augustine, and her anti-Communism gave evidence of a creeping conservatism. Years later in *Heritage,* her son Anthony West's transparent fictional sendup of her career, she appeared as the actress Naomi Savage, who affects a rather snobbish manner when she marries the Colonel (Henry Andrews), who calls her by her family name Emily, just as Andrews took to calling his wife Cicily. Naomi even shakes hands differently after her marriage-- perfecting a frozen, dead hand when it is gripped--and she pronounces certain words differently--all in an effort to elevate her tone. Naomi virtually drops all of her theater friends, considering them too vulgar for her new life. The novel exaggerates, but it echoes Virginia Woolf's impression of West's "silkycareening society voice" at a dinner (December 13, 1932) with West and Andrews. A second encounter in July 1933 did not change Woolf's opinion of the "meticulous fish blooded cultivated Andrews-- Rebecca merely a hard painted woman, that night, living in society." Irene de Selincourt, an old friend, approached the "new" Rebecca West carefully:

> When you spoke at a drawing room meeting in my mother's house, on Woman's Suffrage, you were already Rebecca West then, and beginning to be famous, but of course I can scarcely be said to know R.W. at all. The person I knew was called Fairfield, and she wasn't famous, but only marked "different." I am told you don't like to remember those days, but I hope you can think of me without absolute nausea, for in an odd sort of way we were friends, and recognized each other, all raw and untried as we were.

But West did not forget her friends or her causes. She wrote a major essay on the Pankhursts in 1933, affirming their indispensable place in the history of Woman's Suffrage.[1] She also wrote for the conservative *Daily Telegraph*, it is true, but she often disagreed with its editorial line. She enjoyed working with her editor, Cyril Lakin, the "wisest boss I've ever had except you," she claimed to Irita Van Doren, her editor at the *Herald Tribune*. "God knows you need me, you little bunch of simpletons, not only to teach you about literature, but about life," she lectured Lakin. The *Telegraph* was wrong to attack Harold Laski, a professor at the London School of Economics and an influential political speaker and writer. He was not a Communist--some Left Wingers even considered him "poisonously Right." But she doubted Lakin would listen. "The strong point of the D.T. staff, as I have to confess to my friends, is its beauty. Just its beauty. Nothing else."[2]

By defending Laski, West honored her early pro-suffrage days. She had first seen Laski in 1912, when she was nineteen, at a conference on nonmilitant methods of attaining the vote. He stood up and took charge of the meeting, persuading the group to "cross the road from the hall where it was being held and convert itself into a raid on the House of Commons, which was one of the most militant forms of suffragist action conceivable." In 1929, she and Laski had been colleagues on *The Realist*, edited by George Catlin, Vera Brittain's husband, who had introduced her to Henry Andrews. Wells had also induced Laski and West to sponsor a proposed new world-wide organization, the Federation of Progressive Societies and Individuals.

---

[1]Anthony West, *Heritage* (New York: Random House, 1956); *The Diary of Virginia Woolf, Volume Four: 1931-1935*, ed. Anne Olivier Bell (New York: Harcourt Brace Jovanovich, 1982); Irene de Selincourt to RW, n.d.; on June 15, 1933 de Selincourt replied to a letter from West, remarking that she was grateful "not merely because it was such a very nice and friendly one but because you have really remained a human being!", Yale; "A Reed of Steel," reprinted in *The Young Rebecca*, ed. Jane Marcus (Bloomington: Indiana University Press), 243-62.

[2]RW to IVD, n.d., Irita Van Doren Collection, Library of Congress.

It aimed to formulate a "common creed among all left-wing movements in the world, centering on public ownership replacing private property, the creation of a world monetary system, treaties to control armament, vast educational initiatives, and guaranteed rights of free speech, publication and movement." Not surprisingly, the organization never materialized, but it is revealing that West remained comfortable in this kind of company.[3]

While remaining politically engaged, West continued work on a collection of short stories, *The Harsh Voice*, a novel, *The Thinking Reed*, and a play, *Goodbye Nicholas*, which is set in a villa near Cannes, during the period just after the 1929 crash. The play was true, West told Alexander Woollcott, "every incident, except the motivation of Nicholas."[4] An international financier, Nicholas is clearly modeled after Ivar Krueger (1880-1932) and Samuel Insull (1859-1938). Krueger, a Swedish industrialist and financier, emigrated to America, making a fortune in real estate and construction. He then established the United Swedish Match Company, which cornered three quarters of the world's match trade through a series of acquisitions and combinations. He lent vast sums to foreign governments, thus securing monopolies, but by 1931 he could not satisfy bank demands and committed suicide. Huge irregularities in his business practices were exposed after his death. Similarly, Insull, who began as Thomas Edison's secretary and became manager of his business interests, took control of Chicago's transit system (overcoming competing public utility companies) and through numerous mergers and interlocking directorates, established a three billion dollar utilities empire, which collapsed in 1932.

Such spectacular successes and failures, and the ability of individuals to manipulate and skew the world economy, suggested to many people,

---

[3]Isaac Kramnick and Barry Sherman, *Harold Laski: A Life on the Left* (New York: Allen Lane, 1993), 66, 263, 266.

[4]RW to AW, n.d., Houghton Library, Harvard University.

including West, that capitalism might be doomed, and that it had contrived a system so complicated that even the individuals who profited from it would inevitably become its victims. This is what Nicholas thinks. He has kept his financial empire alive by borrowing more than forty-five billion dollars and using it not to invest but to meet his payrolls and expenses. He has forged government bonds and lived in style, but he has decided to commit suicide and to expose his crookedness, believing that only his forthright confession will finally shock people out of their naive faith in capitalism and in business leaders and drive them to find a better economic system--one that is democratic and respects the rights of workers, giving them a "directer method of access to these goods."[5]

In New York City, Lawrence Langner of the Theatre Guild wanted to produce the play, but he immediately spotted the improbability of West's third act: "Finally, his suicide for the purpose of 'dealing an effective blow at the public's belief in me and my kind as miracle workers' does not seem worthy of a man of Nicholas's astuteness. People are going on doing exactly the same thing at this moment after the death of Krueger, after the exposure of Insull." Over more than two years West revised the play. She gave Clarissa (Nicholas's lover) a stronger voice (she had gushed over Nicholas in the first draft and passively accepted his suicide). "If one's a real woman one knows there's something queer in men that makes them want to spoil things"-- responds Clarissa, echoing a sentiment West would soon explore in her novel, *The Thinking Reed*. Clarissa rejects Nicholas's claim that his suicide will be a lesson, arguing that it is merely a symptom of a world "in love with pain and death." West introduced more dialogue and added a character in the final scene--casting about for ways to enliven and interrupt Nicholas's turgid speeches. She also practiced a sleight of hand by emphasizing his moral position--his desire to expose himself as a crook--rather than the probability

---

[5]Manuscript versions of the play (some of which are unpaginated) are at Tulsa.

that his suicide would actually effect change. The play became his elegy--how a brilliant man, an aviator tortured by his bombing of civilians, who turned to business as a redemptory activity and then found he was still destroying humanity. For his main business partner is a German, a Nazi who believes the world hates and conspires against Germany, and who announces: "we have kept our integrity of soul, we have not betrayed the idea of Nordic domination, we still aspire to drive out the Jews."

Even with improvements in the third act, West never rectified the faults Langner succinctly summarized: the play was diffuse, too much of a tract on the evils of capitalism, with not enough character development, and too much discussion of ideas.[6] But the play is a valuable comment on the kind of hero West valued, a thinking reed, noble because of his effort to contemplate his defeat. In *The Thinking Reed*, Marc Sallafranque would be her most convincing example of the male capitalist as flawed hero, a type she had been trying to realize for more than a decade.[7]

At the beginning of the play, Nicholas's friends virtually worship him. He is seen not merely as a financier, but as a man who "puts things right." He hypnotizes the world with his personality. He is thought to be straight with people. Yet he has apparently abandoned Clarissa, his mistress, who is *chic* but not tidy. Compared to her he is elegant; he is said to take the sloppiness out of life. A mystified Clarissa senses he still loves her, yet he has been seen with another woman, who is quite coarse and obviously beneath him. An angry Clarissa spouts off about how all men are devils, but then she cannot seem to help herself in idealizing Nicholas's good points. It puzzles

---

[6]LL to RW, June 2, 1993, Yale.

[7]Both Nicholas and Marc suit the epigraph from Pascal that West appended to her novel: "Man is but a reed, the most feeble thing in nature; but he is a thinking reed. The entire universe need not arm itself to crush him. A vapour, a drop of water suffices to kill him. But, if the universe were to crush him, man would be still more noble than that which killed him, because he knows that he dies and what the advantage is which the universe has over him."

her that he makes love to her even after he has been seen with the other woman. His confusing behavior and Clarissa's response to it mirror the Beaverbrook-West drama in her letters. As passionate as West, Clarissa wants to kill Nicholas, yet she won't let him go because she persists in believing there must be some point to his actions that she has missed. All is revealed, of course, in the trite third act, when Clarissa learns that Nicholas has wanted to spare her from dealing directly with his suicide.

Clarissa receives in the play what West never got in life from her lovers: a full explanation. There has been a reason for Nicholas's meanness and for his humiliation of Clarissa. He is a man who has gained power but not lost his humanity. He is, in short, everything West wanted Beaverbrook to be. He is, in a phrase West used for Richard Yaverland a "king of the world." Indeed, the structural failure of *Goodbye, Nicholas* is reminiscent of *The Judge* and evocative of West's powerful doubts and her search for faith. She might as well have ended the play by proclaiming "The King is Dead. Long Live the King!"

If modern capitalism is treated as tragedy in *Goodbye, Nicholas*, it is treated as farce in *The Modern Rake's Progress* (1934), a satirical volume produced in collaboration with illustrator David Low.[8] His drawings are a takeoff on Hogarth, whose etchings show the undoing of a young man who succumbs to the vices of his age. Low's satire is lighter than Hogarth's moral exemplum. West complements his purpose admirably, confecting an amusing fable of Young George, a "lesser scion" of an ancient family which had "foredoomed itself to poverty through imprudence" (13). He is suddenly removed from his obscurity as a clerk by inheriting the fortune of an American

---

[8]*The Modern Rake's Progress* (London: Hutchinson, 1934). Page numbers for subsequent quotations will be cited in the text within parentheses. An earlier venture with Low, *Lions and Lambs* (London: Hutchinson, 1928), was a curiously inert performance for her. Its portraits of prominent figures like Beaverbrook lack her usual sparkle.

relation, shot dead in a gunfight between bootleggers and hijackers while motoring on the outskirts of Chicago. Hailed by the press as a new celebrity, George finds himself dealing with "puzzling beings, who demand the secrets of his private life as confidently as the mendicant friars of old used to demand alms." Accustoming himself to this new status, he changes his "clerkish white collar and blue suit" for a "sizzling shirt" and "pyrotechnic sports suit" (17).

West worked into the story all she had learned about being a celebrity. George finds he must employ an interior decorator, buy a Picasso--even though the picture looks to him like the "entrails of a locomotive"--consort with "surly young geniuses," and fawning "lovelies" (17-18). This is an age which "too much in a hurry to develop discrimination, puts a magnifying glass over personalities just to get something to interest it" (26). This kind of social criticism is tossed off so effortlessly that it careens along just as rapidly as George's rise and fall in high society.

George becomes a film investor and engages in the primitive rituals of producers: "They feel that if professions of energy and power and ambition are made before they start a film, it will certainly be a super film. Even so do natives in need of rain beat tom-toms and blow on strange instruments to provoke a storm" (34). His money goes out, but he fails to see a negotiable product. "Of more than the Rake's money may we ask what happens to the rain that falls into the sea, since the sea seems no fuller," West concludes (37).

George's next mistake is becoming a promoter of English heavyweights, who "as time goes on, prove themselves descendants of Wordsworth's Lucy; boxers whom there are none to praise and very few to love" (43). George adores the comradeship of promoters, who are "constantly performing rituals in celebration of friendship." But when he adopts cigar smoking, the favorite activity of a dominating personality, "it seems only a matter of time before it starts smoking George" (45). He loses a pile on his protege, knocked out and lying still on the canvas, a "descendant of Wordsworth's Lucy. No motion has

112

he now, no force; he neither hears nor sees; rolled round in earth's diurnal course, with rocks and stones, and trees. And oh! the difference, the financial difference to George!" (47)

Each of the twelve chapters of *A Modern Rake's Progress* charts the ever hopeful and bedazzled George as he visits night clubs, buys a racing stable and frequents the track, contracts a stylish but loveless marriage, divorces, gambles at casinos, is ruined by investing in a sure-fire product that will replace expensive shoe leather, and loses his friends and his suite at the Hotel Magnificent. He "finds his level" in the last episode, on the dole, trying to explain to the poor why their "labour and leisure are so slightly rewarded." It is so that enough will be left over for the elite who can "develop themselves to perfection" (125).

Although George is a fool, his society is corrupt; it capitalizes on the working classes. West was still enough of a socialist to indict the system as rigged, even while she admired the tenacity of capitalists, such as Sam Hartley in "The Abiding Vision," the fourth and last story in her collection, *The Harsh Voice*. Just when he is about to be destroyed by a congressional committee investigating his companies, he resurrects himself with the ringing phrase: "I am an American and I took risks (239). Walking out on the congressional committee, he becomes an overnight sensation on the strength of press reports. What saves Sam from becoming merely the cruel engine of an economic system seems to be the power of love--the devotion of both his wife and his mistress, who admire him for his manly risk-taking.

West deemed her four short stories in *The Harsh Voice* "a complete guide to the relationship of the sexes."[9] They also demonstrate how her work stands right at the crossroads of predestination and the unconscious. In "The Salt of the Earth," (the third story in *The Harsh Voice*) she assails Alice Pemberton, an interfering, cruel burden to her family, friends, and household

[9]RW to Winifred Macleod, postmarked May 23, 1934, AM.

staff. Always ready to offer advice and to criticize, she is entirely blind to the devastation she wreaks, even when her long-suffering, compassionate husband patiently points out how she has alienated everyone. Alice is forty, but she has the looks and temperament of a wilful child who insists on her own way. Her brother and sister can no longer bear her visits. Her husband Jimmy has lost business because of her. Yet it is Alice who is always finding everyone else "rather vulgar, and ordering them about, as if their destiny is in her hands. Jimmy acknowledges that her intentions have been good, but in effect she tries to "find out what people live by, and you kill it." Her response to Jimmy is that of a "pitiful child," for she is incapable of recognizing her demoralizing impact on others. When Jimmy regretfully points out Alice's faults to her, she accuses him of malignity: "Your lips are full, but you hold them so that they're thin - it's a cruel mouth." A surprised Jimmy replies: "Is it? . . . It may be. It's hard to tell about oneself. I think I hate it when I have to be cruel, but maybe I don't. Probably one never gets into a position when one's forced to do something unless one really wants to do it" (172-73).

Alice's own glimmerings of truth are the dreams that disturb her otherwise placid view of her rectitude: something horrible is approaching her, circling her, and closing in to kill her. It is a premonition of her own poisoning, a self-inflicted truth. "Can't you stop it?" Jimmy asks. "No," she answers, "I have to go on doing the very things that bring it nearer." Jimmy's conclusion joins the determinism of Augustine and Freud: "God, what a life this is . . . full of presciences that don't do us any good, full of self-consciousness that tortures us by telling us what sort of hole we're in but never how to get out of it. It's nothing to cling on to, really" (182-83). The evocation of Alice's moral imbecility and brutality is so effective that the story's improbable ending--Jimmy's poisoning of Alice so that she can no longer torment her family, household, and community--is a relief, an act of mercy to Alice, her family, her household, and community.

Alice would hardly seem a fitting alter ego for West, yet both the author and her character shared an apocalyptic foreboding. As West confided to novelist Fannie Hurst:

> There *is* something going after me with an axe. You know it. You know damn well that nobody you know is so completely excluded from all normal human relationships, that nobody you know has had such unprovoked contacts with madness and cruelty. I know what to think. I'm going to get on with my life, but I'm going to face facts.[10]

The reviewers' praise and reservations suggest why *The Harsh Voice* fails to achieve the highest form of art as West defines it in *The Strange Necessity*. Edith H. Walton notes the "smooth high glaze, a competence of construction, reminiscent of Somerset Maugham." But the style has a brittleness and "occasional meretriciousness." The stories are "contrived for a maximum dramatic effect." For example, in "There is No Conversation" the reasons for the narrator's obsession with the lives of the American businesswoman and the French aristocrat are withheld for a "twist ending" that violates the story's integrity, making the reader exclaim "how clever," not "how tragic." That Walton should use the word tragic is uncanny, for it is precisely the word West would have employed against fiction that forces feelings rather than allowing the tragic nature of human misunderstanding to reveal itself. "There is No Conversation" delivers a shock, as in the game of *boules* analogy she constructs in order to condemn factitious art in *The Strange Necessity*. The adjustments of her fiction are not automatic and organic; instead they call attention to themselves. "We are aware of the teller of the tale more than we should be," Harold Orel observes.[11]

If "The Salt of the Earth" surpasses the other stories, it is because "its trickiness and ingenuity are apparent from the start," Walton concludes. It

---

[10] RW to FH, n.d., Texas.

[11] *New York Times*, February 3, 1935, Yale clipping file; Orel, 145.

generates its own fascination as "one gleefully assents to the murder" of Alice Pemberton, though whether a woman could be as completely blind to the hatred her "busybody benevolence" engenders seemed improbable to Robert Lynd.[12] To accept Alice Pemberton's complete lack of self-consciousness is to accept a diminished, a melodramatic view of human character. To see people in such stark terms is emotionally satisfying, but it does not make for the greatest art. Lynd questions the endings of the stories, suggesting West "deserted human nature for psychological theory," but like John Collier, he finds the stories "vastly enjoyable." The truth is that they have the verve of the second-rate; they are engines of enjoyment, propelled by plots that Collier perceptively notes are "almost too efficient." As Edith Walton concludes, West knows how to keep the pot boiling. Like her letters, her stories seethe with conflict and tension. *The Harsh Voice* proved popular. By late January 1935, West's agent, A.D. Peters, reported that almost ten thousand copies had been sold. It encouraged her publisher, Jonathan Cape, to hope that she could be built up "as an author, rather than as a writer of scattered books."[13]

West could have followed up the popular success of *The Harsh Voice* with her novel, *The Thinking Reed*, well under way by the end of 1934. But when the novel proved recalcitrant, she embarked on a trip to report on Washington, D.C. and the New Deal. West's articles and private letters about her American sojourn seem to confute each other. In public, she was complimentary or at least tactful about the New Deal. In private, she excoriated it. In *The New York Times*, she confined herself to a foreign visitor's point of view, pointing out the differences between Washington and other political capitals such as London, Paris, or Berlin, where governments immersed

---

[12]*News Chronicle*, January 11, 1935; *The Daily Telegraph*, January 15, 1935, Yale clipping file.

[13]ADP to RW, January 25, 1935; Rupert Hart-Davis to ADP, February 20, 1935, Texas.

themselves in the normal functions of the city and its populace. Washington, on the other hand, was a "closed cell of a city," where political personalities burgeoned and had an "endless capacity to amuse." Indeed, the place made "personality grow so lushly that the principles involved are buried like Mayan palaces in tropical forests." Style predominated--she would forget a politician's point, seduced by his oratorical gestures and body language. She admired Franklin Roosevelt's "fine, suave yet vigorous American manners." On Mrs. Roosevelt, she lavished tributes, lauding her "uncontrived charm in the eagerness with which she hurls herself at good works. . . . She goes well with the White House, so full of light and air and grace."

In her role as observer/fact-finder, West did not find "agreement on a common policy and philosophy which one expects from the same administration. . . . I found New Dealers who professed fundamentally different political theories, and even some who seemed to profess different political theories with different parts of their brains." The same official could sound like a "hard-shelled" Tory--saying men on relief should feel ashamed so that they would be driven back to work--and like the "voice of inexpert socialism," claiming that the government could afford any plan of relief because the country was so rich. These incongruities, however, seemed unified by the official's "charm, energy and idealism." She concluded by proclaiming the New Deal the "most hopeful administration to be found in the world today."[14]

But would it work? To her husband, she described Washington as a mess: "a more incompetent administration can never have been seen on earth. Good is being done by letting socialworkers tackle obvious jobs that would have been tackled here long ago had it not been such a vast country - but -!" Andrews should be glad he was not with her: "You would find the New Deal

---

[14]May 12, 1935, 3, 20.

insupportable & you would find the old hard-shelled Republicans just as bad."[15]

That West sounded more negative in private than in public is not surprising. In earlier trips her forthright criticism had been met with extreme hostility and been regarded as English snobbery. (Her articles on the New Deal in England were much more critical.)[16] Then, too, she used letters to vent extreme feelings and to sharpen the edges of her critical mind. Writing for publication in America restrained West and forced her to focus with a more objective lens. After all, she had an audience of thousands to attract-- quite a different thing from her diatribes to a husband or a friend. Finally, she loved America, and she was loyal. Whatever her misgivings about New Dealers, she would treat them publicly in a genial manner.

The American trip and a tour of France in 1935 gave West the impetus to complete her novel, *The Thinking Reed*. It would reflect, in part, her sense of a European crisis. In one of her best essays, "The Necessity and Grandeur of the International Ideal," she pointed out that since the war Europe had behaved like a person "shattered by a traumatic experience: capricious, distracted, given to violence towards the self and others, careless of their environment, and incapable of carrying on a normal constructive life." Fascism had appealed to infantile emotions, the quest for an ideal childhood, in which the dictator as "all-powerful father" provided protection and provision. Organizing the state on "nursery lines" gave many people a "degree of emotional satisfaction far greater than they would receive from participation in political activities, and puts them in an exalted state, comparable to that of young persons in love, when the merest trifles seem of tremendous and

---

[15]RW to HA, May 3, 1935, Yale.

[16]See, for example, "The New Deal, Part III," *Time and Tide*, September 7, 1935, 1268-69.

delicious significance." In normal times, would people take such satisfaction in the fact that the trains ran on time in Fascist countries?[17]

In *The Thinking Reed*, West was determined the explore the psychology of an infantilized world she deemed bent on destruction. It is an international novel about the marriage of a young, wealthy American of French descent to a French-Jewish automobile manufacturer. In her book on Henry James, West had complained that he had not given his heroine, Isabel Archer, the moral intelligence of an adult. Or as the American poet, Louise Bogan, put it: "Rebecca gets very mad at him because his young girls try to act as though they were suitable creatures for marriage, and had never heard of Mary Wollstonecraft."[18] In Isabelle Terry, West sets out to right James and to rewrite *The Portrait of a Lady*.

Isabelle, who has studied at the Sorbonne, has a "competent steely mind." But since her aviator husband's death she has found herself involved in an affair with Andre de Verviers, who likes to make passionate scenes. He has made her the "slave of everything she hated:  impulse, destruction, unreason, even screaming hysteria."[19] Isabelle regretfully detects a masochistic streak in herself, one that is akin to Sunflower's. In order to free herself from Andre, she stages a violent scene, making a public spectacle of herself grinding his flowers into the ground, and thus convincing him that she will be more dangerous than his game-playing can tolerate. Unfortunately, this disgusting incident is witnessed by the fastidious Lawrence Vernon; he immediately drops his courtship of Isabelle, who he had planned to marry.

"To cover her humiliation she accepts the offer of marriage of Marc Sallafranque . . . a clown possessed of industrial genius, a charming disposi-

---

[17]*Challenge of Death*, ed. Storm Jameson (New York: Dutton, 1935), 241-60.

[18]*What the Woman Lived: Selected Letters of Louise Bogan* (New York: Harcourt, Brace, Jovanovich, 1973), 21.

[19]*The Thinking Reed* (New York: Viking, 1936), 5.

tion, a grotesque appearance, and no self-control."[20]  The words are from West's synopsis, and they reveal how strongly the plot is suffused with her own biography. Isabelle (honored not only with the name James gave to his heroine but with that of West's mother) is extraordinarily intelligent, manipulative, and fragile. Another novelist might not have made Lawrence Vernon's rejection of Isabelle quite such a humiliating experience, but for West the very keenness of her heroine's sensibility must mean that she feels mortified. Marc has an exaggerated version of Henry Andrews's physical oddity (West called her husband "the Elk"), and though Andrews did not gamble in casinos as Marc does, he exhibited a recklessness with money and an eccentricity that spelled doom to West as Marc's does to Isabelle. Marc's grotesque, clownish, undisciplined, but warm and acute personality both appeals to and appalls Isabelle. He embodies the contradictory aspects of males who have both built and destroyed civilizations.

Isabelle tends to project her animosity onto others, blaming them for the poor position she finds herself in. After she accepts Marc's proposal at the restaurant where she has just dined with Lawrence Vernon, she suggests that she and Marc announce their engagement to him: "They went out on the terrace, Marc's fingers opening and closing on her wrist, to the man who had brought this on her" (65). Isabelle is also hostile to Marc, especially when she finds that much of their life is taken up with rich, idle people she despises. Writing to a friend about the reviews of *The Thinking Reed*, West commented: "very few people have seen what a hymn of hate against the rich it is."[21]

Isabelle learns to love Marc, for he is devoted to her and elicits from her a tenderness and concern for him that she frankly did not feel when he proposed to her. He shows no trace of the sadism she has come to expect in men, "only tenderness and pity" (139). With Marc at hand, Isabelle is able to

---

[20]"The Novelist's Dilemma," Tulsa.

[21]RW to Doris Stevens, n.d., Yale.

see her "priggish and censorious" nature (220). He helps Isabelle recover the purpose of her life, just as Andrews helped West--which she acknowledged by dedicating the novel to him. Nevertheless, the female must watch over the male: Isabelle tries to keep Marc away from the gaming tables, where his huge losses have jeopardized his relationship with the government which helped to establish his business after the war. Because Marc has not handled his workers very well (there have been labor disputes and strikes), any public action that compromises him is likely to lead to his losing control of his factory.

Isabelle and Marc seem to lose their way among the trifling rich, who "treat life so that it would never form any pattern, to rub down each phenomenon till it became indistinguishable from all others of its kind" (89). As in her baffling attraction to Andre de Verviers, she finds it "odd that she and Marc should find themselves among such ridiculous people" (193). Marc has known only the discipline of his work as an industrialist; outside of that he is immune to criticism and unable to see the consequences of his imprudence. He is sulky and nihilistic: "This damned life, it makes us all the same" (260), he complains to Isabelle.

To save him from a night at the gaming tables that she is sure will ruin his career, Isabelle stages a violent scene, screaming at Marc in the casino, accusing him of infidelity and fainting. In the event, she does reclaim Marc's sensible side, but at the price of losing her child. Her miscarriage, she reflects, "formed part of a society that was itself a miscarriage, that had not cohered into a culture or civilization, that could not cohere into the simplest sort of pattern" (327). This lacerating self-criticism, joined to Isabelle's understanding of the world at large, is what West had found lacking in James's not quite adult Isabel.

*The Thinking Reed* is a dramatization of the world that West deplores in "The Necessity and Grandeur of the International Ideal." It is a world she knew firsthand--as she revealed a few years later to Irita Van Doren, when she wrote a letter of introduction for a young friend:

> partially intelligent - but politically vicious - pro-Franco, pro-Fascist ... typical of a world you may not see in America - the plutocratic international. She is quarter-Viennese, quarter-Serbian, half-English (or Irish. I can't remember which). Her sister (another beauty) is married to one of the leading young Fascists - the Boss of Florence. All over Europe people like her, physically magnificent, fundamentally decent in instinct, quite mentally efficient, utterly undisciplined and uneducated, are running about staying in each other's lovely houses, marrying each other, behaving in time of crisis with superb courage, and bitching things beyond belief.[22]

"I do not for one moment put Isabelle and Marc as admirable people," West notes, but they deserve respect, she might have added, because of their ability to think--however fitfully.[23]

Isabelle almost loses this ability after her miscarriage. She blames Marc for the loss of her child. She even requests a divorce, supposing that a more fastidious man--the bland, second-rate artist, Alan Fielding--would suit her better. But when she sees Alan's bad paintings, from which (he acknowledges) something is missing, she returns home to Marc, realizing that her hatred of him has been sheer self-indulgence: "I got the maximum sensation out of hurting Marc ... I gave way to that impulse without restraint, because I am a rich woman and have never been disciplined" (407). As West puts it in her synopsis, Isabelle "reflects that the tiresomeness in the male has something to do with his power, that Marc's violence has something to do with his industrial genius, and that power and genius are what a woman wants in a man."[24]

---

[22]RW to IVD, n.d., Irita Van Doren Papers, Library of Congress.

[23]"The Novelist's Dilemma," Tulsa.

[24]Ibid.

At the end of *The Thinking Reed*, Isabelle tells Marc: "I want to think of you as being better than I am in every way." She is immediately taken aback by her avowal, admitting

> that sounds abject, but it is not. I want to feel that way about you not because you are a man and I am a woman, but because you are you and I am I. If we were different people and I were really better than you, I should be quite content to think it, it should be possible for a wife to feel that her husband is not superior to her and for the marriage to be all right. (413)

Marc protests the compliment, alleging that Isabelle is superior to him and can no more see it than she can see her whole face. "I have often thought in loving you I love a woman of whom you have never heard, of whom you have not the slightest idea, who is nevertheless entirely real" (415).

Neither husband nor wife is entirely convinced of the other's feelings. If Isabelle's reconciliation with Marc is complete, it is nonetheless one between enemies--as men must necessarily be to women, Isabelle believes. Like West, she has finally found rest with a man after ricocheting from her other lovers, but she cannot help thinking about what Marc has "done to me." Resignation more than celebration mark Isabelle's attitude: "Had you not better learn to put up with men, since there is no third sex here on earth? Or have you made arrangements for travelling to some other planet where there is a greater variety?" (420) The novel's final two sentences unify West's vision of the male and the female, the personal and the public, the individual and society:

> It struck her that the difference between men and women is the rock on which civilization will split before it can reach any goal that could justify its expenditure of effort. She knew also that her life would not be tolerable if he were not always there to crush gently her smooth hands with his strong fingers.

As West explained to her publisher Harold Guinzberg in late November 1935, the ending of the novel had given her trouble. She had completed a draft in September, but she had put it aside as "dead." A month later she came back to it and saw what she needed to do--scrap the "starry-eyed and holding hands" scene in favor of a more sober, more seasoned conclusion. Now she was convinced she had it right.[25]

Elizabeth Bowen called *The Thinking Reed* a "classic novel [with] almost no imperfections . . . It is impossible to think beyond it." The distinguished American poet and critic, John Crowe Ransom, said the novel was "perfect in a form so rare that hundreds of efforts must fail in order that one may be successful." *Time* considered it "among the best novels in the short memory of man." Reviewers saw *The Thinking Reed* as a comedy of manners with a sharp satirical edge. They admired the sensuous evocations of Paris, Antibes, Le Touquet, and her figures of speech--both concise and extravagant. Malcolm Cowley cited the description of Isabelle's face, which had the "pasteurized look of a wealthy orphan," and the description of the gold-digging Poots, who has a habit of drooping her eyelids in an expression that "made her face look like an unmade bed." Nearly all critics acclaimed West's gallery of minor characters, especially Aunt Agatha, Alan Fielding's formidable relative to whom he and everyone else abase themselves.[26]

This extraordinary critical success, plus handsome advertisements announcing "Rebecca West's first novel in seven years," should have encouraged her to write more fiction, for it could be viewed as solidifying her reputation as a novelist. Yet she continued to be dogged by charges that she was more of a critic than a novelist, and that *The Thinking Reed* was actually more of an essay than a novel. Louis Kronenberger, one of her most thoughtful readers, suggested that even the most brilliant and climactic scene in the novel--the dinner party at Le Touquet followed by a night at the Casino--was "at once unreal and overreal, at once too theatrical and too

---

[25]RW to HG, November 26, 1935, Viking.

[26]*New Statesman and Nation*, April 11, 1936, 571; *Southern Review* 2 (1936):399-418; *Time*, March 9, 1936, 79; *The New Republic*, March 11, 1936, 142.

intellectual--the same scene that enthralls us as spectators dissatisfies us as thinking beings." What it amounted to was a "fabulous amount of melodrama."[27]

Other mixed reviews are symptomatic of Rebecca West's problematic place as a novelist. Few reviewers or even her later critics have taken sufficient cognizance of her effort to write novels--each one quite different from the other--which do not easily situate themselves in the English and American tradition. Her brief against James was that he had not been enough of a critic, and that there should be a way to combine what was called essay and novel writing in one form. The French had found it in Proust, and she was exploring his form in *The Thinking Reed*, making both her characters' mentalities and their social scene her subject. Malcolm Cowley came closest to recognizing her ambition by singling out a passage concerning Poots, whom West called in a short essay, "The Novelist's Dilemma," the "crystallization of a lifetime's hatred." But Cowley's introduction of the passage, saying it is an example of the novel's "wise and picturesque generalities," does not do justice to Rebecca West's unification of the social and the psychological:

> [Poots] had the voice which had been fashionable among Englishwomen for some years, a tired and timbreless gabble which made a curious claim to sense, which pretended that though the speaker was late, or in debt, or taken in adultery, it was the very contrary of her fault, since she had been besieged by people inferior to herself, who had urged upon her a delay so great, a financial policy so extravagant, a sexual habit so profuse, that the lesser figure of her actual fault made it appear by contrast a virtue, or at least an unusually practical and restrained way of dealing with the situation. (178)

The Proustian length of her sentences makes extraordinary demands on the reader, but that is because the clauses are like so many layers of social observation the writer must both summon and analyze. The long sentence

---

[27]*The New York Times Book Review*, March 8, 1936,

captures a complex of societal forces working through an individual. In such sentences, the West who writes to Irita van Doren about her Fascist friend, the West who writes essays on the international ideal, and the West who fashions stories that are social comedies, combine to make the highest art. The content of this particular sentence on Poots shows how a class of people can refuse to take responsibility for their own actions. It demonstrates a political sensibility of genius, which can argue not only ideas but can show how, on a daily basis, people can deny the consequences of their own actions and still live quite well, free and clear of any obligation to rectify their own chaos.

# CHAPTER SIX

## 1936-1941

After *The Thinking Reed*, West did not publish another novel for twenty years. She did not stop thinking of herself as a novelist, and she began a new novel in 1941, but journalism beckoned because the "world was changing. Heavens how quickly, how dramatically, how drastically . . . Can you blame me if I ran about the world watching it cast its old skin and put on the new?" she asked her readers. But this traveling troubled her. She would return home with the "pressing conviction that quite soon people would not read novels because human beings would have forgotten how to read, as part of a general amnesia that would leave them with no memories except perhaps the technique for shooting arrows."

The world was going to hell. Moreover, her faith in fiction weakened when it "took a turn which I could not approve." It seemed on its way to obsolescence to her. Except for *Orlando*, she found most of Virginia's Woolf's work "painted with gentility; a clutch at intellectual privilege on the ground of specially delicate perceptions." Of course, there were novelists she admired--such as Henry Green--but they did not have a lasting influence, and the environment for her kind of fiction seemed forbidding.

In her youth, she had looked forward to writing "novel after novel."[1] But in her case, novels did not come easily, since each one had to be a

---

[1] "The Novelist's Voice," BBC Broadcast transcript, September 14, 1976, Tulsa.

product of an imagination that yoked history and psychology, the individual and society--not an easy union to achieve or to understand, as the writing and critical reception of *The Thinking Reed* proved.

In the spring of 1936, West accepted an invitation from the British Council to lecture in Yugoslavia. She had just abandoned a projected book on Finland, a "beautiful example of a small nation threatened by the great powers" struggling for independence.[2] The grammar and pronunciation of Finnish had defeated her. Serbo-Croatian, though a difficult language, yielded to her dogged study, though she would never become fluent in the language and traveled the country with a dictionary in her lap. More importantly, she discovered in Yugoslavia the source of everything that had driven her to become a writer. In March 1937, she would return to the country with Henry Andrews, and again alone in the spring of 1938--each time expanding her notion of the travel book, *Black Lamb and Grey Falcon*, that would work an irrevocable change in her life and career.

When the book appeared in America (1941) and in England (1942), it was addressed to a world at war. Indeed, West's four-year labor on *Black Lamb and Grey Falcon* occurred as she despaired over the Western democracies refusal to check the spread of fascism and her certainty that war was inevitable. She had argued against the pacifists in England throughout the 1930s, giving her support to the Spanish Republic when it was attacked by Franco.[3] Her husband had lost his job at Schroders when he refused to support the firm's collaboration with Nazi policies, and he had risked his life

---

[2]Autobiographical fragment, Yale.

[3]When Ralph Bates, West's colleague at *Time and Tide*, and a supporter of the Spanish Republic, needed money for an American lecture tour on behalf of the Republic's propaganda ministry, West paid his fare. Bates was far left of her in his politics but that did not prevent her from supporting his work or refusing his offer to repay her. It was her gift to the cause. Interview with Ralph Bates. See also Carl Rollyson, *Rebecca West: A Life* (New York: Scribner, 1996), 186-87.

to spirit Jews out of Germany. As one of West's friends put it, "Henry Andrews was a sort of Scarlet Pimpernel."[4]

By mid-March 1938, West had become convinced that the English government had a made a secret deal with Hitler "of the most drastic nature." Confirming her suspicions with Lady Rhondda, the editor of *Time and Tide*, and others, West reported her fears to Alexander Woollcott: the war scare was real enough. She was not being "hysterical"--at least not on her own. "London last week was the most frightened city I've ever lived in. Damned unpleasant," Agnes de Mille, a West confidant, wrote to her mother on March 29.[5] West realized immediately that the Munich agreement in late September had been a sell-out to Hitler.[6] Only England's stalwart defense against German air attacks lifted her spirits, for it showed a greatness the reminded her of the Elizabethans.[7]

But would anyone read a book about Yugoslavia while the war was everyone's central focus? West worried that she would have no readers for a tome of over one thousand printed pages about a land few people in Europe or America had visited or thought important. She knew that she would have to write a dramatic narrative and a spiritual autobiography demonstrating that the personal, the political, the historical, and the contemporary, fused in the record of a journey not only through a specific country but through the sensibility of the western world. *Black Lamb and*

---

[4]Interview with Fleur Cowles. The Scarlet Pimpernel is a character in Baroness Orcyzy's famous novel by the same title. He is an Englishman who rescues innocent victims of the Reign of Terror in Paris. He is an ingenious man and master of disguises. The mild mannered but courageous Henry Andrews made an excellent agent who also reported to the English government on his observation of the German aircraft industry during his many visits to Germany in the 1930s. See Rollyson, 196.

[5]RW to AW, March 14, 1938, Houghton Library, Harvard University; Agnes de Mille to her mother, Sophia Smith Collection, Smith College.

[6]For West's antipacifism and her reaction to Munich, Rollyson, 185-86, 195-96.

[7]RW to Alexander Woollcott, May 22, 1940, HH.

*Grey Falcon* is an exemplification of what West calls "process"--the mind's ability to think through the stages by which it comes to know itself and the world, the process that she first essayed in *The Strange Necessity*.

In bold capitals, the dedication of *Black Lamb and Grey Falcon* reminds West's readers in 1941 that Yugoslavia no longer existed and that the people she wrote about had lost their freedom.

> TO MY FRIENDS IN YUGOSLAVIA,
> WHO ARE NOW ALL DEAD OR ENSLAVED
>
> Grant to them the Fatherland of their desire,
> and make them again citizens of Paradise.

The German invasion had instantly made her travel book into a work of history, the recovery of the past. Her dedication sounded the book's nostalgic note, emphasizing her sense of loss and yearning to recapture a golden age, which had made these people "citizens of Paradise." Their journey was also her's; writing about Yugoslavia meant writing about herself, a writer who constantly sought her own heaven on earth.

### Prologue

The prologue to *Black Lamb and Grey Falcon* begins with a brief scene: West is raising herself on her elbow and calling to Henry Andrews through the open door into the other wagon-lit:

> My dear, I know I have inconvenienced you terribly by making you take your holiday now, and I know you did not really want to come to Yugoslavia at all. But when you get there you will see why it was so important that we should make this journey and that we should make it now, at Easter. It will all be quite clear, once we are in Yugoslavia.[8]

There is no reply to her reassuring words because her husband has gone to sleep. It is "perhaps as well" West remarks, for she "could not have gone on to justify my certainty that this train was taking us to a land where everything

---

[8](New York: Viking, 1986), 1. Page numbers for subsequent quotations will be cited in the text within parentheses.

was comprehensible, where the mode of life was so honest that it put an end to perplexity" (1). That she should feel this way is amazing to West, since this is 1937, she had visited Yugoslavia for the first time the year before, and she had spoken the country's name for the first time only two and a half years ago, on October 9, 1934.

*Black Lamb and Grey Falcon* begins like a 1930's movie. A wife asks her husband (her reluctant audience) to humor her; she is polite and solicitous, but also slightly guilty about hauling him off on a trip at an awkward time. That he has fallen asleep is not treated just as a little joke but as an opportunity for West to think through her motivations. What is this "land where everything was comprehensible"? It is paradise, of course. But human beings are such that they might easily sleep through it, miss it entirely--as West herself did until her journey to Yugoslavia in 1936. But to explain her sudden awakening, she must shift to an even earlier moment, which brings her to the third paragraph of her prologue--another scene, this time in a London nursing home.

In the first two paragraphs, West builds a mood of suspense, of mild humor, and of curiosity--not unlike what is found in a Hitchcock film.[9] Yugoslavia has made its appeal precisely because it is not familiar; it will take a good deal of explanation to get the point of this exotic locale. Each stage of her feelings will be explored by delving further and further into the past and then reeling it back into the present. As in *The Strange Necessity*, West's model for this looping back in time in order to advance the action is Proust. Her prologue is comparable to his "overture" in *Remembrance of Things Past*, in which his method, themes, and characters are encapsulated.

On October 9, 1934, West had been in a nursing home, getting prepared for an operation. The doctor assured her that "it would be all quite

---

[9] This opening is also a more accessible version of her first paragraphs in *The Strange Necessity*.

easy," but her unconscious, "a shocking old fool, envisages surgery as it was in the Stone Age, and I had been very much afraid. I rebuked myself for not having observed that the universe was becoming beneficent at a great rate" (2). Readers of the whole of *Black Lamb and Grey Falcon* can recognize the irony of this scene, for it is the book's mission to show that the universe is not "becoming beneficent at a great rate," and that, indeed, the settled, complacent, English view of history is largely an illusion.

Recovering from her operation West hears that King Alexander of Yugoslavia has been assassinated in the streets of Marseilles. She imagines the worst will happen--war and the loss of her husband and son. She attributes her fears to the "archaic outlook of the unconscious," but, again, the phrase is ironic, because it is precisely the unconscious that alerts her to the imminence of a world war, in which everyone will find themselves through aerial bombing in the "breachless unity of scrambled eggs" (2)

It is characteristic of her book's style that it interweaves characters, dramatic scenes, dialogue, description, reportage, literary criticism, philosophical, theological, and feminist analysis with mundane metaphors; her insights are grounded in everyday reality and in the colloquial as much as they are in art history and figurative language. Her book has been used as a travel guide; it is also a primer on how to take the modern world. She provides an account of civilization and its discontents. The book might seem tiresome and pretentious if it were not punctuated by story after story, reflecting on the teller and the told. Some of the stories tell against West, and she is not afraid to reveal her most deep-seated prejudices, but there are so many stories--enough for a thousand and one nights--that no opinion she offers should be viewed in isolation, no thesis of hers need mar her novel of history. She writes, in short, a self-correcting masterpiece.

No sooner is the King of Yugoslavia's assassination announced than she remarks: "We had passed into another phase of the mystery we are enacting on earth" (2). This religious statement (reminiscent of *A Letter to a Grandfather*) cuts across her rational, modern, scientific views; it does not negate them, but it qualifies the idea of progress and that everything will be "quite easy."

West's nurse is at a loss to understand her patient's agitation. Why trouble herself with the King of Yugoslavia, the nurse wants to know, if he is not personally known to her? The nurse is an "idiot," a word that comes from a Greek root meaning private person. Idiocy, West claims, is "the female defect," the penchant of women to absorb themselves in private lives untouched by history. It is the reverse of the male defect, lunacy; men are "so obsessed by public affairs that they see the world as by moonlight, which shows the outline of every object but not the details indicative of their nature." West tries to explain to the nurse: "Assassinations lead to other things." She is thinking of the beginning of World War I, but also of a childhood memory. She is five and looking up at her mother and cousin, standing side by side looking down at a newspaper on a table in a "circle of gaslight, the folds in their white pouched blouses and long black skirts kept as still by their consternation as if they were carved in stone" (3) West is describing the dawn of her historical consciousness in this pre-modern era, explaining how at the earliest possible age she became aware that what happens elsewhere also happens here, at home, immobilizing her family, who were reading about the assassination of Elizabeth, the Empress of Austria.

The descriptions of the womens' clothes, their posture, and the gaslight all serve to emphasize the particulars of the past, which is, in one sense, irrecoverable; but the recreation of detail is so vivid that the past seems present; indeed it has made the present, as West will later say in her book of history.

Elizabeth's death heralds the death of the Austro-Hungarian Empire, which perishes in World War I; her demise is one of the seals on the fate of Europe; it signals a century of warfare. For Elizabeth is the last Habsburg who might have solved the "problem of the Slav populations under Habsburg rule," the last imperialist to work for the autonomy and self-government of the Empire's subject peoples, and to show some understanding of the Slavs, "a people quarrelsome, courageous, artistic, intellectual, and profoundly perplexing" (4) History is presented as a tragic Shakespearean family drama, with the Slavs figuring as a noble house divided against itself and dominated by one aggressor after another.

Elizabeth's is the first of hundreds of biographies in *Black Lamb and Grey Falcon*, each presented with passion and commitment, as though West were describing members of her own family. Indeed, Elizabeth is thwarted by the Archduchess Sophie: "She was the kind of woman whom men respect for no other reason than that she is lethal, whom a male committee will appoint to the post of hospital matron" (5). West speaks of the "blunt muzzle" of Sophie's stupidity, using animal metaphors recalling her rejection of her own odious Aunt Sophie (6).[10] The Habsburg Emperor Franz Josef, is treated like the privileged yet incompetent males West rails against in *Family Memories* (56-94). He is obstinate and lacking in imagination, one of those old men who mismanages his business so that "it falls to pieces as soon as he dies." Yet people say, "Ah, So-and-so was a marvel! He kept things together so long as he was alive, and look what happens now he has gone!" (10) What makes *Black Lamb and Grey Falcon* such an engaging book is that you are made to feel that there is no scene, no character, without an equivalent in your own time and family.

Nevertheless, history is something that happens to us without our knowing it. We are like Eliot's patient etherized on a table. Or as West puts it, under an anesthetic "I was cut about and felt nothing, but it could not annul the consequences. The pain came afterwards," West says of her surgery (14). The historical pain comes in the form not only of Elizabeth's assassina-

---

[10]For West's memories of her bossy, condescending Aunt Sophie, see Rollyson, 28; see also *Family Memories*, ed. Faith Evans (New York: Viking, 1988), 5. Page numbers for subsequent quotations will be cited in the text within parentheses.

tion, but in the mysterious death of her son Rudolph, and the assassination of King Alexander--the collapse of a chain of personalities who might have contributed to the solution of the Slav problem, which unresolved led to World War I.

West repeatedly watches a film of King Alexander's assassination, and she is struck by his "immense nobility" and how it gives the lie to the epithet "Balkan," meaning a savage, unstable, ungovernable person, a barbarian. The death of such men has left no buffer between the Austrians ("violence in imperialist form") and Fascists ("violence in totalitarian form" [21].

How the world has come to such a sorry pass is the theme of *Black Lamb and Grey Falcon*. Quoting the words from Pascal that she had used for *The Thinking Reed*, West suggests that "we must learn to know the nature of the advantage which the universe has over us, which in my case seems to lie in the Balkan peninsula" (22). To understand the history of what has become Yugoslavia is to understand the forces of history. This cannot be done in England, as she makes clear in a dialogue with her husband at the end of her prologue:

> "Is it so wonderful there?" he asked. "It is more wonderful than I can tell you," I answered. "But how?" he said. I could not tell him at all clearly. I said, "Well, there is everything there. Except what we have. But that seems very little." "Do you mean that the English have very little," he asked, "or the whole of the West?" "The whole of the West, I said, "here too." . . . I stumbled on, "Really, we are not as rich in the West as we think we are." (22-23)

West is hard put to explain because she has had what amounts to a religious experience and words simply will not do. One definition of paradise is surely a place where "there is everything there. Except what we have."

### Journey

**Journey** continues the opening scene on the train. Surrounded by Germans, West confesses she cannot understand them. She admires their conviviality with themselves and with strangers--something not permitted to the formal English--but they are chauvinistic and contemptuous of Yugoslavia, refusing to believe her praise of the land, its people, its art, and its cuisine. They are at once extraordinarily aggressive about things German and curiously meek and passive in so far as taking control of their own lives. One man complains of the Nazis and the "unforeseeable taxes" they have imposed on businesses like his. "They were all of them falling to pieces under the emotional and intellectual strain laid on them by their Government, poor Laocoons strangled by red tape," West concludes. Her image of totalitarian torture is arresting. In *Laocoon*, the Hellenistic sculptor portrays a magnificently muscled, powerful priest twisting in torment, attacked by two serpents, entwining themselves also about his two sons. "The young people, they are solid for Hitler. For them all is done," the German businessman says (32).

Because Germans lack a historical sense, of how change occurs over time, they seem fated, like Laocoon, to suffer. As West says of the German businessman, "he seemed quite unused to regarding anything that the state did as having a cause or any but the most immediate effect" (34). It horrifies her to think that there are sixty millions like this man in the center of Europe, passive and with a "special talent for obedience" (37). Approaching her first stop in Yugoslavia, Zagreb, West notices a young man running along the train platform calling out to his beloved, "Anna! Anna! Anna!" It is raining, but he does not use his umbrella. Because he holds it at arm's length West concludes he has brought it for Anna. He does not lose hope when he cannot find her in the long train; he trots a third time looking for her. It is the sight of this persistent, loving man, out in the "strong spears of the driving rain," that provokes West to conclude: "I was among people I could understand" (38).

### Croatia

Constantine, the Belgrade press bureau representative of the Yugoslav government, (Stanislav Vinaver) greets West and her husband on the train platform in Zagreb, the capital of Croatia.[11]  He is an extraordinary intellectual and sensualist who becomes nearly a mythic figure whose head resembles the "best-known satyr in the Louvre" (41). West lauds his nobility, great physical courage, and dedication to the idea of a unified kingdom of South Slavs (Serbs, Slovenes, and Croats), which is the only way to resist the continual pressure of the Italy and Germany to the West and of Bulgaria to the East.

Constantine is accompanied by two colleagues--Valetta, a young Croat poet who opposes the central government in Belgrade and favors an autonomous Croatia, and Gregorievitch, a revolutionary who has fought to free Croatia from the Hungarians. Valetta complains about the corruption in Belgrade and the wasteful building up of that capital while Croatia languishes. The only tyranny he knows is the tyranny of Serbian Belgrade. Thirty years older than Valetta, Gregorievitch has endured "poverty and imprisonment and exile" during the tyranny of the Austro-Hungarian Empire, which suppressed the Croatian language and Croatian aspirations toward self-government. He has been inspired by the Serbs, who have freed themselves from foreign oppressors and have a history of self-government. To him, uniting with his Slav brothers in Serbia is the "Kingdom of Heaven on earth," and Valetta is "quite simply a traitor" (42).

Different in appearance, in age, in politics, Constantine, Valetta, and Gregorievitch argue constantly. They embody the shaky structure of the Yugoslavia born out of the death of the Austro-Hungarian Empire. Yet, as West observes, they are all Slavs; they are "all the same." A door opens, and all three men "twitch and swivel their heads" in the same way. "These enemies advance on each other" moving to the same tempo (43). She has again detected the tragedy of a family drama working itself out across several

---

[11]Constantine is based on Stanislav Vinaver, a poet and Yugoslav government official. See Rollyson, 178-80, 187-91, 207, 213.

generations, overlapping and yet distinct from each other, so that even the ten years that separate the older Gregorievitch from Constantine make for different political perceptions.

It is to West's credit that she plays these argumentative scenes against her anti-Croatian bias. To be fair, she finds much to admire in the mobile and sensitive faces of Croatia's "cultivated townspeople" (47) and in what her husband excitedly calls "this raging polyglot intellectual curiosity" (63). She examines carefully Bishop Strossmayer's biography--"one of the most beautiful lives in modern history," her husband remarks. Strossmayer "risked every-thing" to wrest the Croatian people from the Austro-Hungarian Empire while working against anti-Austrian and Hungarian feeling, opposing anti-Semitism, and working to reconcile the Roman Catholic and Eastern Orthodox Churches, which divide between them the loyalties of the Croats and the Serbs (109). But West is troubled by the German influence that, she alleges, has corrupted indigenous traditions; the poorly designed handwork and peasant dresses are greatly inferior to what she had found in her earlier trip to other parts of Yugoslavia. Although she cites instances of Croat resistance to the Germans, her history emphasizes Croat collaboration, "a burning, inde-structible devotion to the Habsburgs" (52) Even when the Croats fight to save the Habsburgs during the revolution of 1848, defeating a Hungarian army marching on Vienna, the Habsburgs deny Croatian demands for autonomy and make them subject to the central government. Later, to placate Hungary and to establish a dual monarchy, the Habsburgs negotiate a deal which delivers the Croats as chattels to the Hungarians. In a characteristic aside, West says these transactions have a "kind of lowness that is sometimes exhibited in the sexual affairs of very vulgar and shameless people: a man leaves his wife and induces a girl to become his mistress, then is reconciled to his wife and to please her exposes the girl to some public humiliation" (54).

Croatia is the girl who has never grown up. The Croats have been extraordinary soldiers, courageous and enduring, yet they have been treated like jilted mistresses and the victims of impotent lovers, "never summoned to command or been given any opportunity for success or failure." The trouble with Croatia, West concludes, is that its history has no form; there is no art to it. "If one's existence has no form, if its events do not come handily to mind and disclose their significance, we feel about ourselves as if we were reading a bad book" (55). Such comments can be read not merely as historical analysis but as autobiography. For West, events had to cohere; in her glummest moments when she could not make sense of her own life, she acted as though it had been a bad book. What she sought, as she moved away from Croatia and toward the South and the East, was redemption, a reading of history, of lives and biographies, that would justify human suffering. This is her hope; this is her elation, though at periodic intervals she checks herself with sober pronouncements, the first one coming after a few days in Croatia: "It is not comfortable to be an inhabitant of this globe" (50). Such universal statements are constantly at war with her feeling that she has found in Yugoslavia an "intensity of feeling," an "immense and exhilarating force," that stems from "whole belief," a spirituality that will work her salvation (58).

In the village of Shestine, she does catch a glimpse of what she is seeking. On their heads women wore red handkerchiefs "printed with yellow leaves and peacocks' feathers, their jackets were solidly embroidered with flowers, and under their white skirts were thick red or white woolen stockings." Similarly, the men sported sheepskin leather jackets with "applique designs in dyed leathers, linen shirts and fronts embroidered in cross-stitch and fastened with buttons of Maria Theresa dollars or lumps of turquoise matrix, and homespun trousers gathered into elaborate boots." Their singing in church is as splendid as their clothing, and such a contrast to Western church music "almost commonly petitioning and infantile, a sentiment cozening for remedy against sickness or misfortune, combined with a masochist enjoyment in the malady." Here the service is a rejoicing, and singing is simply to be adored for its own sake. People think "not what they might ask for but what they might give. To be among them was like seeing an orchard laden with apples or a field of ripe wheat, endowed with a human will and using it in accordance with its own richness" (64-65).

It is a divided congregation--men on the right, women on the left:

> At a ceremony which sets out to be the most intense of all contacts with reality, men and women, who see totally different aspects of reality, might as well stand apart. It is inappropriate for them to be mixed as in the unit of the family, where men and women attempt with such notorious difficulty to share their views of reality for social purposes. (65)

This is the first of many scenes in which West will explore what men and women mean to each other, and whether this should be the same in all places and at all times.

### Dalmatia

From Zagreb, inland and close to Germany, West and her husband travel south to Dalmatia, along the Adriatic coast. This is one of the great battlegrounds of Balkan history, territory that has changed hands repeatedly over hundreds of years. She finds many angry and volatile Dalmatian men: "In such a shambles a man had to shout and rage to survive" (119). Dalmatia's periods of stability have been brief and rare, as in the colonial administration of Napoleon's Marshal Marmont. Its natives, such as the Uskoks, a stalwart people of military genius, are eventually corrupted through constant warfare and become pirates. Both Italy and Austria have degraded this beautiful area with their imperial intrusions. "It is sometimes very hard to tell the difference between history and the smell of skunk," West concludes, employing pungent expressions to show how paradise has been perverted (127).

Approaching the isle of Rab she is blissfully overcome with the scent of myrtle, rosemary, and thyme--as "soothing a delight as sunshine." One of the most "beautiful cities in the world," it is set on a ridge overlooking a harbor. Depending on the time of day, the stones of Rab seem silver, rose and golden, blue and lilac, the different colors determined by the quality of light reflecting off the underlying whiteness. Dominated by four campaniles, situated in perfect relationship with each other and the city, Rab's "horizontal oblong with four smaller vertical oblongs rising from it," form an equation that Euclid could not have fashioned more simply (129).

The point of such descriptions, beyond the sheer delight conveyed by a traveler to travelers, is that here is a world that is intact and meant to be self-governing, "a focus of culture, a fantasy made by man when he could do more with his head and hands than is absolutely necessary for survival" (130). Closely examining one of the campaniles her husband details how it is perfectly divided along Euclidean lines and exclaims:

> How did the man who built this tower seven hundred years ago know that these severe shapes would affect my eyes as a chime of joy-bells would affect my ear? He must have been a man of incredible cunning to make this stony promise of a fluid world, this geometric revelation of a universe in which there is not an angle. (132)

One of Henry Andrews's functions in West's epic tragedy is to act as her chorus.

Rab is a crucial stop because it exemplifies the spirit of the Slavs who resisted the Ottoman Turks. "These people of Dalmatia gave the bread out of their mouths to save us of Western Europe from Islam," West asserts (137). Her quarrel is not merely with history but with her contemporaries, for behind this statement is her anger at those who think the Nazis are not worth fighting--not even to prevent an invasion of Britain.

Dalmatia is ancient. West finds in Split Roman facades and portals similar to what she has seen near her flat in Portman Square--her way of linking the English with a people they would just as soon forget, let alone defend. She spends pages on Diocletion and his rule in Dalmatia in the days when the Western Roman Empire was beginning to crumble. One of her grandest characters, Diocletion is comparable to Hegel's world historical individuals, a man she suspects of killing himself with poison, having judged the empire ungovernable. "There is no denying the horrible nature of our human destiny" (148) she concludes, in a statement calculated to shock and alarm her English audience, which has "an unhistoric attitude" (153).

In Dalmatia, events of hundreds of years ago define the present and are felt to be part of it. In England, "every generation has felt excitement over a clear-cut historical novelty, which has given it enough to tell its children and grandchildren without drawing on its father's and grandfathers' tales." In Dalmatia, history has not changed since the Roman occupation; in fact, the history of Dalmatia is the history of occupation. Imagine, West urges, "if the last clear-cut event in English history had been the departure of the Roman legionnaires in 420," followed by hundreds of years of invasion and internal disorder. Diocletion's reforms had been the last effort to "restore the earth." The people of Dalmatia have looked upon every other effort to govern as tyranny, so it is no wonder that "their instinct is to brace themselves against any central authority as if it were the enemy." To them this is not "petulant barbarism" but self-preservation (153).

An imminent world war provokes West's apocalyptic rhetoric. Diocletion does not merely reform government; he attempts to "restore the earth," for she is writing an allegory of her own age, which can be seen more clearly in cities like Split than in what she calls "our diffuse Western towns" (160). It is this apocalyptic mode that accounts for the shifts between light and dark in her narrative. Not surprisingly, she is fascinated with the Manichean influence in Dalmatia, calling it "an extremely useful conception of life"--the idea that the world and human beings are made up of light and dark elements, good and evil (172). It is a good allegory, for it explains much about history and human behavior: Napoleon before 1806--a figure of light, actually interested in reforming the world; Napoleon after 1806--largely a tyrant who would not supply Marmont, his man in Dalmatia, with the resources to govern wisely and humanely the Slavs he had come to love.

This extraordinarily romantic view threatens to overwhelm the book's authority as history, a conspicuous example of West's psychologizing of everything until it takes on the sheen of her histrionic self. Approaching Korchula, she praises it for its Balkan quality of visibility; it represents what she had promised her husband, that he would *see* the world much clearer in Yugoslavia. On the spot, however, she has a moment of doubt; perhaps it won't seem quite so beautiful as she had supposed. Arriving there, however, she announces confidently that she was "perfectly right about Korchula." To which her husband responds: "And let that be enough for you. . . As for your other demands that from now on every day will be an apocalyptic revelation, I should drop that, if I were you. You might not like it even if you got it" (203). One of her husband's functions in *Black Lamb and Grey Falcon* is to serve as her disputant.

Andrews represents, among other things, the rational, level-headed Englishman. Often his reservations, questions, and arguments clarify even as they take issue not only with West but also with Constantine and other Slavs. By constantly referring to Andrews as "my husband" she emphasizes their marriage as a union of opposites. When she is tired, he announces he will sit and look at their maps, for he is "much given to that masculine form of auto-hypnosis" (203). It is a dig but a tolerant, even amused one. Emotionally and intellectually, they are quite different yet compatible. He argues in principle for empires and central adminstrations--admitting their corruption and inhumanity but also contending they are often necessary in regions where diverse peoples simply cannot federate among themselves. She argues in principle against empires because they subjugate the genius of individual peoples while conceding many specific instances where empires have done good, established sound laws, and reconciled warring peoples to each other.

Husband and wife play in different keys, reversing the major and minor chords of each other's arguments.

Nowhere is this clearer than in Dubrovnik, an exquisitely beautiful city (her husband points out) that West refuses to admire. Why? Because in her view it embodies the "worst of England" (231). As an independent republic Dubrovnik thrived on a policy of appeasement; she detests its "readiness to rub along" with the Turks, its shunning of the Orthodox Church (246). It is too beautiful to allow her to use the word skunk, so she settles for saying that its stratagems evoke a "smell not of the rose" (247). This somewhat awkward, indirect phrase, aptly captures her condemnation of appeasers, who sidle out of conflicts and commitments.

"But the Republic worked . . . you cannot deny that the Republic worked," Andrews protests (267). Yes, but at the cost of denying its own Slavic nature, which rests on a faith that there will be a Messiah, that human suffering will be redeemed, West replies. What she really detests, he suggests, is that those in power have to exercise it as though they are infallible. Perhaps no one can rule without the presumption that "he knows all that is to be known, and therefore cannot make any grave mistake." West would have it, then, that governors admit they are inferior to those whom they govern, "for it is the truth that we are not yet acquainted with reality and should spend our lives in search of it." Of course, this is the meaning of her journey. "But perhaps you cannot get people to take the responsibility of exercising power unless you persuade the community to flatter them," says her husband. The argument continues with no resolution, except for Andrews's last words, which have the effect of resuming the journey: "I think, my dear, that you hate Dubrovnik because it poses so many questions that neither you nor anybody else can answer" (268).

### Herzegovina

The argument between West and her husband reaches a crescendo in their visit to Herzegovina. Without the Austrian Empire, he argues, the

Turks could not have been defeated. Certainly, West rejoins, but afterwards Austria wasn't needed. She is forgetting the Russians, he points out. Who would be afraid of a "rotten state"? she asks. "That, oddly enough, is something that no nation ever knows about another," he notes, giving examples of how nations have repeatedly misinterpreted each other's preparedness for war. (His statement seems even sounder since the collapse of the Soviet Union.) "But how absurd the behaviour of nations!" West exclaims. They don't know the simplest things that individuals must know if they are to survive. This is, of course, Andrews's point; nations do not act and should not be judged like individuals. "I suppose that I was being, in my female way, an idiot, an excessively private person, like the nurse in the clinic" West concedes. But she cannot resist having the last word: "But it is just to admit that my husband was indulging his male bent in regard to international affairs, and was being a lunatic" (281). In other words, if one looks only at the outlines of events, of how power politics functions, one completely loses sight of the inhumanity, the monstrousness of international relations.

There has been a tendency to read these dialogues between husband and wife--and the emphatic statements West makes about men and women--in isolation from the narrative of *Black Lamb and Grey Falcon*. Yet the baldness of her propositions is constantly clothed in a much more sophisticated and evenhanded language, which suggests that in the dialogues West is creating herself as a character with sentiments that do not always square with her narrator-self. Because *Black Lamb and Grey Falcon* is both novel and history, both fact and imagination, her own voice shifts between the emotional, opinionated person she is and the history she writes. She constantly reminds us she is a woman with all the prejudices of her time and of her family and cultural background, but she is also a historian capable of rising above them. Thus after arguing with her husband, she reviews Napoleon's career, and reaches a conclusion that transcends their quarrel and her character's voice: "Yet without doubt he was a genius till the turn of the century. It would seem that empire degrades those it uplifts as much as those it holds down in subjection" (284).

Herzegovina is on West's itinerary because it is an introduction to those Slavs who "have so often suffered a real degradation under their Turkish masters." Slavs who have not been held down in subjection find it difficult to comprehend this enslavement, and it is one reason why modern Yugoslavia has had trouble cohering as a state. West puts the problem in the form of an analogy (one of her favorite ploys), showing how what appears to be exotic is not actually so when conceived in terms of English geography: "It is as if the North and East of England and the South Coast were as they are now, and the rest of our country was inhabited by people who had been ground down for centuries by a foreign oppressor to the level of the poor white trash of the southern states or South Africa" (274).

The Turks, who are so often villainized in *Black Lamb and Grey Falcon*, receive some acknowledgement here for building beautiful towns and villages. West admires the bridge in Mostar as an example of "medieval Turkish workmanship. It is one of the most beautiful bridges in the world. A slender arch lies between two round towers, its parapet bent in a shallow angle in the centre" (288). It speaks to the cruel relevance of her book that this bridge, which was not destroyed in the Second World War, has been shelled into oblivion in the recent war.

"Here in Mostar the really adventurous part of our journey began," West announces. Here she finds the true individualists, who think and speak without the conformity she sees in people walking to work over London Bridge. Mostar faces reveal thoughts that are "never fully shared, of scepticism and satire and lyricism that felt no deed to have been yet finally judged." The "smallest village, or, in a town, a suburb or even a street, can have its own fantasy of costume" (289-90).

Yet even here, her Manichean and restless feminist spirit strains against the traditional Mostar costume which engulfs and hobbles women. It consists of a black or blue man's coat much too large for a woman, cut with a stiff military collar, eight to ten inches in height, embroidered on the inside with gold thread. When a woman pulls the huge coat over herself, the collar projects forward like a visor, hiding her face like a veil. With sleeves that hang loose or are stitched up, and a skirt that trails on the ground, she is virtually swallowed up.

West reads this clothing as a work of art, a dream, a fantasy of culture. It playfully emphasizes the contrast between heaviness and lightness, between coarseness and fragility, between what breaks and what might be broken but is instead preserved and cherished, for the sake of tenderness and joy. It makes man and woman seem as father and daughter. The little girl is wearing her father's coat and laughs at him from the depths of it, she pretends it is a magic garment and that she is invisible and can hide from him. Its dimensions favour this fantasy. This empathic response to the traditional arrangements of society gives way to suspicion and rebellion as she sees how the clothing presents the female also in a more sinister light: as the male sees her when he fears her. The dark visor gives her the beak of a bird of prey, and the flash of gold thread within the collar suggests private and ensnaring delights. A torch is put to those fires of the imagination which need for fuel dreams of pain, annihilation, and pleasure. Veiling women perpetuates man's "league with death," fomenting his special hatred for the "instrument of birth." On the frontiers of paradise, West cannot help ending her section on Herzegovina with a troubled vision of its women. Even as they are "hastening toward secret and luxurious and humorous love-making, they hint of a general surrender to mortality, a futile attempt of the living to renounce life" (292).

## Bosnia

West compares the fate of Bosnia to a woman who resists by yielding. She allows herself to be occupied by a man, seems pliant to his requests, and yet reserves an uncompromising individuality that he cannot conquer. This is to state baldly what she takes hundreds of words to elaborate in one of her most fascinating psychological analogies. The facts she is interpreting, on the other hand, can be stated in a sentence: "The heretic Bosnian nobles surrendered their country to the Turks in exchange for freedom to keep their religion and their lands, but they were aware that these people were their enemies" (302). It is the visceral sense of history she captures when she declares that Sarajevo was "plump in insubordination," when she gives the sultans and viziers a plaintive voice: "But when did we conquer these people? Alas, how can we have thought we had conquered these people? What would we do not to have conquered these people?" The Turk is unappeased; the Slav is "never subject, not even to himself," she concludes (304-06).

"Extremely tall and sinewy," Bosnian males appear to her as manic, black Highlanders: "Their darkness flashes and their cheekbones are high and their moustaches are long over fierce lips." In dark, heavily braided, homespun jackets, crimson belts and headgear, "they seem to clang with belligerence as if they wore armour." They are a throwback to the Middle Ages, dashing knights, but in homespun that suggests the Wild West as well (327).[12]

*Black Lamb and Grey Falcon* is a pastoral, a yearning for an idealized past, where men were men and women were women--West actually uses a variant of this phrase, which has alarmed certain feminist readers, who deplore what they regard as her abasement before men. They fret over what seems to be an endorsement of a traditional society, a flouting of West's own early feminism. Yet there is nothing in her book that suggests men are the superior sex. She does admire Bosnian men extravagantly, and she does not

---

[12]In *Family Memories*, 174, West traces her father's ancestry back to a German or Wendish Serb, "a member of a Slav enclave in East Germany. . . His genes must have been powerful, for my father was strongly Slav in appearance with high cheekbones and bright eyes. When, as a middle-aged woman, I went to Bosnia, I was amazed to see my father walking down every town and village, but the resemblance was not perfect: my father was well-made but not tall, and the Bosnians were a giant people."

discount the virtues she sees in this pre-modern environment, but she is not advocating it for the modern world. She is suggesting, however, that the modern world has lost certain things and become confused in its quest for equality between the sexes, and that we would do well to understand how it is that men and women of the past reached an understanding about their roles vis a vis each other and society. In this respect, she is doing what the pastoral has always done, critiquing the present by honoring the past--in the process simplifying that past in order to make a point. Here she is writing not so much history as polemics; if *Black Lamb and Grey Falcon* were put into verse, no one would have difficulty recognizing it for the pastoral poem it is.

West's pastoral is more than a myth, however, because it is held together by reportage. She does not forget her feminism, but she describes a setting entirely different from early twentieth-century industrial England. Her Bosnian women are just as responsible as the men are for creating their traditional world. In fact, to West the women look "heroes rather than heroines, they are raw-boned and their beauty is blocked out too roughly. But I will eat my hat if these women were not free in the spirit." They are not passive types; on the contrary they are as "handsome and sinewy" as their men. They do not look oppressed; they seem happy. They have wit, they guffaw, and jeer. She finds a female "Voltaire of this world," alert to its peculiarities and amusements, voluble, critical, and satiric. None of these women can read, and they lose very little by it, West insists--a shocking attitude for a feminist? Perhaps, although she evinces a wonderful lack of sentimentality, refusing to smugly suppose that what she knows, what the West has, would benefit these women. For better and worse, it is a self-contained, fully functioning world--not the kind of world Rebecca West or any modern feminist would care to inhabit, but one that Rebecca West does not choose to impose upon or to use for a lamentation that it is not more like her own. As she puts it, "these women were their own artists and had done well with their material" (327-29). She pays them the respect of not condescending to them. Of course, they form a fiction of her own making--we may wonder if these women are as content with their own lives as West surmises--but *Black Lamb and Grey Falcon* has already established the fallible, problematic aspects of her vision in her debates with her husband. The very life of the book inheres in this Arabian tension between the teller and the told.

Even more controversial today is West's suspicion that as a way of preserving their spiritual freedom these women have pretended to an inferiority to men in certain matters. (This ruse is parallel to the feminine one she claims the Bosnian nobility perpetrated on the Turks.) Her argument is that in such a society men may need to feel superior by claiming certain activities as exclusively their own. With more than a little sarcastic humor she supposes the male ego is fragile and needs this kind of bolstering. She acknowledges that the women are taking an enormous risk, because their deference to men includes "an abnegation of economic and civil rights." No such bargain can be made in the modern industrialized world, "for it can hold good only where there are no other factors except the quality of women threatening the self-confidence of men." If modern women were to withdraw entirely from the male sphere of work, for example, it would not guarantee that men would be restored to their "primitive power," because the insecurity of employment built into the economic system would not change. It troubles her that even in a traditional society women would have to practice fraud; they win only her qualified approval: "Still in this world of compromises, honour is due to one so far successful that it produces these grimly happy heroes, these women who stride and laugh, obeying the instructions of their own nature and not masculine prescription" (330).

The centerpiece of **Bosnia** is West's treatment of the assassination of the Archduke Franz Ferdinand, which became the pretext for Austria's declaration of war on Serbia, and the beginning of the First World War. His visit to Sarajevo on St. Vitus's Day (June 28, 1914) confirms her sense that men desire death as much as life. It is perverse that he should visit on a day of "immense significance to the South Slav people" (343). This feast day of a saint is also a day of mourning, for it commemorates the defeat at Kossovo in 1389, when the Serbs lost their kingdom to the Turks. In 1914, it was, as well, a day of pride, for the Serbs had defeated the Turks in 1912, and Franz Ferdinand would have to know that his presence--accompanied by Austrian military maneuvers--would be taken as a provocation to a people "seething with revolt."

Any account of this section of *Black Lamb and Grey Falcon* would be hard put do justice to the psychological intricacy of West's approach--her magnificent exploration of Franz Ferdinand's biography and that of his assassin, Gavrilo Princep, a young Bosnian. She portrays Franz Ferdinand as a repulsive creature, a devotee of death, who makes his hunting forays, for example, into killing grounds of mass extermination. Yet his morganatic marriage to a woman who was deemed unworthy of the Habsburgs elicits West's sympathy because of the couple's devotion to each other: "their natures must certainly have been to some degree beautiful" (346). She believes he is human after all; still he chooses death over life. Princep, on the other hand, is portrayed as a very young, even bumbling assassin, filled with the rage she has seen in the behavior of many young Bosnians who detest the tyranny of the Habsburgs and yearn to be united with their brothers in Serbia. His terrible deed is no isolated act. West quotes Franz Ferdinand's dying words: "Sophie, Sophie, live for our children!" Then she addresses him directly, as though they were on the same historical stage: "So was your life and my life mortally wounded, but so was not the life of the Bosnians, who were indeed restored to life by this act of death." This is Shakespearean drama, this yoking of the private and public, the husband and wife and their assassin, with West putting herself at the center of the action, for it is her conceit that these events in Sarajevo shook the whole world, undoubtedly making her life different from what it would otherwise have been. What

Princep has attacked is the representative of "a society which adored death, which found joy in contemplating the death of beasts, the death of souls in a rigid social system, the death of peoples under an oppressive empire" (350)

West is at pains to show that Princep is not a fanatic: "He never made a remark throughout the trial that was not sensible and broadminded" (376). He endures the brutal treatment of a long imprisonment--he dies from neglect of his medical condition--with tranquility. Indeed, he is presented as the saint of St. Vitus's Day, celebrated in religious language: "He offered himself fully to each event in order that he might learn in full what revelation it had to make about the nature of the universe" (378) This echo of Pascal fuses with West's paean to the Slavs, who do not shirk suffering, who take their dose of reality without an anesthetic.

The assassination she terms the Sarajevo *attentat* is "mysterious as history is mysterious, as life is mysterious." A "complete deed," it has the virtue of freeing a people from the "inertia we all feel in the universe, the resistance life puts up against the human will, particularly if that is making any special effort." Like so many seemingly vast generalizations in *Black Lamb and Grey Falcon*, this one is anchored in the narrative, for West has just shown how many of Princep's colleagues ran away and botched their own opportunities to kill Franz Ferdinand. Princep himself had failed on his first try and lost his nerve. West is well aware of how this glorifying of a murder must appear to her contemporaries:

> I write of a mystery. For that is the way the deed appears to me, and to all Westerners. But to those who look at it on the soil where it was committed and to the lands east of that, it seems a holy act of liberation; and among such people are those whom the West would have to admit are wise and civilized. (381)

She can neither dissociate herself from the assassination nor completely accept it, emphasizing both the otherness of the culture she interprets and its links to her own.

The Sarajevo *attentat* becomes "an apt symbol of life: which is loose and purposeless, which weaves a close pattern and doggedly pursues its ends, which is unpredictable and illogical, which follows a straight line from cause to effect, which is bad, which is good." It is a mystery because, West concludes:

> the sum will not add up. . . . The soul should choose life. But when the Bosnians chose life, and murdered Franz Ferdinand, they chose death for the French and Germans and English, and if the French and Germans and English had been able to choose life they would have chosen death for the Bosnians. (381-82)

Informing this statement is her rueful reading of the reports of nineteenth century English travelers who praised the Austrians and Turks for civilizing unruly Slavs.

### Serbia

Part of the extraordinary length of *Black Lamb and Grey Falcon* is attributable to West's conviction that the West has never given the Balkans a good look. It has lauded the Habsburgs because it has not been willing to recognize the humanity of the Slavs. Gerda, Constantine's stout middle-aged German wife, who has joined them for their tour of Serbia and Macedonia, comes to personify the worst aspects of Western ethnocentrism. She is a sloven so far as her understanding of history is concerned and shows it in her appearance: fair, abundant, but formless hair and light, grey eyes that "look almost blind, vacant niches made to house enthusiasms" (457-58). She stocks her mind not with what she sees, but with what she wants to believe. In her grand manner, Gerda dismisses everything about the Slavs. In her vehement detestation of Jews, and in her constant clashes with West and Andrews whenever they admire anything Slavic, she reveals herself to be no better than a Nazi--even though her husband is part-Jewish. Indeed, Constantine encourages her expressions of contempt by playing the comical Jew, a stage

154

stereotype who amazes West because it is so at odds with the urbane poet of her first Yugoslav trip.

West's petulance often shows through in her portrait of Gerda, who is rarely given redeeming qualities. It is one aspect of the book that troubled her American publisher and some critics. To Marshall Best, her editor at Viking, she replied that she was "staggered" at his criticism, for she had "toned down" Gerda, who was all too typical of the German and Austrian attitude toward Slavs. To Harold Guinzberg, Andrews acknowledged the criticism as "an important one," but he did not promise any substantial revisions. "The fact is that what is recorded did truly take place," no matter how "grotesque" it might seem. Indeed, the marriage of Constantine and Gerda, of a Jewish writer to an anti-Semite, bears a striking resemblance to the story of Franz Werful and Alma Mahler. Gerda's real name was Elsa Silex, and she was the sister of Karl Silex, "now well known as a Nazi journalist," Rebecca revealed to critic Clifton Fadiman.[13] The issue, however, may be regarded not merely as historical, but esthetic. Some readers have simply tired of West's systematic demolition of Gerda.

In **Serbia**, West is moving toward the heart of the Balkans, showing why for her it has become a metaphor of history itself. She describes how against extraordinary odds Serbia destroyed the Ottoman Empire in the Second Balkan War (1912) and achieved its dream of independence, which she treats as a work of art, a quest for form, composed by Serbs over centuries of struggle against the aggressor: "the poem had completed itself." Overwhelmed in the First World War by a German fortified Bulgarian army, "it was now necessary for the country to die." The religious overtones, the dirge of tragedy is unmistakable in one of her most moving passages describing the slow, agonizing Serbian retreat, "fighting a rearguard action,

[13]RW to MB, May 8, 1941; HA to HG, May 8, 1941; Viking; RW to CF, November 10, 1941, courtesy of CF.

leaving the civil population, that is to say their parents, wives, and children, in the night of an oppression that they knew to be frightful." Out of the monasteries monks come following the soldiers, "carrying on bullock-carts, and on their shoulders where the roads were too bad, the coffined bodies of the medieval Serbian kings, the sacred Nemanyas, which must not be defiled." They also transport the rheumatic King Peter, paralyzed by the autumn cold, and Prince Alexander, recovering from an appendectomy "packed in bandages wound close as a shroud, and put in a stretcher and carried in the procession of the troops. It is like some fantastic detail in a Byzantine fresco, improbable, nearly impossible, yet a valid symbol of a truth, that a country, which was about to die should bear with it on its journey to death, its kings, living and dead, all prostrate, immobile" (584-85). How is it possible that this magnificent canvas of a civilization, complete in a paragraph, has never been filmed? It constitutes only one of the many moments in *Black Lamb and Grey Falcon* in which history appears whole, emerging in this case out of her rapt rehearsings of the Obrenovitch and Karageorgevitch dynasties.

With the poem "now written" (587) with Yugoslavia established as a state after the First World War, West recounts the noble yet terribly flawed effort of King Alexander to unite the Croats, Slavs, and Slovenes. A superb diplomat, he is nevertheless inept in dealing with his own people and with contentious political parties. He eventually declares a dictatorship, punishing several prominent politicians with jail terms. Yet his assassination is not treated as the end of a tyrant but as a mortal blow against a kingdom, which has struggled to realize itself, however imperfectly. For Alexander had been more than a ruler; "he had been fundamentally the priest of his people" (615).

## Macedonia

This religious note is sustained in West's view of Macedonia as the repository of the Byzantine tradition, a "supremely beautiful civilization" in which people continued to live the "fullness of life" even as they conceded their doom (638). "They are what the Serbs were before the battle of

Kossovo" Constantine claims for these fierce and fervent people (677). Enchanted by the Serbo-Byzantine icons in the monasteries and by the "tragically sculptured mountains and forests," West announces: "It is a land made for the exhibition of mysteries, this Macedonia" (704-705).

One of the two central events of **Macedonia** is Bishop Nicholai's Easter Service, his working of what Rebecca calls "magic," a yoking of earth and heaven, body and spirit, which expresses itself in the "double quality of his voice . . . grand and yet gutteral," suggesting he can speak to "gods and men and beasts. He had full knowledge of what comfort men seek in magic, and how they long to learn that defeat is not defeat and that love is serviceable" (720) She likens him to Prospero, who acts as a "conduit for a force greater than himself" (722). People gather around him to celebrate the idea of goodness and resurrection, that "death had been cheated, and the destroyed one lived" (723). For West, Macedonia is the "bridge between our age and the past," in that it preserves this hopeful and pristine message of Christianity (765).

But Macedonia also provides West with Christianity's opposite message, the Atonement, which she had opposed in her first published article on religion more than a decade before she started work on *Black Lamb and Grey Falcon*:

> That a father should invent the laws of a game knowing that they must be broken, force people to play it, sentence the players to punishment for breaking them, and accept the agony of his son as a substitute for the punishment, was credible enough to people who believed that hate might be the ultimate law of life. To us who have been given the Christian idea of love and mercy as an essential part of divinity, it is not credible.[14]

In Macedonia, West approaches a sacrificial rock, where the lambs are sacrificed, the cocks' heads are severed, and the women pitch jars to the "red-

---

[14]"My Religion," in a collection of the same title (New York: D. Appleton, 1926), 24.

brown and gleaming" ground, she confronts the "body of our death . . . the seed of the sin that is in us . . . the forge where the sword was wrought that shall slay us." The shameful rite is a "beastly retrogression," re-enacting the "dawn of nastiness" as it had first broken over "infant minds." To her, it is a scene of sadism; men put their hands on "something weaker than themselves and prod its mechanism to funny tricks by the use of pain, to smash what was whole, to puddle in the warm stickiness of their own secretions." The ceremony at the rock is the equivalent of a "penny-in-the-slot machine of idiot character. If one drops in a piece of suffering, a blessing pops out at once. If one squares death by offering him a sacrifice, one will be allowed some share in life for which one has hungered." It appeals to those with a "letch for violence." This is what Western thought has done to the Crucifixion, pretending that "this repulsive pain is the proper price of any good thing" (823-26) West rejects the Atonement as a nonsensical yet convincing ploy, allowing even figures as great as Augustine to indulge in their appetite for agony.

This perverse scene provokes West to say of Augustine: "He loved love with the hopeless infatuation of one who, like King Lear, cannot love." Calling Shakespeare's play, the "supreme work of art produced by Western civilization," she sees in it the failure of love and of Shakespeare's insistence that only love will do, only love will save humanity. *King Lear* tells us that the knife is at our throats, and that we are to be sacrificed in a world gone mad with death at the absence of love (828).

*Lear* is West's touchstone here--as it often is in her letters--because it brings her back to the family, her family, the father and his three daughters, a kingdom rent asunder, a paradise lost. Unreconciled to the rock, West continues on her quest for reality, unable to accept the notion that suffering is necessary, that it is a kind of spiritual payment owed to God the father. This she could never accept, not being certain of his love, not being certain that he *could* love.

## Old Serbia

The old kingdom of Serbia, made great by Stephen Dushan (a magnificent monarch West compares to Queen Elizabeth I), is also where the Serbs suffered their greatest defeat--on the plains of Kossovo, where Tsar Lazar's army failed to turn back the Turks. This event in 1389 is commemorated in the great poem, known to all Serbs, which Constantine recites to West. Tsar Lazar is visited by a grey falcon (Saint Elijah) offering him the choice of two kingdoms: heaven and earth. Lazar chooses heaven (eternal salvation) rather than earth and accepts the sacrifice of his soldiers and his kingdom in the battle against the Turks. Lazar's choice is the desire to be pure, to make a sacrifice of oneself, rather than be implicated in evil. West denies the thesis of the poem, that Lazar could redeem himself without considering the fate of his people, for his redemption meant five hundred years of domination by the Turks and the enslavement of millions of people.

"Lazar was a member of the Peace Pledge Union" West tells Constantine, realizing that the "poem referred to something true and disagreeable in my own life" (911). The poem evinces an attitude she had protested earlier in the left wing and in the pacifist movement: the desire to be defeated, to evade the responsibility of worldly power. The left-wing has wanted to be right, not to do right. It has not spoken as though power would be its someday, as if it was "predestined to rule" (912) On the contrary, "they would prefer to divert themselves from it and form a standing pool of purity. In fact, they want to receive the Eucharist, be beaten by the Turks, and then go to Heaven" (913). She does not absolve herself of this terrible judgment, for she is speaking of herself and her friends in the most self-lacerating passage she was ever to write:

> I looked into my own heart and I knew that I was not innocent.
> Often I wonder whether I would be able to suffer for my
> principles if the need came, and it strikes me as a matter of the
> highest importance. That should not be so. I should ask myself
> with far greater urgency whether I have done everything

possible to carry those principles into effect, and how I can attain power to make them absolutely victorious. But those questions I put only with my mind. They do not excite my guts, which wait anxiously while I ponder my gift for martyrdom. . . . I began to weep, for the left-wing people among whom I had lived all my life had in their attitude to foreign politics achieved such a betrayal. They were always right, they never imposed their rightness. (913)

In Yugoslavia, which "writes obscure things plain, which furnishes symbols for what the intellect has not yet formulated," she concludes that the "black lamb and grey falcon had worked together." Through a "senseless and ugly magic rite" sacrifice is endorsed as essential to the continuance of life; only suffering will anneal sin, so that humanity is put into a passive position, supine in its spiritual immobilization. The rite of the black lamb exalts in cruelty; the annunciation of the grey falcon authorizes surrender (914). "We had regarded ourselves as far holier than our tory opponents because we had exchanged the role of priest for the role of lamb, and therefore we forgot that we were not performing the chief moral obligation of humanity, which is to protect the works of love." West herself had been "imbecile enough" to believe she might secure her salvation by "hanging round a stinking rock where a man with dirty hands shed blood for no reason" (915).

Constantine does not merely recite the poem of the grey falcon, he has lived its message, marrying Gerda and binding his loving heart to this woman of hate so that he might be defeated and innocent. Constantine and Gerda, in fact, suggest the alternative to West and Andrews. Whereas the latter couple are complimented many times on their compatibility (they provide pleasure for one party who observes how close they sit together even though they are not young [718]), the former are the very epitome of the forces rending Europe apart. Watching what West calls beautiful Macedonian boys and girls dancing in the open air with clothes as lovely as flowers, Gerda takes out a cigarette and declares that she must smoke to disinfect herself, for she feels contaminated by people she does not consider civilized Europeans.

Gerda sees no order or culture but only a mish-mash of different and primitive peoples (660). It is her view that is putting all of Europe to the knife even as West writes her book.

Perhaps even the great Stephen Dushan, who might have reunited the disintegrated Byzantine world, succumbed, in the end, to a desire for death and defeat, West speculates. For he died in his prime, having acknowledged that he had sometimes acted out of fear when he had it in him to exert his strength. Yugoslavia, a country so full of life, has been tormented by the deaths of its many heroes--like Stephen Dushan who "stepped back from the light of his doorway, he retreated into the blameless world of the shadows; and Constantinople faded like a breath on a windowpane." So much of human achievement can fade, West concludes, in "this infatuation with sacrifice" (917). It is a form of masochism that she struggled against in her own life, and which becomes visible to her in Yugoslavia--as palpable as the black lamb's "cold twitching muzzle" on her bare forearm, put there by an Albanian amused at her outcry.

### Montenegro

What Gerda denies is the "mystery of process," that life is a journey, a quest for reality, which yields only partial answers (1012). West arrives at this formulation--the "mystery of process"--on the heights of Montenegro, a land of heroes, of human beings who have never failed in nerve, who never stop aiming for the summit, so to speak. Their perfect physiques (symmetrical features and figures, lustrous hair, eyes, and skin) strike her as almost a surfeit of grace--like choking the eye with cream. She meets a woman wandering on the heights, wondering over her family tragedies, speculating on the mystery of process. It is this refusal to be "dismayed by complexity" which recommends this woman to West, for unlike Gerda she has not clammed up in an impregnable superiority (1013).

Yet as so often in *Black Lamb and Grey Falcon*, such triumphant passages which redeem West's view of Yugoslavia's uniqueness are not allowed to stand unchallenged. In the most harrowing section of the book, she and her husband are guided up a steep mountain by a Montenegran who refuses to acknowledge that he has lost his way. Reaching the summit, he orders them in the fading light of day to descend the other side by negotiating the tiny ruts made in a cliff. Confused, then alarmed by his dangerous summons, West rushes back toward her starting point, only to learn from an outraged Constantine that the Montenegran was too proud, too much of a "hero" to admit his error, and would have had them descend in an area known to be unsafe (part of it has crumbled into the sea) and where they would surely have met their deaths. Thus the courage which made these Montenegrans invincible also spells their doom, for as Constantine points out, the Montenegran guide would have countenanced his own death rather than turn back to admit defeat. This episode and others prompts West to revise an earlier estimate: "The woman we had met walking on the mountains that afternoon seemed not such a consoling portent as I had thought her. On the great mountains she was so small; against the black universal mass of our insanity her desire for understanding seemed so weak a weapon" (1022). *Black Lamb and Grey Falcon* is itself, an example of the "mystery of process," an extraordinarily fluid and open-ended masterpiece.

## Epilogue

The **Epilogue** is actually a series of endings to West's gargantuan work, just as the *Prologue* is a series of beginnings. It is a summation of her life, the nature of her career, her reading of history, and her devotion to art. Her Easter journey ended, on her way back through Croatia, she meets with a Croatian student wishing to write a thesis on her work. It cannot be done, West tells her, because she has made no continuous revelation of herself as a writer, and the interstices between her works are too great. Not only does this student not understand what it has meant for a writer like West not to confine herself to a conventional literary career, West finds that the student has no understanding of herself and would deny her Slavic roots, sullenly identifying herself with Vienna--the seat of the Empire which has suppressed her Croatian heritage. Hence, the student cannot see the irony of studying a writer whose career repudiates the status quo and the discontinuities of history perpetuated by empires (1084-88).

Belonging to an empire herself, West is ambivalent, recognizing that its claim to bring order to the disordered parts of the world has been "more than half humbug." Yet colonization has released in Britain a "love of action" and a desire to reform the world that had not been mere humbug and that led to the institution of laws and actions on the behalf of other peoples that could be deemed chivalrous (1090).

West's ambivalence, as well as her sense of estrangement from her left-wing friends--many of whom had proved hostile to small states such as Yugoslavia liberated by the First World War--provokes her into charging that they have lost a grip on what it means to be free and self-determining. Entranced by the bogus internationalism of the Soviet Union, confusing the nationalistic aspirations of Yugoslavs with imperialism, and "choked with our victory in the last war, we now have an appetite for defeat," a craving for a "blanched world" without blood (1103). For her, there are worst things than the shedding of blood in the Balkans. England and France anesthetized themselves as Hitler and Mussolini, appealing to the rootless and restless urban masses suffering in economic depressions, commit murder after murder, destroying national traditions with an immature "baby ferocity" (1112).

During these fascist depredations England has forsaken its "bustling polychrome Victorian self" for a death-like slumber, as though it were "locked fast in frost" (1115). It longs for annihilation, hankering after a perverse peace that elicits from West a passage often quoted:

> Only part of us is sane: only part of us loves pleasure and the longer day of happiness, wants to live to our nineties and die in peace, in a house that we built, that shall shelter those who come after us. The other half of us is nearly mad. It prefers the disagreeable to the agreeable, loves pain and its darker

> night despair, and wants to die in a catastrophe that will set back life to its beginnings and leave nothing of our house save its blackened foundations. (1102)

How else to explain the acceptance of Hitler's and Mussolini's "baby ferocity"? Kossovo in 1389 and England in 1939 are as one. Just as the Nazis prevail in Europe with an air force that shows off their technical superiority, the Turks subdued Europe with a "ferocious and ingenious use of cavalry." The English in 1939, no more than the Slavs in 1389, have provided "appropriate counter-forces." Just as Serbia collapsed only thirty-four years after it has reached the height of its power in the reign of Stephen Dushan, so England is on the edge of oblivion only thirty-seven years after Queen Victoria's funeral. It is West's dread that England will experience the same moral and material squalor under the Germans that the Slavs suffered under the Turks and Austrians (1119).

West reaches this low point at what might be called the second act of her **Epilogue.** Although she makes no such division in her text, it is clear that she has modeled her book's ending on her country's greatest work of literature when she conjectures:

> Perhaps there is a balance in our souls which is hung truly between life and death, and rights itself if it swings over too far in the direction of death. Such an equipoise can be noted in Shakespeare's *King Lear*, which above all other works of art illuminates the sacrificial myth: he set out to prove that the case for cruelty is unanswerable, because kindness, even when it comes to its fine flower in love, is only a cloak for ravening and treachery, and at the end cries out that love is the only true jewel in the universe, that if we have not found it yet we must go on mining for it till we find it. (1125)

The message of this art outlasts the bombs, which may twist the bowels, but which cannot sustain the attention as art does, reliving experience and imposing on it a form.

It is art in the form of the poem about the grey falcon which sustains the people of Yugoslavia, reinforcing their decision to resist the Nazis even after much of Europe has capitulated, and to refuse terms of surrender, preferring their own destruction, save for a remnant that repairs to the mountains. At first, their devotion to this poem puzzles West, for she has read it as sanctioning defeat and welcoming death. Then she recurs to two lines which suddenly yield not only a new meaning, but one contrary to her earlier interpretation: "An earthly kingdom lasts only a little time,/ But a heavenly kingdom will last for eternity and its centuries" (1146) Although she does not put it this way, West suddenly realizes that the "heavenly kingdom" can be taken not as a reference to heaven but to Gregorievitch's vision of Yugoslavia as the "Kingdom of Heaven on earth." This is the kingdom for which Yugoslavs fight; the same one she came to find on her Easter journey.

What West has effectively done is turn the poem and her book inside out. There is precedent for this, she points out, in the

> complex nature of all profound works of art. An artist is
> goaded into creation on this level by his need to resolve some
> important conflict, to find out where the truth lies among
> divergent opinions on a vital issue. His work, therefore, is
> often a palimpsest on which are superimposed several incom-
> patible views about his subject; and it may be that which is
> expressed with the greatest intensity, which his deeper nature
> finds the truest, is not that which has determined the narrative
> form he has given to it. The poem of the Tsar Lazar and the
> grey falcon tells a story which celebrates the death-wish; but its
> hidden meaning pulses with life. (1145)

*Black Lamb and Grey Falcon* excoriates the West, especially England, for its death-wish, yet its hidden meaning pulses with life. As West wrote the *Epilogue*, English fighter pilots had turned back the Luftwaffe; the stalwart Yugoslavs had been defeated but had set back Hitler's timetable for invading Russia by a crucial month and blocked his plans to take over Turkey. Studding her praise of Slavic courage throughout her book are analogies to English history, to those supreme moments when England, especially under Elizabeth I and Victoria, stood for greatness. Written into her palimpsest of a book is the idea that all great works of art subsume their own contradictions, present argument after argument in layers like a medieval parchment, written and erased, written and erased, with the layers imperfectly visible and yet seemingly within our grasp, reflecting the dramatic and dialectical nature of a great mind. *Black Lamb and Grey Falcon* is ultimately about the greatest incompatibles, about life against death. It is about division and the human equation, written at almost unbearable length, and yet as elegant in conception as a Euclidean problem.

The final image of the **Epilogue** occurs in France, where people bring flowers to the grave of King Alexander, whose assassination in 1934 first brought Yugoslavia to West's full consciousness, and whose grave receives the tribute meant for his brave countrymen and women as well. The final words of *Black Lamb and Grey Falcon*, however, are reserved for her husband, named for the first time in her bibliographical note, in an expression of love also embodying the values her book imparts:

> As for my husband, Henry Andrews, it is true that whatever is best in this book is his, and that during the years of its writing he never flagged in his desire to relieve me of all the drudgery he could take on his shoulders. Most of all I thank him for the patience with which he watched me as I engaged on what seemed till very recently the curiously gratuitous labour of taking an inventory of a foreign country. It took great faith, for which I am most grateful. (1158)

Old friends wrote to West express not only their pleasure in *Black Lamb and Grey Falcon* but to show they recognized its uniqueness. "Nobody but a woman could have written that book, so personal and so scholarly, so full of intuition and knowledge," declared journalist Dorothy Thompson. Novelist Storm Jameson marveled at its rich picture of a "country and a people, peoples, living, at so many depths, on so many planes of feeling." Coupled with the "stored-up richness" of West's own experience, the book was "as wholly satisfying as a very good poem. . . No fear enters anywhere into this book. Or into your writing. . . as rich and supple as any I have ever read

. . . an extraordinary and very beautiful freshness about it." Critic Lewis Mumford captured the spiritual dimension of the book, calling it in a letter to West "one of the few thoroughly mature books that has been written in our time . . . one from which a lost soul might get his bearings in the present world."[15]

Paul Fussell's excellent *Abroad: British Literary Traveling Between the Wars* quotes Rebecca West on D. H. Lawrence's travel writing but does not remark that she is also describing her own: he "traveled to get a certain Apocalyptic vision of mankind that he registered again and again, always rising to a pitch of ecstatic agony."[16] Fussell notes that a reviewer once said that Lawrence might have written a good book on Italy "if he had been content to see things simply, and to see no more than he really saw." Fussell's response to the reviewer on Lawrence's behalf serves West as well:

> But what Lawrence really saw in things and places was the Infinite. Like all literary travelers worth reading, he played a spume of imagination upon empirical phenomena, generating subtle emotional states and devising unique psychological forms and structures to contain them. He "felt and urgency to describe the unseen so keenly," says Rebecca West, "that he has rifled the seen of its vocabulary and diverted it to that purpose." (155)

"To perceive this," Fussell concludes, "is to notice that there is no way, ultimately, to distinguish his travel writing from his fiction except by its insistence that it is a 'true' account of real, verifiable places" (155-56). West treasured and had framed an appreciate letter from Lawrence, in which he declared their affinity: "I always like you when you are on the war path." Perhaps sensing how much it cost both of them to maintain their independent, questing spirits, he added: "The battle is here below and it's too soon for us

---

[15]DT to RW, October 12, 1942, Yale; SJ to RW, March 29, 1942, Tulsa; LM to RW, September 28, 1944, Tulsa.

[16](New York: Oxford University Press, 1980), 147. Page numbers for subsequent quotations will be cited in the text within parentheses.

to look on from the heavenly balconies. So I am once more spitting on my hands--so no doubt are you. Then a war whoop. . . . I hope you are renewing your energy like the eagle."[17]

Journalist John Gunther compared *Black Lamb* to Velazquez, to the third act in *King Lear*, and to all nine symphonies of Beethoven:

> I was revolted by most of the reviews I saw because they missed the two things I thought most admirably notable: 1) the application of the book's theme -- that is the conflict between love of life and love of death -- to every kind of human problem; 2) the fact that it surely contains some of the finest description of *nature* in the English language. And it somehow pleased me too that it was not so much a book about Jugoslavia as about Rebecca West.

As critic Lesley Chamberlain puts it, "West needed an object equal to herself in extent and complexity to explore and analyse, and found it in Yugoslavia where East met West."[18]

---

[17]DHL to RW, April 15, 1929, Tulsa.

[18]JG to RW, October 6, 1944, Tulsa; "Rebecca West in Yugoslavia," *Contemporary Review* 248 (1986):262-66. For a discussion of the critical reception and contemporary relevance of *Black Lamb and Grey Falcon*, see Rollyson, 212-16.

# CHAPTER SEVEN

## 1941-1947

Rebecca West and Henry Andrews spent much of the war years helping Yugoslav refugees. They believed that the Serbs should take the lead in Yugoslavia (as they had done before the war) because of their tradition of self-government. They also attacked the Croats for being divisive and oppositional by nature: "I don't like Croats very much," West wrote to historian Phillip Guedalla, "they resemble the Irish."[1] Because the Irish had not taken an active role in defending Britain against the Nazis, they were as good as Nazis so far as she was concerned. West did not believe Croats could govern themselves any more than the Irish could. Reports of Croat collaboration with the Germans and Croat massacres of Serbs only strengthened her prejudice.

Since November of 1941, during Henry Andrews's two-year tenure in the Ministry of Economic Warfare, he had worked diligently with members of the governments-in-exile on the postwar economic development of Central Europe. He composed several memoranda outlining a complex structure of agreements protecting the sovereignty of individual countries but acknowledging that only through various "joint organs of administration" could the whole region flourish. He treated Central Europe as an attractive market for both Great Britain and the United States, one that Germany had heretofore

---

[1]June 5, 1944, Tulsa.

dominated, but he was not proposing a revival of British imperialism: "We are not the sahibs, and we are not dealing with 'natives.'"[2]

After Andrews left the Ministry of Economic Warfare in 1943, Jan Masaryk, the Czechoslovak Foreign Secretary, invited him to join a committee of Czechoslovak, Greek, Polish, and Yugoslav members, which had agreed to pursue the development of Central Europe along the lines Andrews had proposed. Masaryk welcomed the fact that Andrews was not a government official, for it enhanced the expression of the committee's "personal esteem" for him.[3]

Andrews realized that Russia might oppose his plans. Not only did it want to secure Central Europe as a buffer against Germany, it also sought to curb Western-style economic growth, which after all would be another kind of challenge to Soviet hegemony. The impoverishment of these countries, Andrews argued, not an improvement in their standard of living (which is what he promised) would work in the Communists' favor. The best line of defense against the spread of Communism in Western Europe would be strong Central European economies. In effect, he was proposing a Marshall Plan, including massive investment in public works such as road building, housing, and electrification, reversing the Great Powers' traditional neglect of the region. He hoped for "frank cooperation" with Russia but did not suggest how Britain's wartime alliance with Stalin could be perpetuated given his concerns about Communism. He hoped it would be enough for the Soviet Union to see that strong governments in Central Europe, in alliance with both the Soviet Union and the West, would check German militarism.

In January 1944, Churchill changed horses in Yugoslavia, provoking an eruption in West's life and work with aftershocks that lasted almost to the day

---

[2]Henry Andrews memorandum, November 1941, Postscript January 1942, Notes 1 & 2, June 1942, Yale.

[3]JM to HA, August 23, 1943, Yale.

she died. Since April 1941, when Yugoslavia was attacked, Churchill had been supporting General Mihailovic, the leader of the loyalists, often referred to as the Chetniks, supporters of King Peter and the Yugoslav government-in-exile in London. It had been the natural choice for Churchill, a fervent anti-Communist before the war--although he did not want to upset the Soviets, his valuable ally, by appearing to oppose Communists in Yugoslavia. The other option had been to back Tito, head of the Yugoslav Communist Party since 1937 and leader of the resistance (the Partisans) in the western part of the country. Before the war, the Yugoslav Communist Party had a negligible following. A paid Soviet agent, Tito had followed Stalin's line slavishly, even approving the Hitler-Stalin pact in 1939 and calling the war an imperialist enterprise that Communists should shun.

For over two years Churchill had stood by Mihailovic, even though he received reports that Tito was engaging in an effective guerilla campaign against the Germans. Mihailovic, hampered by lack of supplies and arms, conducted fewer attacks on the Germans; there were reports from the SOE (Special Operations Executive) in Cairo that he was collaborating with the Germans and the Italians, although British and American officers who were with the loyalists saw no evidence of this.

Historians Richard Lamb and David Martin take a position close to West's, condemning Churchill for going over to the Communists. Franklin Lindsay provides a first-hand view of Tito and the Partisans and argues that Churchill was right. Boris Todorovich, a member of Mihailovic's forces, and Michael Lees, a British liaison officer with a Mihailovic unit, and others, have published memoirs defending his policies and claiming that his refusal to fight stemmed from strategic and humane considerations (Germans killed one hundred Serb hostages for every German killed) and that his failures to engage the enemy were exaggerated. One of the key arguments of Mihailovic's defenders is that Communist infiltration of the British services, including the Foreign Office, SOE, and BBC, ensured that Tito's successes were overstated and Mihailovic's were underplayed, and after 1942 often knowingly maligned. In August 1943, Sir George Rendel, British ambassador for the Yugoslav government-in-exile, became disturbed at the anti-Mihailovic tone that crept into conversations about Yugoslavia. By 1943, the British had found it easier to send supplies and arms to Tito than it had ever been able to do for Mihailovic. Support for Tito, Rendel noted in his memoirs, had more to do with seconding the efforts of Britain's Russian allies, now touted in the British Left's campaign for Tito.[4]

West believed in Mihailovic's staunch anti-Fascist record before the war, and even if he had parlayed with the Germans, she said it would have been for temporary strategic purposes. Such shifting of position was common fare in Balkan history, she emphasized.[5] She relied on reports from Yugoslav friends and a considerable flow of correspondence from Slavs who admired *Black Lamb and Grey Falcon* and wanted to apprise her of what was happening to their country. She also had access to information from contacts in the Foreign Office.

West's friends, R. W. Seton-Watson and A. J. P. Taylor, historians of the Austro-Hungarian empire and of the Balkans, questioned Mihailovic's motivations. Seton-Watson observed: "It is not a service to the Yugoslav cause to exaggerate his role or to treat him as one who can unite all

---

[4]Richard Lamb, *Churchill as War Leader* (London: Bloomsbury, 1991), 250-75; David Martin, *Web of Disinformation: Churchill's Yugoslav Blunder* (New York: Harcourt Brace Jovanovich, 1990); Boris Todorovich, *Last Words: A Memoir of World War II and the Yugoslav Tragedy* (New York: Walkner and Company), 1989; Michael Lees, *The Rape of Serbia: The British Role in Tito's Grab for Power, 1943-1944* (New York: Harcourt Brace Jovanovich, 1990); Sir George Rendel, *The Sword and the Olive: Recollections of Diplomacy and the Foreign Service, 1913-1945* (London: John Murray, 1957).

[5]In "Prospects in Yugoslavia" (a manuscript notebook article at Yale), West wrote: "Now I think it very unlikely that Mihailovic did not sometimes come to an understanding with the Germans and Italians, that he didn't say on various occasions to the Italians that if they allowed him to do this he would allow them to do that. Such understandings are a recognized part of ancient warfare, and have always been carried on in places outside the Western convention."

Yugoslavs behind him." Reports of Mihailovic's collaboration with the Italians and of his forces' burning of Croat villages disturbed Seton-Watson. Tito had contributed at least as much to the resistance as Mihailovic, and he had the "active sympathy of our Russian allies," Seton-Watson concluded.[6] But he made no mention of the massacre of thousands of Serbs by Croat and Moslem Ustase (Fascist collaborators).

A. J. P. Taylor put the case directly to West:

> You don't seem to have made up your mind whether Mike [Mihailovic] is right because he is trying to preserve Yugoslavia or whether he is right because he has despaired of Yugoslavia and is going back to great Serbia. All you insist on is that somehow he is right, but you can't have it both ways.

Taylor predicted that the post-World War I effort to combine Slavs into multi-ethnic national states was doomed to failure. The Serbs would be better off without the Croats because federations of Slavs would never be stable enough to defend themselves from the great powers. Russian influence was inevitable in the Balkans, and West should make her peace with it. West's response to Taylor's letters is unknown, but she would surely have scoffed at this sentence: "The Russians are not democratic now, but there is a chance they may become so; there's not much chance for us." She wanted Russians to become defenders of Western virtues, Taylor alleged, virtues the British were "too corrupt and feeble to do anything about." In a passage that could only have maddened her, he deplored Russian ruthlessness while excusing it as an inevitable historical process, one that Great Britain itself had done much to promulgate: "The peasant must disappear; that is the lesson of all civilisation. Nasty for him, but it can't be helped. And, in the long run, the Russian way of liquidating him is no worse than our way in the eighteenth century, which has made us the civilized people we are."[7] West had made it

---

[6]Letter to *Time and Tide*, July 24, 1943, p. 609.

[7]A.J.P. Taylor to RW, March 7, [1942], Yale.

clear in *Black Lamb and Grey Falcon* that British imperialism, as bad as it had been, was not anywhere near as evil as Nazism and Communism. To relativize all forms of imperialism in this way was to lose one's moral compass--which is what she saw happening in the move from Mihailovic to Tito.

With Churchill's change in policy, West felt increasingly isolated and threatened. On March 15, 1944, she attended an afternoon party at Buckingham Palace. She met Sir Orme Sargent, Assistant Under-Secretary of State for the Foreign Office, who had told her earlier that British recognition of Tito had been due solely to military necessity. She now disbelieved his "version of military necessity" and regretted that the Soviet Union had "won the war politically." West eyed Anthony Eden, Foreign Secretary, uneasily, wondering whether he was successfully turning over Great Britain and Europe to Russia. She did not like Eden's "soft handsomeness," or his manner of laying his arm across the shoulders of the men he spoke to. British Conservative Party M.P. Kenneth Pickthorn had pointed out this "insincere and unpleasant" detail to her.[8] Pickthorn had earlier told West that he had become disturbed at how the government apparently viewed his and West's efforts on Mihailovic's behalf: "You and I could easily find ourselves in prison for a year if we continue our activity."[9] As one of her Yugoslav friends suggests, West was caught between factions: "The Right wouldn't say Churchill was wrong, and the Left followed their own policies." She felt herself to be a pariah. "There were others who were sympathetic to her position but they kept quiet."[10]

To West, Churchill had decided, before the end of the war, to consign Yugoslavia to Communist tyranny. She had predicted before Munich that

---

[8]RW diary entry, Tulsa.

[9]RW to Aleksa Gavrilovic, February 18, 1976, courtesy of Aleksa Gavrilovic.

[10]Interview with Aleksa Gavrilovic.

either the Nazis or the Communists would dominate the small countries in Central and Eastern Europe. By picking Tito, Churchill had made his choice. His short-term goal might be winning the war, which meant supporting Stalin and Tito, but in the long term he had already lost the peace. By the end of January 1944, she had completed a satirical story, "Madame Sara's Magical Crystal," which exposed Churchill's crime. She sent it to Sir Orme Sargent with a note saying she would not publish the story, "thus giving guarantee of my willingness to sacrifice myself to the needs of my country."[11] West's politics are inseparable from her literary development, and this suppressed story suggests the beginnings of her postwar investigations into the history of treachery.

Madame Sara is a poor medium--about all she can summon through her powers of divination are a series of contemporary newspaper reports. She is a convenient device, allowing West to point out the absurdity of the way Tito is lionized and the way history is told. Instead of Yugoslavia, the setting is France; instead of Marshal Tito, the hero is Marshal Pierrot--an apt name for a historical clown, a figure in a historical farce. The narrator claims that what Madame Sara has to report is absurd but nevertheless disturbing: "It is plainly impossible that we should ever impose on France first an unauthorized Commander-in-Chief and then a puppet government. Yet, somehow, the whole thing seems to remind me of something. But I will let my readers judge for themselves" (168).[12] West is not impartial, of course. She wants readers to realize that Tito is an outlaw, a self-appointed ruler, and that by

---

[11]Quoted in Rebecca West, *The Only Poet and Short Stories*, ed. Antonia Till (London: Virago, 1992), 167. "Madame Sara" is printed for the first time in this volume. Page numbers for subsequent quotations will be cited in the text within parentheses.

[12]By making the country France, West emphasized British lack of interest and empathy for Eastern Europe. She understood that Churchill would not stand for such a fraud as Tito governing in Western Europe.

recognizing him Churchill has endorsed an illegality that will result in a postwar government following the Soviet line.

Once the switch to Tito had been made, West noticed that the BBC began to tout him. In response, she skewers its fatuous propaganda, disguising it only slightly as an excerpt from a newspaper called the *Daily News-Lamentations*--a particularly fitting title with its allusion to "The Lamentations of Jeremiah" and the dirges over the fall of Jerusalem, for Yugoslavia had been West's Jerusalem:

> The one source of satisfaction in an otherwise gloomy land-scape is the emergence in France of what seems to be likely to be a real popular leader, in the person of Marshal Pierrot. His partisan troops have apparently done valiant work all over France, which it may be hoped will act as an inspiration to the British and the French regular armies. His firm and manly proclamations, which declare that he and his men, who number about a hundred thousand alone, can claim to represent France, strike a sound democratic note. (169)

Thus a tyrant is legitimized and made to seem heroic.

But the truth manages to filter in from foreign correspondents, including a dispatch describing an encounter between Marshal Pierrot and regular French troops: "The regular French troops hailed them as friends, but the guerrillas opened fire and killed and wounded many of them" (169). Historian Richard Lamb unequivocally states that Tito's partisans were the first to attack Mihailovic's Chetniks. American OSS officer Franklin Lindsay suggests the Partisans and Chetniks attacked each other, aware that they were battling for the future of their country, which often meant ceasing operations against the Germans so that they could fight each other. For West, there was no ambiguity. Communists would not cooperate with anti-Communists; indeed their *raison d'etre* was to establish a one party state.

Mimicking Tito's charges against Mihailovic and his staff, Marshal Pierrot accuses "certain French generals" of collaborating with the enemy; he says he has the documents to prove it. Relying on reports of Tito's slaughtering of Chetniks, West has Marshal Pierrot accuse the French general of his own crimes, of ambushing and torturing Pierrot's men with "utmost barbarity" (170-71). *The New Simpleton* repeats Pierrot's claims and concludes "all this seems very credible" (171). Even the *Sunday Tory* rationalizes Pierrot's opposition to the war in its early stages by noting he "revised his opinion of how to serve the real interest of France, and ever since has been the life and soul of all that was significant in French resistance" (171). The last sentence reveals how the effort to build up Tito soon separated itself from any contact with reality. Of course, Mihailovic detractors would say that West conveniently forgets that the media had done the same for Mihailovic until the turn against him in late 1943.

The language used to describe Marshal Pierrot is akin to that used to transform Stalin into "Uncle Joe":

> This interesting career had made a truly magnetic personality. He is strongly built, with penetrating eyes and a firm chin, and his manner is at once simple and commanding. He is adored by his men, being stern but just. He rides on a white horse and is said sometimes to walk on water. (172)

In fact, Tito was often photographed with a white horse--a nice example is to be found in Lindsay's book.

"Madame Sara's Magic Crystal" includes a cable from a distinguished Frenchman on behalf of Frenchmen in England protesting the British government's backing of Marshal Pierrot:

> WE ARE UNABLE TO UNDERSTAND WHY THE FUTURE OF OUR GREAT COUNTRY SHOULD BE DECIDED BY REPORTS DRAWN UP BY YOUNG ENGLISHMAN WHO SPEAKS RUSSIAN FLUENTLY AND WEARS KILT AND BY CANADIAN INSURANCE AGENT" (172).

West's targets are Fitzroy Maclean and William Deakin, who she regarded as two of the evil geniuses that persuaded Churchill to switch sides. It is characteristic of her to think that these two men were decisive, and that Churchill had not gathered information from other sources but was merely a dupe, or worse, an appeaser of the new winning power, the Soviet Union and its lackey, Tito.[13]

As West later told her sister Letitia, "the same sort of Conservative who approved of Munich is now absolutely infatuated with the idea of offering the whole of Eastern Europe to Russia."[14] For her, biography, not geopolitics, was destiny. History pivoted on personalities. To change sides was to betray the loyalty of Churchill's and England's most fervent supporters. The cable concludes:

> WE BEG YOU TO REMEMBER THE FREE FRENCHMEN
> WHO IN THE DARKEST DAYS OF 1940 DID NOT
> ABANDON THE STRUGGLE AGAINST THE NAZIS AND
> WERE PROUD TO STAND SHOULDER TO SHOULD
> WITH THE BRITISH" (172-73).

She is referring, of course, to the Serbs, who did not mouth Tito's anti-imperialist pieties and who stood against Hitler even though it meant catastrophic losses. West knew that Mihailovic was careful about the timing of his engagements with the Nazis because the Nazis had killed ten Serbs for every Nazi soldier's loss.

Madame Sara's running stream of newspaper quotations carries her into the autumn of 1944 (West was accurately predicting the course of British propaganda from the viewpoint of January 1944). The claims for Marshal Pierrot become more and more ludicrous:

> All those in the area controlled by Marshal Pierrot have been taught to read and write during the fourteen months during which Marshal Pierrot has been in power. Indeed he has visited many of the schools where these illiterates have been taught, and has personally given them their lessons. On these occasions, of course, he leaves his horse outside. (173)

---

[13]For a sympathetic biography of Maclean, see Frank McLynn, *Fitzroy Maclean* (London: John Murray, 1992), and Maclean's autobiography, *Eastern Approaches* (New York: Penguin, 1991).

[14]RW to Letitia Fairfield, n.d., AM.

What is literal and what is fiction have become completely confused and absurd.

What would West have Churchill do? She makes that clear at the end of her story. That it is her point of view is coyly introduced by noting Madame Sara's confusion; she is not sure if the statement is a newspaper article or a letter. At any rate, it constitutes a summing up of 1944, suggesting the British government might have told the truth about Marshal Pierrot, that he was part of a civil war, with good people on his side and good people against him. Probably the best man would win, and France should be left to work out its destiny. This position, by the way, is essentially the one put forward by historian Richard Lamb, who argues that the British government should not have taken sides.

Instead, West contends, the Left did not oppose the Right, who got the idea of elevating Pierrot and "worked it out to the last detail . . . played him up as if all conceivable kinds of right were on his side and all conceivable kinds of wrong on the other side" (177). Both Left and Right sold this fiction to the public, a great shame to the gullible Left, she thinks:

> Honest, it was a shame to take their money. There wasn't a silly story they wouldn't believe, on evidence that wouldn't justify hanging a cat; and I don't think it ever struck them that most of those stories were told them by Government officials. No, we don't worry about Left-Wing intellectuals any more. (177)

The last sentence carries on West's quarrel with the Left begun with the advent of the Russian Revolution, Emma Goldman's trip to England, and continued in *Black Lamb and Grey Falcon*. Both Left and Right played a curious game of appeasement--this is the story's final point. Appeasement is always an easy out, justifiable because it seems to prevent bloodshed. The trouble is that it only puts off the day of reckoning, the day when "we will have to defend ourselves in the real situation" (178). Ultimately, in West's book, the sellout of Mihailovic and the embrace of Tito, meant a sin against reality, a sin that would be committed again and again in the postwar years, when she would see Communist agents at work everywhere. Churchill had provided the model of how the West could be bamboozled. It was an unforgivable act, and she would never let him or his adherents forget it.

In February 1945, Louis Adamic, editor and publisher of *Today and Tomorrow*, a pro-Titoist journal, accused West and Andrews of organizing a conspiracy of industrialists and financiers to exploit the Balkans. Adamic reported that they had enlisted in this intrigue friends such as Milan Gavrilovic, head of the Serb Peasant Party in pre-war Yugoslavia, and the tin manufacturer, Sir Robert Barlow, as well as other reactionary Yugoslav exiles. Adamic alleged that this group counted on General Mihailovic to restore a monarchical and autocratic government in Yugoslavia favorable to British imperial interests. He also noted that Andrews's own family had grown rich on its colonial investments in Burma (now lost in the war), and that *Black Lamb and Grey Falcon* touted Andrews's devotion to the Balkans while virtually ignoring the lives of the Yugoslav masses. West reacted to Adamic's attack as another Communist effort to discredit her.

West believed in national purposes and traditions--not in supranational ideologies and criminal conspiracies such as Communism and Fascism that led, as she argued in *The Meaning of Treason* (1948), to the betrayal of rational, democratic values. Thus she condemned British scientist Alan Nunn May, a spy for the Russians, and rejected the extenuating argument that he had acted out of idealism, wishing to share with the Soviet Union atomic secrets that should not be monopolized by the West. Nunn should be tried like any other criminal for breaking a contract with his government, she concluded.[15]

---

[15]See the final revised edition of *The Meaning of Treason* (London: Virago, 1982), 179-190. Page numbers for subsequent quotations will be cited in the text within parentheses.

West's early and persistent criticism of Communism cost her dearly. As Doris Lessing observes, West was

> consistently and bravely critical of communism, at a time when this meant she was subject to the usual denigration and slanders. I remember it all too well. It wasn't just a question of "the comrades" but a climate of opinion which extended far beyond the extreme left. Orwell was a target and so was Rebecca W. It must have been hard to stand up to it, particularly as she was sensitive and hated being considered negligible, yet she did, standing by her guns. And of course she was right, and her critics so very wrong.[16]

On her first trip to America after the war, West encountered liberals doing unwitting work for the Communists. She argued with poet Archibald Macleish who disputed her claim that Fascism and Communism were essentially the same. The quarrel may have been provoked by one of her treason articles that claimed Communism was Fascism with a "geographical and glandular difference." She disliked the *Vogue* and *Harper's Bazaar* glamour that seemed to surround Communism. It had a prestige that liberals found hard to resist.[17]

In June 1947, Soviet pressure had prevented Czechoslovakia from accepting Marshall Plan aid, and after six months of agitation and intrigue, the Communists took over the government in February 1948. In March, Jan Masaryk, the Czech foreign minister, was found dead in a Prague courtyard. Whether he had committed suicide or been pushed from a window, there was no doubt that his death marked the end of Czech independence. Masaryk had been not only Henry Andrews's friend and collaborator, he had also helped Maxim Kopf, the husband of West's old friend, Dorothy Thompson, find asylum in America. West wrote to Thompson, another staunch anti-

---

[16]Doris Lessing to the author, December 30, 1995. See also Carl Rollyson, "Rebecca West and the God That Failed," *Wilson Quarterly* 20 (Summer 1996):78-85.

[17]RW to Henry Andrews, May 13, 1947, Yale.

Communist, just before Masaryk's death: "Well everybody told us that Czechoslovakia was handling Russia beautifully. It's time they started trusting you and me, President and Vice-President of the Pessimists' Club." Her attacks on the Progressive Party and their presidential candidate, Henry Wallace, for pursuing a pro-Soviet line further aggravated the Left. She began receiving letters accusing her of being anti-Democratic, anti-Semitic, and anti-Negro.[18]

West's postwar studies of treason trials brought her much acclaim, but they also contributed to a feeling, even among her friends, that she had succumbed to "treasonmania" while she exorcised her personal demons. John van Druten, who had dramatized *The Return of the Soldier,* and who had been close to West for several years, distrusted her "recherche bits of free association," and he satirized the way she psychologized everything, tracing the traitor William Joyce's actions "back to some obscure snub delivered to his father at an Irish garden party by an English country lady in 1903."[19]

It is true that just as she projected much of herself into Augustine as modern man for the 1930s, she found in William Joyce (1906-1946)--popularly known as Lord Haw--her alter ego and a symbol of the 1940s postwar world of treachery. He grew up in a home rife with religious conflict but devoted to the British Empire. William's father, Michael, had made himself most unpopular in his native Ireland because of his pro-Unionist politics, and William adopted his father's allegiance--even enlisting in the British army before he was of age. There was something extraordinarily pure and touching about William's patriotism. During his brief army stint, his fellow recruits

---

[18]RW to DT, February 28, 1948, Syracuse; West covered the Progressive Party Convention for the *Evening Standard* and the *New York Herald Tribune.* See, for example, her *Tribune* articles of July 24, p.3 and July 26, p. 2. West believed these articles incited a smear campaign against her, as she wrote to Evelyn Hutchinson, September 13, 1948, Yale. For an example of her critique of a pro-Soviet historian, see ""The New Carr," *Time and Tide,* March 24, 1945, pp. 241-42.

[19]JVD to G. B. Stern, January 18 [no year], BU.

made sport of his earnestness by whistling "God Save the Queen," knowing that he would jump out of bed and stand to attention. Yet William knew there was something suspect in his family history that cast doubt on his allegiance to the British Empire. He had been born in Brooklyn, New York, and feared that the British authorities would consider him an American citizen. It has never been proven whether or not William also knew that his father had become an American citizen, for Michael Joyce destroyed evidence of his American citizenship and claimed to be a British subject after he moved back to Ireland when William was still a young boy. William's treason trial would hinge on the issue of his citizenship. Did England have the right to try him after his American citizenship was established?

William's pro-British fervor revealed itself in a remarkable manner. At the age of sixteen he wrote to army officials expressing his desire to draw his sword for the Empire. His patriotism had been sharpened by a bitter awareness that he was in the despised minority in his native land; a love of the British was tantamount to treason. He was the product of mixed parentage (a Protestant father and Catholic mother), precocious, alienated from his native land, possessed of a sharp and eloquent tongue that often got him into fights--all qualities reminiscent of Rebecca West, but a West gone awry, so to speak, becoming involved with the British Fascists and indulging in a love for street fighting.

West's earliest memories of her father's conservatism, of reading writers such as Kipling, of revering the Royal Family (memories that came flooding back to her when she met the Queen during the war), equipped her to amplify Joyce's biography. She, presented him as a sincere soul, an excellent tutor of young children, who perverted his own desire for distinction into an identification with totalitarianism, made necessary when England did not recognize his abilities, when its own Fascist leader, Oswald Mosley, failed to treat his deputy, William, with the respect William had worked so hard to earn. Joyce turns on England as if turning on a lover who has spurned him, and West imagines him leaving England at the beginning of the war to serve Hitler as a means of seeking a way to return triumphantly to London.

Exactly how William Joyce transformed himself from British patriot to traitor, from a Conservative to a Fascist, has never been fully explained. West succeeded in her biography of him because with psychological brilliance she extrapolated a convincing narrative, in which she equates the intensity of his desire to be accepted by the British with the intensity of his Fascism, a powerful new ideology that would restore an effete England to William Joyce's idealized and heroic version of it, a version England had failed to achieve during William's youth.

In West's biography, Joyce becomes Britain's insidious alter ego, invading British homes with an intimate, cocksure radio voice. She heard the plaintive tone of someone whom society had not taken unto itself. In Joyce's voice, she heard, no doubt, the sounds of her own sense of rejection. His passionate ambition was to exercise authority. West's passion had always been to thwart the authority others seemed to exercise over her. She compared the grief of Joyce's followers during his treason trial with the mourning of the early Christians--a particularly apposite analogy, since she found in Joyce a saintly devotion to his cause, even when he knew he was going to be executed.

For West family life determines the individual, and in her evocation of Joyce's background she remarks that he was being "strangled by the sheer tortuousness of his family destiny" (40). For her, it is fated that this man's life should end on the gallows. His problem is that he wants to govern, not to be governed, West concludes, speaking again not only for Joyce but for herself and her vision of a humanity which is constantly straining against authority. Like West, Joyce was the "apple of the family's eye," and like her, he reacts to his family's confidence in his exceptional abilities with an extraordinary rebelliousness, as if his own genius is paradoxically inhibited by the family's claim on him (58). Joyce invested Fascism with an international character, she argues, so that Fascism sanctioned his betrayal of family and country in a way that other British Fascists, such as Mosley, could not abide.

Those passages in which Joyce's character melds with West's become apparent when she shifts to suppositions. She has him embarking for Germany: "One day his little feet twinkled up the area of his basement flat near Earl's Court. His eyes must have been dancing" (91). Such passages are bereft of evidence but full of her utter identification with her subject, her ability to show what joy it must have been to Joyce to turn traitor. Her prose is infectious, making readers also speculate on what "must have been."

West calls William Joyce a "revolutionary" a term she uses to define one who both hates order and loves it, who will destroy so that he might create a superior order (98). It is here that West took her stand in the postwar world against revolution, reaffirming what she had said twenty years earlier about the Russian Revolution--that it was bound to restore the tyranny of tsardom. One cannot murder society in order to save it. That William Joyce is transformed into the quintessential Rebecca West character is revealed in a single sentence: "He was not going to be king" (137). Every dynamic character in her fiction and nonfiction sooner or later is measured in terms of royalty. Joyce's kingly attributes suggest to West that he is a symbol of humanity, that he has it in him to want simultaneously to live and to die. Like one of Shakespeare's heroes, his struggle is tragic. His example marks an "end to mediocrity" (144).

It is an empathetic portrait, yet West affirms the court's decision that William Joyce must hang. All of her later writing is an effort to reconcile herself to authority and to study how badly things go wrong when those like Joyce will not submit to be governed. Even though he was not a British subject, she thought it right that he should be tried as a traitor. She carefully threaded her way through the legal arguments, affirming the rightness of the principle that allegiance draws protection and protection draws allegiance. William Joyce, in other words, conducted himself as a British citizen, traveled abroad on a British passport, had a claim to be protected by British laws and the British government--and by the same token was liable to be tried by them.

The very lengths to which West goes to justify this conclusion, however, suggest that it was a near thing in her own mind, that her own sympathies and the court's judgment could have gone the other way; that is, a part of her also believed that the individual has a right to throw off allegiance, a matter the lawyers debated for days during Joyce's trial. West concedes at the end of *The Meaning of Treason* that there is a case for the traitor and that all men should have a drop of treason in their blood. Otherwise, how can the status quo be challenged, how can a nation avoid the fatal complacency that could lead to its demise? Thus West presents herself as a hanging judge, with qualms. No more than Joyce did she ever see herself as acceptable, an Establishment figure.

West's fusion of the psychological and the political, and her effort to read the postwar trials as a narrative of the contemporary world, reached a climax in her report from Nuremberg. She arrived on July 23, 1946, in the eleventh month of the trials, which had become a "citadel of boredom," grinding down the spirits of nearly everyone and so diminishing the personality of the defendants that it was difficult to tell which was which--except for Herman Goering. He fascinates her. She fastens on his "smiling wooden mask." He is a bit of a fake but also considerably like a demonic force. He is a man of enormous appetite. West imagines:

> If he were given the chance, he would walk out of the Palace of Justice, take over Germany again, and turn it into a stage for the enactment of his governing fantasy, which is so strong that it fills the air around him with its images, so madly private that those images are beyond the power of those who seem them to interpret them.

West finds something soft and peculiarly sexual about Goering--not homosexual, she adds, but when his humor is good, he recalls the madam of a brothel."[20]

Like so many of West's characters, in her fiction and nonfiction, the Reichsmarschall is full of life and death:

> Sometimes he wore a German Air Force uniform, and sometimes a light beach suit in the worst of playful taste, and both hung loosely on him, giving him an air of pregnancy. He had thick brown young hair, the coarse bright skin of an actor who has used grease paint for decades and the preternaturally deep wrinkles of the drug addict. He looked infinitely corrupt, and acted naively. (5-6)

When Goering balloons in importance, West brings him back to earth. The air of depravity, of everything for sale, pulses with life in her imagery. Goering has made a whore of history, and he has the figure, the dress, and the makeup for it.

West believed in Nuremberg's importance, but she could not gainsay its failures. In *A Train of Powder*, which contains her most important writing on postwar Germany, she transforms Nuremberg into the story of the German imagination, of its penchant for fairy tales and overbuilding, its Wagnerian dreams of grandeur, which contribute to the excesses of Nazism. In a Schloss, an old nineteenth-century mansion, she finds a metaphor for this Germanic need to overproduce and to dominate. She expects the mansion's greenhouse to be like the English variety, "A desert place of shabby and unpainted staging, meagerly set out with a diminished store of seed boxes" (26). Instead, it is neat, clean, full of plants, and perfect, flourishing in the hands of a crippled gardener's single-minded devotion prophetic of Germany's rebirth. The scene at the Nuremberg Schloss becomes West's own tribute to and

---

[20]West's Nuremberg report, "Extraordinary Exile," first appeared in *The New Yorker*, September 7, 1946. I quote from the much revised version included in *A Train of Powder* (New York: Viking, 1955), 3, 6. Page numbers for subsequent quotations will be cited in the text within parentheses.

warning about the self-dedication and dynamism of German culture, which she regards as a great force for both good and evil. She knows that Germans are perfectly capable of transforming their fairy tale desire for a happy ending into "Lear's kingdom of loss" (35).

West believed that the trials made a profound statement, settling once and for all that crimes against humanity should be punished. Yet the Nuremberg judges, she realized, were compromised. Some of the indictable crimes, such as unrestricted submarine warfare, had also been committed by the Allies. American and British judicial procedures baffled the German attorneys, who did not understand the role of cross-examination, as did the relatively passive Allied judges, because German judges took a far more active role in questioning witnesses. "The trouble about Nuremberg was that it was so manifestly a part of life as it is lived; the trial had not sufficiently detached itself from the oddity of the world," West concludes (51).

# CHAPTER EIGHT

## 1948-1966

Rebecca West's political isolation in the late 1940s and early 1950s resulted in her disaffection from much of the literature of the period as well. Estranged from the American temper, she castigated its indulgence in self-pity and sensationalism--two aspects of *Death of a Salesman* and *A Streetcar Named Desire* that repelled her. She also felt alienated from the British literary and journalistic community, dominated by males who she said hated her and circulated slurs that were beyond her power to repair. She suspected that she had not been asked to be a regular reviewer for *The Times* because of her politics.[1] Meeting with her French counterpart, the redoubtable anti-Communist Raymond Aron, she was not surprised to hear him say that he would have found it very difficult to maintain his position as an anti-Communist were it not for his job on *Le Figaro*. Even the non-Communists could not bear to hear Communism attacked.[2]

Intellectuals such as Noel Annan and Isaiah Berlin shared West's anti-Communist views, but Berlin thought "she had gone somewhat round the bend," and Annan later concluded: "I think if one conducts crusades against people for their beliefs (as opposed to denouncing them for ignoble, mean and dastardly actions), one closes one's mind and to a minute degree becomes

---

[1]RW to Emanie Arling, April 28, 1953, Yale.

[2]RW diary entry, April 23, 1953, Tulsa. For a detailed account of West's anti-Communist articles, her position on McCarthyism and the attacks on her politics, see Carl Rollyson, *Rebecca West: A Life* (New York: Scribner, 1996, 284-94).

infected by the very poison that one hates." Annan has a point. West's friend, Emily Hahn, once asked West what she thought of her meeting with the extreme anti-Communist, Frieda Utley. West said, "I think she goes too far." About West, Utley said to Hahn: "Charming, but she goes too far." West despised both Berlin and Noel Annan for what she deemed to be their overly tolerant positions. She might well have replied to them in words from her review of the *Gulag Archipelago*: "Let us remember that 25 years ago a large part of the Western European and American population of intellectuals were, with disgusting singlemindedness, pimping for Stalin." In West's mind, the very notion of the intellectual (an independent thinker) had been corrupted by her fellow intellectuals. She reviewed Berlin's *Russian Thinkers*, finding it insufficiently critical of its subjects and written in a repetitive, almost gushing style, that "shames the cuckoo."[3]

In the late 1970s, at a literary dinner West was aghast to find herself pinioned between Berlin and Annan. She knew that Berlin had not appreciated her review, and he bowed out of a conversation with her, but Annan chatted about the exposure of Anthony Blunt as a Communist spy, an exasperating topic for West because she had been receiving letters saying, "Well, we always thought that you were dotty, thinking there were Communist spies in England, but it seems to have been true." West regarded Annan as having been "passionately left most of his life," although he was now "ratting." She suspected he was trying to see how much she knew about Blunt even as he emphasized that he had not known Kim Philby, Guy Burgess, or Donald Maclean, Blunt's accomplices. Annan's belief that the Blunt coterie were the successors to the hard-line Fabian socialists intrigued her.[4] Annan later shrewdly suggested that after Bernard Shaw and Beatrice and Sidney Webb

---

[3]IB to the author, May 31, 1993; NA to the author, September 25, 1993; Interview with Emily Hahn; "Soviet Camps: who's guilty," *Sunday Telegraph*, June 25, 1978, p. 12; "Sir Isaiah's Brand of History," *Sunday Telegraph*, January, 1978, p. 14.

[4]RW diary entry, November 29, 1979, Tulsa.

defeated Wells's effort to make over the Fabians into a broader based, democratic organization, West had "turned against anything that could be said to be authoritarian."[5] The Webbs and Shaw, as West frequently noted, eventually became apologists for Stalin's Soviet Union.

Since completing *Black Lamb and Grey Falcon*, West had struggled to write a novel that would incorporate her Shakespearean sense of the treacherous nexus between family, politics, and art--abandoning one sizable manuscript, "Cockrow," in 1943, and beginning another, "Cousin Rosamund" in early 1949, both of which would eventually be completed as *The Fountain Overflows* (1956) and *The Birds Fall Down* (1966). But contemporary politics kept diverting her attention, for she saw herself engaged in an apocalyptic battle against the spread of Communism. She was quite aware, as she put it in one letter, that certain editors had decided she was "literally insane" on the subject.[6]

Institutions like the monarchy seemed more precious to her than ever-- as was evident in her article on the coronation of Queen Elizabeth II. She took enormous satisfaction in the pageant, calling it "an opera with real people." A year earlier her report on King George VI's death treated him as a Shakespearean hero. Her admiring portrayal of the royal family--it had not "lost its Eden"--derived from her quest for paradise lost, a theme that pervaded her nostalgic novel/saga-in-progress, "Cousin Rosamund."[7]

The work had grown to over 90,000 words as she reworked her sense of "the strange necessity," the importance of art in apprehending the world. She took inspiration from a set of drawings Picasso had done in his early seventies. They were unified by the subject of the painter and his model and

---

[5]Interview with Noel Annan.

[6]RW to Leonard Russell (her editor at *The Times*), March 8, 1954, Tulsa.

[7]"Rebecca West: The Coronation," *New York Herald Tribune*, May 3, 1953, p. 1.

were obviously related to his recent breakup with Francoise Gilot--although West made only the briefest, indirect allusions to that tumultuous event. She interpreted Picasso's drawings as saying that "It is necessary that the model should be painted as that she should be loved. It is as much a vital function as sex." The drawings were wonderfully comic and dealt with a theme dear to her: the "manifold imperfections of our sexual destiny." She explored Picasso's central metaphor of the circus:

> There the beautiful and the strong and the dignified collaborate with the deformed and the comic, and with the animals. Into the ring go the equestrians and the strong men and the acrobats, the dwarfs and the clowns, the horses and the performing dogs and the monkeys. Out of their incongruity they make a whole.[8]

She was demonstrating her argument for art in sentences that carried the pith of *The Strange Necessity*, the carnival of human desire and religious quest she had created in the figure of her Negro carnival barker in *A Letter to a Grandfather*. Her essay on Braque, which is just as masterful and even more playful than her Picasso piece argues:

> Braque, always interested in form, slows down his bull so that he can have a good look at him, while Picasso is fascinated by his thrust and speed. Braque's bull would be a better husband than Picasso's and not such a good lover. Picasso's bull has literary associations and takes part in controversies whereas Braque's bull has never seen its name in print.[9]

Both esthetically and biographically, West's *jeu d'esprit* works. Picasso wrote poetry and associated among the literati; his pictures have a literary allusiveness that Braque's do not. West had an affinity with Picasso. As she

---

[8]Pablo Picasso, *A Suite of 180 Drawings*, with an appreciation by Rebecca West (New York: Harcourt, Brace, 1954 [no pagination]).

[9]"The Private and Impersonal Notebooks of Braque," *Harper's Bazaar*, November, 1955, p. 195

confided to a friend, her husband "often thinks I rush at gates like a bull instead of a decent cow."[10]

When West offered her most sustained interpretation of literature, history, and politics in *The Court and the Castle: A Recurrent Theme in Shakespeare, the English Novelists, Proust, and Kafka* (1957), she showed no sign of letting up. In her Augustinian mode, she set centuries of Shakespeare criticism aside, contending that *Hamlet* was not a sympathetic psychological study of a sensitive, introspective man, but rather a stern and pessimistic revelation of humanity's imperfections embodied in Hamlet's rather crass behavior. Ophelia did not love Hamlet and she did not kill herself. Where was the line in the play in which Ophelia expressed this love? Polonius and Claudius had used her as a pawn. As Queen Gertrude said, Ophelia's drowning had been an accident, provoked no doubt by Ophelia's great distraction and fear. Now that Hamlet had killed her father, she had no protector at court and the cruel Claudius had no use for her. Critics had missed the point: *Hamlet* was about politics and power.

West reaffirmed that she had thrown off the influence of her early mentors, Shaw and Wells, who believed in the perfectibility of man and of society, in revolutions which could raze society and build it again better from the ground up. West had become a disciple of Edmund Burke, who believed in reform not revolution, and argued that tearing down time-honored institutions did more harm than good, because it destroyed the partial regard for human rights painfully gained over the ages.

West suggested that in Trollope, for example, social institutions, no matter how unjust they might be to certain classes of citizens, were absolutely necessary to civilization's survival. Even bureaucracy, the bane of Kafka's life, was also his mainstay. It could crush individuals, level illogical and unjust

---

[10]RW to Norris Chipman, November 9, 1955, Tulsa.

charges against K. in *The Trial*, but society could not function without bureaucracy. Kafka knew this quite well, having been trained in the Hapsburg Empire's bureaucracy..

*The Court and the Castle* is one of West's most impressive books. Frank Kermode, one of the century's most distinguished critics, extolled her power, the "full pressure" of intelligence and experience rarely seen in literary criticism. He thought her Trollope chapter "exceptionally fine" and the ones on Proust and Kafka the best he had ever read. But he admitted his "discomfort" with the alien mode of her thinking. Like many reviewers, he took issue with her "Calvinist *Hamlet*."[11]

Reviewer John Wain concluded that *The Court and the Castle* "is too profound and densely packed for me to be able to assess it until I have had time to live with it, to keep it beside me as a companion to my reading, as one keeps *The Sacred Wood* or *Countries of the Mind* or *The Wound and the Bow*." It constantly challenges the way we read--a "book with a bite."[12]

*The Court and the Castle* dovetailed with West's publication of *The Fountain Overflows*, the first part of her Aubrey family trilogy, "Cousin Rosamund." Charles Fairfield makes his appearance in the novel as the journalist Piers Aubrey, a magnificent monarch of a father, an aloof but dazzlingly Byronic figure, brooding over the great events of his day, exciting both the reverence and the irritation of his colleagues, who do not know how to cope with this brilliant yet irascible and profligate man, who is a gambler and a spendthrift.

West often said she had Edmund Burke in mind when she created Piers Aubrey. As a child she had heard her father in argument honor Burke

---

[11]"Literature and Statecraft," *The Spectator*, July 25, 1958, p. 146.

[12]*London Magazine*, December 1958, pp. 62-65; Peter Wolfe, *Rebecca West: Artist and Thinker* (Carbondale: Southern Illinois Press, 1971), 56.

as though he were a god, and she claimed kinship with him through one of her great-grandmothers.  She had grown up with this prophetic figure in the back of her mind.  Like Burke, Aubrey is an opponent of revolution and reveres tradition.  Completely out of sympathy with the modern world, however, he is an isolated figure.  He rues the fact that he is widely and respectfully read and yet exerts no influence--a position West knew only too well.

Piers and his wife Clare (a physical and mental ringer for Isabella Fairfield) dominate their daughter Rose's consciousness.  She is the novel's narrator, who portrays her parents as Olympian figures with the same "eagle look about them" which prevents them from living on easy terms with their fellow human beings.[13]  Clare, for example, is at a loss as to how to treat Miss Beevor, her eldest daughter Cordelia's violin teacher, who has ludicrous musical standards.  Because Clare exists in an esthetic realm so far above what Miss Beevor or the incompetent Cordelia could contemplate, she inevitably hurts their feelings.  Unlike her husband Piers, however, Clare has compassion for those whom she estranges, and she practices a tolerance and decency that Piers can exercise only in the abstract, when he is defending political principles, or taking up the cause of a woman accused of murder.  It is as if his interest in humanity can never focus narrowly enough to take in the plight of individuals unless some great issue is involved--in this instance a judge's abuse of power.[14]  Much is made of the way he hand-makes Christmas presents for his children, because it is one of the few signs of affection he displays--aside from his stimulating conversations with them.

Although Rose and her sister Mary have promising musical careers ahead of them, they remain fixated on their father--as West and her sister

---

[13]*The Fountain Overflows* (London: Virago, 1984), 102. Page numbers for subsequent quotations will be cited in the text within parentheses.

[14]A judge's abuse of power was the plot West had intended to pursue in *The Judge*.

Winifred were on Charles Fairfield. Like Charles, Piers is his childrens' greatest joy and their profoundest disappointment. Or as Rose says, "I had a glorious father. I had no father at all" (274). The family kindles in his presence, and his wife exclaims: "We are all less than Piers" (353). He fills his daughters with stimulating ideas, but he also fails to bring them up in a world to which they belong. He is as much myth as he is man: "He walked as if he had no weight, as if no limitation affected him" (197). Father can walk this way in memory, especially for a child who feels favored: "for it was I whom he had loved the best," Rose assures herself, after Piers abandons his family (337).

Exactly why he does so is never made explicit--anymore than West was ever certain why her father left home. Both Piers Aubrey and Charles Fairfield seem world weary; there is an air of hopelessness about them. Though Charles painted watercolors that West treasured all her life and occasionally wrote about art exhibitions, she believed that he grew contemptuous of her mother's dedication to music, and that his coarsened and corrupted nature rejected the life of art to which Isabella remained committed. This is a very grave sin, since art is a means of salvation in a flawed world. As Clare puts it, "art is so much more real than life" (62). Human beings who deny the art in them--like Uncle Jock, who plays the flute beautifully but assumes a vulgar demeanor and tongue--perversely reject their own redemption. Rose speaks of her mother's "access to the vein of imagination in my father which he was now repudiating, but which must have been what made him fall in love with her in spite of her inconvenient genius and integrity" (64). This wonderful sentence encapsulates the idea that in Clare, Piers fell in love with the best in himself, his imagination. When he leaves Clare, it is tantamount to a repudiation of his best self, the one he leaves at home, so to speak, in the care of his children. He flees, in other words, before they can witness his final degradation, his utter loss of hope for himself and the world. West could never know if her own father had reached such a low point, but fiction provided her with a way of filling the gap left by his absence, of endowing it with an Augustinian significance which did not ease her pain but at least made some sense of it.

West professed surprise that readers wondered why Piers Aubrey went away. She seconded Professor Anthony Cockshut's view that the subject of her novel is the difficulty of leading an artist's life. Although not an artist, Piers had an artist's vision, seeing "more of the truth than is convenient." Consequently, "he could not live at all. . . . He just could not bear life, and his family was part of it."[15]

It is significant that throughout the many years of writing her family memoirs, West never got beyond the time between her father's departure and death, between the ages of eight and thirteen. As Rose confesses later in *Cousin Rosamund*, the last volume of the never completed trilogy: "My father's desertion of me had never ceased to happen."[16]

*The Fountain Overflows* is a book about the struggle to grow up and about the forbidding realization of impending disaster. Piers divines that the twentieth-century will be a calamity. He rejects the Edwardian faith in a "law of progress." One of his colleagues tells Clare: "Your husband puts down in black and white the idea that we're not going forward, we're going backward. He says that civilisation's going to collapse. It's going to shrink instead of spreading. He says that country after country is going to be taken over by common criminals" (316).

Rose has some of the gift of prophecy herself, which she displays at a party by placing her hands on childrens' foreheads and reading their minds. Poltergeists assault the house of Rose's cousin, Rosamund, who becomes the focal character of trilogy, destined to experience the century's worst atrocities,

---

[15]RW to AC, August 19, 1957, Tulsa.

[16](New York: Penguin, 1987), 128. Page numbers for subsequent quotations will be cited in the text within parentheses.

including the concentration camp. West's trilogy is Pauline in its occult portrayal of the world as seen through a glass darkly. In notes for her projected trilogy (eventually she thought it might be four novels), West listed her characters according to their prophetic roles. Thus Piers "saw only a little way prophetically." Clare actually saw more but "got confused in life." Richard Quin, the perfect brother Rose and Mary dote on--and the idealized brother Rebecca never had, based on Isabella's brother, Joey, who died in his twenties--is described as lacking ambition because he knows he will be killed in World War I. Cordelia is "denied her gift of prophecy." Rosamund will become the "perfect priestess" and also the most enigmatic character--in part because she is powerless to prevent the awful vision of the holocaust she harbors. She is compared, in one passage, to an elusive, immobile Greek goddess.[17]

In her multi-volume family saga, West set herself nearly an impossible task: to resolve her feelings about her own family, while integrating those feelings into her interpretation of the twentieth century. She had an ambition worthy of Augustine, who also used autobiography to express his understanding of God and man and to reveal the meaning of history.

The novel was a popular and critical success, doing much to rehabilitate West's reputation as a novelist; it had been twenty years since the publication of her last novel, *The Thinking Reed*. One reviewer called her "today's finest English stylist." Several reviewers recorded their pleasure at reading a novel so packed with characters and incidents worthy of Dickens and of the great Edwardian novelists, Wells and Bennett.[18]

West began almost immediately on *This Real Night*, the sequel to *The Fountain Overflows*, completing much of it and several chapters of a third

---

[17]West's notes for her trilogy are in a manuscript notebook at Tulsa.

[18]John F. Sullivan, "Seeing Beyond the Lattice of Flesh," *The Commonweal*, January 11, 1957, pp. 387-88.

volume, posthumously titled *Cousin Rosamund*. But she would never complete her grand scheme, interrupting it to write her memoirs and to try several other long nonfiction and fictional narratives, as well carrying on a full schedule of reviewing for the *Sunday Telegraph* and producing articles for many other publications. *The Fountain Overflows* proved prophetic, in that its concern with how families and the world nurture but also destroy the artist--applied all too closely to West herself.

Nearly half of *This Real Night* remains fixated on the missing father: "colours do not seem as bright to me as they did when Papa was still alive," Rose laments.[19] She struggles to emerge in her own right as a person and an artist. The father's absence and the death of the artist in him almost fatally disables his daughter. The novel is full of beautiful images of arrested development:

> A family of ducks swam up, self-possessed in their smooth and shining, close-fitting feather suits, some in brown tweeds, others in a birds' version of men's black and white evening clothes, only with the shirt-front right underneath them, so that their yellow paddling legs struck out of its whiteness. Then they landed on the strip of grass in front of us, and waddled about suddenly grown simpletons, stupid about their balance, not certain where to go. They were myself. Often I felt at ease and then, suddenly, I did not know what to do. I was a fool for all the world to see. (63-64)

The alternating senses of equilibrium and disequilibrium, of being in one's element and then becoming ill-at-ease is reminiscent of West's own preco-cious but unbalanced and fitful career.

Complicating Rose's development as a woman and artist is her acute sense of male prerogatives and of the way women are held back. When her Uncle Len bawls out her brother Richard Quin for allowing her and her cousin Rosamund to witness the aftermath of Uncle Len's fight with an unruly

---

[19](New York: Macmillan, 1984), 108. Page numbers for subsequent quotations will be cited in the text within parentheses.

customer at his tavern, an enraged Rose comments "there was no difference in courage between men and women" (89). In words reminiscent of *Sunflower*, Rose concludes: "men find a special pleasure in rejecting women" (167).

*This Real Night* ends with the death of Rose's mother--at a point equivalent to when Isabella Fairfield died and West was preparing to leave Wells and pursue her independence. The effort to come this far in the saga, with virtually the whole of Rose's mature life and her concert career to be covered is perhaps what convinced West that she would need not only a third but a fourth novel to work out the fate of Rose's cousin, Rosamund, whom Richard calls the "Rose of the World" because she represents a spirit that art tries to express and that the world tries to crush (241). It is Rosamund who speaks up when Uncle Len lectures Richard: "Why should we not have been here?" (89) It is a prophetic question, for there is no place that Rosamund will not go, no part of the world that is foreign to her. She is the worldly counterpart to the artist, the person of spirit who acts so as to bring the world to account. She makes concrete a concern for the world what Piers Aubrey only felt in the abstract. It is Rosamund who must bear direct witness, who must die in a concentration camp--as Rose and her sister Mary were to learn at Nuremberg if West had completed her family saga.

In West's saga, in her life, she was plagued by the spiritual question of why art did not save the world, and why artists could not continue to create. West's contemporary, Edith Sitwell, also turned to blending the theological and the personal in her later poetry, especially in the *Canticle of the Rose*. Stuck in one of the manuscript notebooks of "Cousin Rosamund" is West's letter to Sitwell, thanking her for sending a signed copy of *Canticle of the Rose*. West told her that she had been reading nothing else while she was working on her novel. Just then she had been writing an impossible chapter-- "simply an attempt to describe the battle between all angels and all witches as manifested at a children's party." Receiving the *Canticle* made it seem to

West as if Sitwell had "joined in the conversation." To West, it was as uncanny and as prophetic as the fiction she was trying to write. Like Milton's *Paradise Lost*, West's book tries to explain the nature of evil, the role of art and of human will. West's effort was like lifting the world, and it was exhausting. "So often, reading you, I think, 'How hard she works!'" West confided to Sitwell. "The thing is that to write one needs the constitution of a navvy and if one had one wouldn't write. It is the artistic dilemma. How strange that you who are so fine seem to have overcome it."[20]

West's own inability to finish the saga and other projected novels in her later years seemed not merely an individual failure to her but a metaphor of the constant human dereliction of art, of how to maintain the creative vision, the appreciation of form that Henry Andrews expressed in Yugoslavia, that Clare Aubrey evokes in *The Fountain Overflows:* "life is as extraordinary as music says it is" (210). Similarly, Richard Quin in *This Real Night*, going off to be killed in World War I, tells Rose: "And believe me when I say that I shall be all right. In the same strictly truthful sense that it's true that the two angles at the base of an isosceles triangle are equal. No fancy, no frill. Not symbolically, not mystically. Just all right" (241).

A wrought-up Rebecca West often did algebra problems at night to cope with her insomnia. Pages and pages of her notebooks are filled with her solutions to equations, which represented to her the crucial human quest for form and balance. During work on the saga she took a cruise to the Greek Islands and gave a lecture aboard ship that exemplifies the theme of her saga. She spoke about the beginnings of civilization, and about the need for human beings to contact each other and to trade. Going to Greece was like going half-way back to our origins. She praised the Greek gift for self-con-sciousness, which stimulated the human effort to gain control over the environment. The civil service, laws--all stemmed from this Greek aptitude

---

[20]RW to ES, October 5, 1949, Tulsa.

for measuring the pleasure and pain government could provide its citizens. Greeks made the discussion of government common knowledge. But the Greeks also exemplified the dangers of intellectual life--its inclination to game-playing with minds interested only in scoring points against each other. Intellectuals did not have to confront the consequences of their ideas; intellectual frivolity contributed to Greece's decline.[21]

Rosamund, the most non-intellectual character of West's saga confronts the consequences of ideas. While Rose and Mary live rather privileged artists' lives, Rosamund is the "ground we lived on" (86), Rose explains in the last part of the saga West was able to finish. Rosamund is the family's "moral genius" (263). If Piers Aubrey has had a grim augury of a violent twentieth century and retreats from his family and the world, Rosamund is prepared to embrace that holocaust--not because she is an ascetic or a martyr, indeed she makes what West calls a "mercenary marriage" to a crass millionaire in Germany and shows, as Victoria Glendinning puts it, the "ruthless and cunning that have been remarked in many saints. In her synopsis for the saga, West notes that Rosamund is all that art cannot give Rose and Mary. Rosamund is "religion."[22]

In the denouement to their lives, Rose becomes estranged from her pianist-sister, Mary, who decides to give up art for a comfortable life that art has given her. Rose's ambivalence is not unlike what West sometimes felt about her sister Winifred, a closet poet, and the older sister who had first taught West to appreciate fine poetry. Treachery within the family, the forsaking of art, and the treachery of the century were to cohere in the completed saga, though as Glendinning astutely notes, the plan for the saga

---

[21]Manuscript notebook [c. 1962], Tulsa.

[22]Afterword to *Cousin Rosamund*, 290-91. West's synopsis is included in Glendinning's afterword.

was so ambitious that it is difficult to see how West could have come to closure within a reasonable novelistic structure.

In October 1941, West had faced a similar problem: how to encompass her heroine's life beyond youth and middle age in a novelistic structure. She abandoned her novel "Cockcrow," two years later, and took it up again in the 1960s as her commitment to "Cousin Rosamund" flagged. Set in 1908, it focused on fourteen-year-old Laura Rowan, the daughter of a Russian mother, Tania, and an English father, Edward. Laura accompanies her mother to Paris on a visit to her grandparents, the Diakonovs. Nikolai Diakonov, a Tsarist minister, is living in Paris in disgrace, unjustly suspected of divulging information that led to the assassinations of several government officials. When Laura accompanies Nikolai on a train excursion into the Parisian countryside, they are accosted in their carriage by Chubinov, a revolutionary who announces to Nikolai that his trusted friend and aide, Kamensky, has been a double agent, betraying both the government and the revolutionaries. The shock proves too much for Nikolai, who dies before returning to Paris and to Russia, where he had hoped to submit himself to the Tsar's judgment, even at the risk of dying first at Kamensky's hands.

Laura witnesses the male public world Rebecca West criticizes in *Black Lamb and Grey Falcon*. Although Nikolai treats Kamensky as a trusted subordinate and even condescends occasionally to show Kamensky some affection, he has not really known his man; he misses the details that make Kamensky not only an individual but a traitor. The inquisitive Laura picks up Kamensky's spectacles, sees that they are made of clear glass, and concludes he is a pretender. Her discovery provides one of the details that convinces Nikolai that Chubinov has correctly identified Kamensky as a double agent, whom Chubinov knows as the master revolutionary, Gorin. (Ford Madox Ford told West of such a case, of the double agent Azeff, whose story is the inspiration for the novel.)

It devolves on Laura to see that Kamensky/Gorin has loved and betrayed Nikolai just as he has loved and betrayed Chubinov and the other revolutionaries. As Gorin he is a father figure to Russian radicals, and Chubinov's attitude toward him is nothing less than reverential. At the same time, Chubinov is the son of one of Nikolai's oldest friends, and although Chubinov detests Nikolai's politics, he comes to warn Nikolai and to confess that he has regarded Nikolai, as well, as a father figure. Thus treachery is deeply imbedded in family relations. Although it seems incredible that Kamensky/Gorin could endear himself to opposite sides of the political spectrum, in fact those opposites are kin to each other--just as in *Black Lamb and Grey Falcon* the Serbs and Croats argue against each other but use the same accents and gestures.

West invests Laura with a version of herself. West detested being treated like a child and regarded childhood as a "state of disequilibrium" (*This Real Night*, 4). Both Nikolai and Edward Rowan are reminiscent of West's autocratic Anglo-Irish father, whose mother's name was Arabella Rowan. Like Charles Fairfield, Edward Rowan is a snob: "his voice always sounded as if he were making fun of someone."[23] Nikolai regards himself as a "pillar," almost literally holding up the Tsar's kingdom. Edward Rowan is "strongly and slenderly built." Laura admires him as a "symbol of calm," but he is "too arrogant," and prone to "Irish malice." He stands with "too artificial an alertness," in a position appropriate only to a "fencer in play." In fact, he establishes his authority by verbal fencing: "Her father liked to play at tyranny, it was his nature to argue." Nikolai never accepts anyone's opinion without an argument. He is "like a mad king out of a play." Indeed, he is Rebecca West's version of King Lear, blind to the treachery in his own family. Laura's mother Tania has chosen to marry a tyrant similar to her father. In

---

[23]All quotations are from the manuscript versions of "Cockrow" and West's notes on her novel at Yale and Tulsa. Much of the dialogue and narrative closely matches *The Birds Fall Down*, but "Cockrow" is more like a schema than a fully fleshed out novel.

many respects, Edward Rowan establishes a household with a brilliant but submissive wife resembling Charles Fairfield's household. Edward Rowan even comes from County Kerry. He has grown up in a privileged home Laura hears about but never gets to visit, and in her deprived state she deplores his "cold pedantry and lack of ordinary feelings." Edward Rowan is also an adulterer, another kind of family traitor.

Laura's rebelliousness make her as much of a traitor as Kamensky, whom she cannot help liking even after she learns of his treachery. Kamensky treats her like an adult, an equal, saying "the trouble with both you and me is that we are both poets." Yet with his tenderness, it might be said that he is fatherly, giving her the attention that neither her father nor her grandfather knows how to provide. When West revised the novel and titled it *The Birds Fall Down*, she made it clear that Kamensky also wanted to be Laura's lover. He was to embody the all encompassing and understanding maleness which West had always sought.

Nikolai reveals that he is only half a man when he announces: "It is public life which should matter to a man." Kamensky is his erotic other half, the man of intimacy and tete a tetes, where confidences can be exchanged and where spies can discretely transact their business. Eroticism and espionage are linked not only in Kamensky's personality but in Chubinov's voluptuous evocations of Gorin's (Kamensky's) hold on his comrades. The central metaphor of "Cockcrow" and its final version, *The Birds Fall Down*, is Nikolai's fable of the "cocks-at-war"--the males vying with each other for mating privileges, so intent on fighting that they do not hear the firing guns, which bring them down. Nikolai extols the "indescribable fascination in seeing a system, perfect in itself, and in some way very beautiful and ingenious being destroyed at the very moment when it reaches its climax by another system, just as perfect and more ingenious. . . ."[24] This eroticism of destruction recalls West's tour-de-force descriptions of Franz Ferdinand's game shooting. There is a love of killing and a love of what is killed--the human paradox that is stamped throughout *Black Lamb and Grey Falcon*. Nikolai himself is repulsive and lovable, as West found her own father, as she found most men. As she points out in her notes on "Cockcrow," Nikolai's "career is divided between mysticism and careerism." He justifies everything, including murder, in terms of his allegiance to the Tsar, God's representative on earth, yet his actions are no better than those of the revolutionaries. Each side spies on and violates the privacy of the other. "How strange it is that one of our lives should be a noble poem and the other its parody, and that we should not know which was which!"

When Laura has trouble following the argument between Nikolai and Chubinov and begs Chubinov to stop bothering her grandfather, he replies: "Mademoiselle, try not to be wholly English, try to be somewhat Russian, try to believe that the relationships which compose the tissue of life are not always perfectly obvious at the first glance." "Cockcrow" is an assault on English complacency, on Edward Rowan's fatuous declaration on the eve of World War I: "Throughout the last hundred years civilisation has become more and more firmly established, and one can hardly conceive the process should be reversed."

Chubinov's exposure of Gorin is treated like treachery by his revolutionary organization because he has attacked the foundations of its faith, the pillar it has found in Gorin, who like Nikolai, has never wavered in the cause. Yet by harboring Kamensky and by failing to detect his duplicity,

---

[24]Nikolai is also describing hunting and shooting in terms of the Hegelian dialectic of thesis-antithesis-synthesis, which he has, in a sense, fathered. He has much in common with Kamensky (Gorin) as a father figure, since it is Kamensky who teaches Chubinov how to be a good revolutionary. Yet Chubinov, taught to be a good shot by Nikolai, kills Kamensky (Gorin). Also, Kamensky (Gorin), in serving both the tsarists and the revolutionaries is himself a personal example of the Hegelian dialectic--as he hints to Laura.

Nikolai has betrayed the Tsar and himself, just as surely as the revolutionaries have betrayed themselves by venerating Gorin, who has exploited their love. This is the perfect circle of crowing cocks that mesmerizes Nikolai, a seemingly self-sufficient male world that is actually self-destructive.

More than politics is at stake, Chubinov admits, when he sets out to unmask Gorin:

> I also felt the exaltation of a child who is secretly doing something nasty which its parents have forbidden it to do, which was equally ridiculous. I remembered I had felt the same blend of inappropriate emotions when I was a young man and had been obliged to lie to my family about my connection with the revolutionary party.

In each case, as revolutionary and counter-revolutionary, he attacks father and family. His motives, like West's own, are a profoundly conflicted blend of fealty and treachery to the familial ideal--as are Laura's in the second part of "Cockcrow," in which she angers her father by refusing the marriage he wishes to arrange for her. She tries to goad him to confess his feelings, which he finds repugnant, because he would have to acknowledge her desperate desire to have him share his feelings with her. A traitor to Charles Fairfield's views, West knew the anguish of having an absent father who could not accept hers. Allied to Gorin but attracted to Nikolai, Chubinov expresses his tormented dualism by crying out to Nikolai: "I would have liked to prostate myself before both of you and confess all my sins." Like Gorin, Chubinov has become, in a sense, a double agent--as all human beings seem to be in Rebecca West's story of divided feelings.

In such moments, Chubinov looks "as lost as any child," but he is bolstered by Laura's ability to cite the details that confirm that Gorin and Kamensky are one and the same. "Now, mademoiselle, you are pushing us towards reality, as your sex so often does, when we intellectual males turn our backs on it." The novel's long monologues and dialectical exchanges are the equivalent of the male/female debates in *Black Lamb and Grey Falcon*. "We had to find the truth," Laura exclaims, as her grandfather groans, not really wanting to admit that Kamensky has deceived him. Indeed, the train excursion is the first time she is able to exercise her gift for observation, remembering the "hard inflexible courtesy of her father who from the time she had been a little child had treated her as if there were some restraining bar between male and female which could not be lifted." Nikolai is no better than Edward, when he refers to Laura's half-English parentage, which makes her "corrupted by the West." He credits none of her perceptions.

Chubinov's psychological interpretation of the revolt against the father is paralleled by Nikolai's religious explanation, which he tries to keep consonant with his devout Russian Orthodox faith. Kamensky

> believed himself to be God, and therefore he has sought to frustrate me as only God has the right to frustrate a man; but he reverenced me so much that he sinned a second sin, for he thought me God, and he has conspired to overthrow me as it could be worthwhile only to overthrow God. If the little one had known that we were man and man, and servants of God in our very different capacities, he would have been preserved from this guilt.

In such speeches, West reveals her debts to Dostoyevsky and Freud.

But West did not get very far beyond the intensity of the first part of "Cockrow." Much of the argument between Laura and her father, which opens part two, has to be read back into part one, which is easy enough to do for a reader of *The Birds Fall Down*, but which would not be clear to the reader of "Cockrow," where the strands of Laura's train trip with her grandfather and her family life in London are too widely separated. In other words, the novel needed a stronger beginning, one that clearly impressed Edward Rowan on the reader's consciousness and prepared the reader to see the duel between Chubinov and Nikolai as parallel to Laura's duel with her father and family, with Kamensky/Gorin serving as her proxy as well as Chubinov's. Not until family and political life, the private and the public, were absolutely entwined would the novel maintain its tension. That West did not see this in 1943--that the train journey had to encompass her novel just as a journey encompasses *Black Lamb and Grey Falcon*--is clear from her effort to project a future for Laura beyond the Kamensky/Gorin/Chubinov/-Nikolai plot to other lovers and periods beyond World War I. Attempting to write past the logical conclusion of her novel, she finally had to stop, having stymied herself by taking a wrong turn.

The revised novel presents an older (her age changes from fourteen to eighteen) and tougher Laura, one who learns to practice the game of treachery well. The setting is moved to 1900 in order to avoid entangling historically with the 1905 revolution and the rise of the Bolsheviks. Laura develops acumen as a player in the game of treachery that is modern life and politics. She is an extraordinary creation--at once a kind of feminist heroine and potentially as corrupt as the male world with which she duels.

Like "Cousin Rosamund," *The Birds Fall Down* is the novel as prophecy. West's novel bears comparison with the great political novels in English--those by Joseph Conrad and Henry James--but her point of view is distinctly feminist in that she shows how women have been shunted aside in men's political plotting and how women are capable of taking action, when they become conscious of the plots that have excluded them. Yet Laura is also fatally obtuse: she does not understand Kamensky's love for her, and she suspects that she herself is in danger because at any moment Kamensky will discover that she is aware of his double identity. Laura believes that if she does not cooperate with Chubinov's plan to assassinate Kamensky, she herself will be murdered.

*The Birds Fall Down* is an extraordinary amalgam. It contains elements of suspense, spy, and political novels. In the long train conversations between Nikolai and Chubinov, West manages not merely to convey the revolutionary ferment taking place in pre World War I Russia and on the European continent, she is able to show how human character evolves out of the practice of politics and political intrigue. When Chubinov confronts Count

Nikolai, two different interpretations of the world collide. What Chubinov tells the Count, the Count regards as inconceivable, for he trusts neither Chubinov's unstable personality nor his political judgment. Thus it is up to Laura to filter through Chubinov's long, agitated speeches exactly what she can accept. Yet the very length of the conversation, and its twists and turns, builds suspense. Will Count Nikolai finally admit he has misplaced his trust in Kamensky? How will Laura be able to contend with the welter of information Chubinov showers upon her?

Although Laura has her own firsthand experience with Kamensky in Paris, when she visits her grandfather, that experience occurs before Chubinov's revelation. Consequently, she has to rethink Kamensky's actions and her impressions of him through Chubinov's description of Kamensky's other life. The result is a fascinating re-enactment and dissection of what has been presented at the outset of the novel. In the very act of listening to Chubinov, Laura and the reader of the novel have to re-evaluate everything that has been presented thus far. This technique of telling and then retelling events through the eyes of a new witness provides extraordinary insight into what it is like to function in a world on the verge of war and revolution.

Laura discovers that she quickly becomes enveloped in the logic of events, the chain of actions set in motion by a conspiracy. When she decides to abandon Kamensky as he abandoned her grandfather, she does not tell her father, and she concludes that she has no choice to do otherwise. Like Augustine, she thinks of life as making the choice for her. *The Birds Fall Down* is not about which side is right--the Tsar or his opponents--but about a world divided, perpetually split because human beings cannot remain loyal to each other and cannot trust each other. Laura believes that she can confide her secret in no one. She is not even sure she can trust herself, that what she is feeling is right. Yet she is compelled to act. As Chubinov, an arch plotter acknowledges: "We always believe that what we did we had to do. Other men have free will, we ourselves live in a determinist universe."

He also confesses, that after all the rationalizations devised for his actions, "each man is a mystery to himself." This inscrutable quality in human actions, the spring of motivations that eludes even the finest minds, is a theme that transcends the political discussions of the novel and allies West's work with that of one of her major influences, Joseph Conrad.

*The Birds Fall Down* is a most unsentimental novel about the relationship between men and women. It is about the rituals and ceremonies of courtship and loyalty which mean so much to human beings but which they nevertheless betray. Women have been the victims of these ceremonies, but they also been willing participants and are as implicated in good and evil as are the men. This troubling truth is what Laura herself learns, and it is the dramatization of that truth which makes *The Birds Fall Down* West's greatest novel.

Reviews of *The Birds Fall Down* were good to excellent, with a few notable exceptions; some reviewers seemed irritated by the book's long conversations and the hoopla surrounding its publication--an author's tour in October and several flattering notices and interviews. V.S. Pritchett, the most perceptive reviewer, observed that Rebecca's Russians "majored in being Russian."[25] He admired her beautiful evocations of the French countryside, through which Nikolai and Laura travel--a product of West's reverence for things French. As she told several interviewers, she had had a French career, combining journalism and fiction in a way that seemed natural to her Gallic colleagues but foreign to the British. Similarly, her novel reflected a continental blend of ideas and action, characters and arguments. She pointed out that the exchanges some critics found improbable were commonplace in 1900. As her last book would show, her imagination remained fixed, to an extraordinary degree, on the turn of the century that had given her life.

---

[25]"The Climate of Paranoia," *The New Yorker*, December 3, 1966, pp. 225-33.

CHAPTER NINE

## 1967-1983

West celebrated the success of *The Birds Fall Down* with her first trip to Mexico. She planned to write an article on Leon Trotsky's stay in Mexico (she had visited his house and talked with his grandson). But eventually her fascination with the country developed into an idea for a book as grand in scope as *Black Lamb and Grey Falcon*, an evocation of a culture and a vision of history. It would include her patented dialogues with her husband, digressions on his family background and hers, a detailed interpretation of the Aztecs, Mesoamerican art, the Spanish conquest, and a discourse on Cortes and other great men, including Napoleon. She made detailed notes on Aztec social structure, read copiously on the Pre-Columbian civilizations, consulted scholars. There would be a section on the artists Diego Rivera and Freda Kahlo. To refresh her memory and to gather new material, West returned to Mexico twice, in 1967 and 1969. She began her book at the age of seventy-four; it would have taken at least five years to finish at a time when she also wanted to complete "Cousin Rosamund" and to write short stories. It was an enormous, astonishing pyramid of a book to consider scaling at this late stage in her career. It is not surprising that she did not complete it; what is remarkable is that some of the sixty thousand plus words she produced approach the level of *Black Lamb and Grey Falcon*.

In some ways, West's truncated Mexican epic is even more fascinating than her published work, because its multiple drafts reveal how hard she worked at achieving her autobiographical/ historical/psychological effects. The false starts, the repetitions, the occasional confusions in the ordering of words and phrases--even the illegible words--have a mournful, cryptic fascination. They are her own Mayan ruin. All the rigging has been maneuvered into place for a might-have-been masterpiece.

In the human sacrifices of the Aztecs, West found a worthy parallel to the scene of the black lamb on the rock. In both cases, the gods had to be appeased, and human beings were haunted by the need to sacrifice, to atone for their very existence. The sculptures of the angry, hideous-looking Aztec gods overwhelmed West, for in them she saw the malign faces of fate that she had always believed was against her, and a metaphor for this, one of the bloodiest of centuries. She put the argument of the Mexican book in the form of a liturgy or set of moral axioms, which fit together like a chant:

> The human race wishes to die: to kill is to offer up a substitute.
> It wants to live (but not much).
> It wants to be moral.
> It wants a moral excuse for killing.
> It kills if that is to remove something likely to make it die.
> It is happy if it can find a creed which sanctifies killing.
> It is happy if it can find a creed which kills but does not appear to.[1]

She was impressed with the Aztec belief that blood renewed the universe and that copious amounts of human blood might prevent the world from self-destructing as it came to the end of the fifty-two year cycles in the Aztec calendar. What looked like a ritual of death actually contributed to salvation. She rejected this logic, but she saw it operating everywhere, East and West, among the Aztecs and their Spanish conquerors.

This is perhaps why Trotsky receives her sympathy. He is one of the slain modern gods, a victim of a revolution that fed on the blood of its makers, a renegade priest of a contemporary creed. As Andrews puts it to West in her notes, Trotsky and Stalin "quarrelled over a matter of faith."

---

[1]West's manuscripts of her Mexico book are at Tulsa.

West portrays Trotsky as a king-in-exile. To be sure, he is a usurper, but a man of such brilliance that he deserves Shakespearean treatment--the usurper as Macbeth, the revolutionary whose genius entitles him to power even as it provoked him to traffic in evil. Trotsky, like Napoleon, opposes hereditary power, and stands for the human effort to transform ideas into action.

West admits that her love for Trotsky is "irrational," although she does not explain this emotion in the incomplete draft. Surely one reason for her love is what she calls his "Shakespearean character," his ability to observe "exactly what was happening round him, and put its essence into language." Another clue to her affinity with Trotsky is that he is named as one of the survivors, one of the many exiles welcomed to Mexico, a land seeking social justice, no matter how elusive this ideal has proven. Trotsky is one of those whom history is bound to get, yet he eluded Stalin's blood lust for more than ten years.

West's Mexican epic contains riveting scenes that fuse history, art, and politics. A friend shows her a photograph of Freda Kahlo and Diego Rivera, great artists who had a troubled marriage, followed by a divorce and a remarriage. They are standing in Freda's garden, near her creation of a thatched pyramid with a four-tiered altar on which idols are staked in a "congestion which, granted the fiery nature of Aztec gods, should have led to a seismic disturbance." West compares the look the couple gives each other to "that look of slow pneumatic expansion always displayed by lovers in opera, which suggests that, like balloons, they have to be subject to a certain degree of inflation before they can get off the ground." History as theater, artists with a sense of their historical mission, wrests from West some of her most startling figures of speech.

West does not downplay the cruelty of the Spanish conquest, but she admires Cortes's audacity and political genius; her narrative encompasses both his esurience (one of her favorite words) and his piety, his lust for gold and his promise to win souls for his church. She relates the Spanish gifts to

Mexico "beyond counting": wheat, barley, rye, oats, bananas, oranges, limes, apples, pears, sugarcane, horses, mules, hogs, sheep, goats, cattle, and the introduction of the wheel. History suggests to her that it is futile to blame the Spanish for empire-building when Ferdinand and Isabella were themselves just managing to push back Islam and needed colonies to make their economy grow. Her anti-Turk bias shows when she suggests that it would have been worse if the Turks had occupied Mexico as they had the Balkans, making a "mess that brought on us the turbulence of Europe and the two World Wars." Instead of Our Lady of Guadalupe, she asks us to imagine a mosque, and women in veils, revealing not faces but "black snouts," the men "looking their worst in that most unbecoming of male headgear, the fez," a fashion that "might have been running up all over North America." She admired Ataturk because he made Turkey modern, outlawed the veil and the fez, and turned his country's face westward.[2]

The Spanish exploitation of the Indians, West recognizes, is an appalling record, but it ranks no worse than what the Egyptians, Greeks, and Romans did to their slaves--especially the miners, who in every culture seem to excite a peculiar sadism from their masters. Although she concedes that Freudian and Jungian explanations of history often seem detached from reality and incapable of verification because they are founded on a faith in the unconscious, she is attracted to the notion of mining as a raping of mother earth and the association of metals dug out of the ground with excrement. She notes that the Aztecs had a conception of gold as the excrement of the gods. She ponders why miners who extract such treasure from the earth should receive punishment rather than reward. She speculates that miners violate some fundamental taboo so widespread that it has been adopted by peoples as different as Afrikaners and Mormons. But West does not press her point so much as she reveals the sheer inadequacy of any

[2]"Triumph of a Proud Turk," November 8, 1964, *Sunday Telegraph*, Yale clipping file.

rational explanation for the harshness of the miners' treatment. Teasing meaning out of her history, her prose becomes almost incantatory.

Montezuma is presented as Cortes's equal--in some ways as his superior, for the Aztec emperor sensitively encountered an unknowable figure in Cortes. Was he the ferocious god, Quetzalcoatl, returned to earth as Aztec religion prophesied, or was he simply a man? Montezuma put several delicate, tactful questions to the Spaniard meant to establish his true identity, but nothing in Cortes's replies could satisfy the Aztec emperor, who was loathe to offend a god or to put himself at a disadvantage with a man. The Aztecs, West points out, had founded their civilization on the remains of several others--the Mayans, the Olmecs, the Toltecs, the Miztecs, each of which had perished from some unknown cause, perhaps for some grave sin that the Aztecs feared they might themselves commit. Thus isolated, they could be compared to the British, if they had experienced not only the Norman conquest, the fall of Rome and Byzantium, but also (before the sixteenth century) the annihilation of France, Germany, Spain, and the Low Countries. In effect, Montezuma's position would be like a British or American government suddenly faced with "phenomena which might be either a hostile expeditionary force of space-men or the Second Coming of Christ."

West's epic fragment on Mexico is a congeries of brilliant narratives broken up by sections of notes, sketches of argument and character, and bald statements of theme. How the Trotsky section would have been hooked to Cortes, Mexico to Spain, West and Andrews to the history they confront, and that history to West and Andrews, is not clear, but their potential nexus impregnates her text as she walks us through her visit to Trotsky's house, her conversation with his grandson, her dialogue with her driver, her tour of the Archeological Museum in Mexico City. One of her working titles for the book, "Survivors in Mexico," alluded to the linkage she never finished forging between her characters, who are, like herself and her husband, doomed on the main highways of history, and yet survivors nonetheless.[3]

West worked fitfully on her Mexico book through the first part of 1967. She kept going over the same sentences. Even writing letters seemed difficult, and she sought relief in composing "rather odd poetry" about Mexico.[4] Rereading what she had written, she thought it good but disorganized; she could not construct the joints.[5]

Other promising novels and stories remained stillborn--the most interesting of which, "The Only Poet," West returned to with some regularity in the early 1970s. She liked the dialogue--there were quite remarkable scenes between Leonora Morton and her lover Nicholas, a probing of the sex and love nexus that went considerably beyond what had been essayed in *Sunflower*. Indeed, in some ways, "The Only Poet" rewrites that abandoned novel, for it too is haunted by the figure of Max Beaverbrook, now called Gerard March, who woos Leonora, then abruptly drops her. "He used you," Nicholas remarks, "as a cover for something. Either he's a pederast or impotent."[6] More than any other Rebecca West work, "The Only Poet" focuses on the physicality of lovemaking, of the one unique thing (it is never described) that Leonora is able to do for Nicholas. Yet he cannot remain faithful to Leonora, and she cannot accept his plea that she is more important than any of his other women. Eighty, and sensing her imminent death,

---

[3]In *Family Memories*, ed. Faith Evans (New York: Viking, 1987), 223-243, West includes a chapter on Henry Maxwell Andrews and his part-Scottish, part-Danish family, with close ties to Burma and Germany. This polyglot ancestry appealed greatly to West, and at one point she considered placing this chapter at the head of her memoirs, perhaps as a metaphor for her own diverse identities.

[4]RW to Kit Wright, June 10, 1967, courtesy of KW.

[5]For further details on West's book on Mexico, see Carl Rollyson, *Rebecca West: A Life* (New York: Scribner, 1996), 353-60.

[6]*The Only Poet and Short Stories*, ed. Antonia Till (London: Virago, 1992), 327. Page numbers for subsequent quotations will be cited in the text within parentheses.

Leonora ranges over their affair, still trying--as West continued to do in her diaries and letters--to fathom the male psyche.

Leonora lives in London but longs for her country home, which bears some resemblance to West's country home, Ibstone. She misses her walled garden, the change of the seasons, her labradors, who are "like the ideal family solicitor, chasing the woodland smells as if they were getting concessions out of the Inland Revenue" (297). But London is convenient for Leonora, as it was for West--especially for its indoor swimming pools. "One got something of what one had got from love-making, from that first thrust into the water, the surrender of the whole body to an unusual element" (298). Like West, Leonora still yearns for a lover "who is strong as men are, who gives a sense of protection" (330). But obedience is not the word for Leonora's attraction to the powerful Nicholas: "For a woman to obey a man is horrible, to surrender her will, her sense of right and wrong, it is the sort of thing a prostitute does to curry favour with a man" (345).

How Leonora was to die baffled West. "It has to be seen whether I have still the physical strength necessary for the exercise of the imagination," she confided to her diary. She had "wonderful notes" for the novel, but she feared she had lost her "capacity for fiction." When she wrote, however, she felt happy and hopeful, feeling Leonora hopping around in her mind, a figure "not unlike myself," but part of a work that seemed to West "unlike anything else I have written."[7]

West made progress on "The Only Poet," but of a curious kind, announcing that she had achieved "the real right beginning."[8] She sought the same perfection of origins in her memoirs. Nearly every ambitious project she attempted in her last years showed the promise of a brilliant beginning, which was constantly rewritten. She would go back, go back, go back to first

---

[7]Diary entries, February 26 and 28, 1973, Tulsa.

[8]Diary entry, April 28, 1973, Tulsa.

causes, never clinching her arguments or developing her notes for the later parts of her novels. Her dreams followed the same pattern of reversion: a combing over of the past, then an abrupt halt, like her heroine Leonora, who dies still sorting out her history. In her eighties, West tired easily and her book drafts sputtered.

West spent her last productive decade writing reviews for the *Sunday Telegraph* and working on her memoirs. In 1977, some of her best work was collected in *Rebecca West: A Celebration*, and in 1982, the year before she died, *The Young Rebecca*, a collection of her early, irreverent journalism appeared, and *1900*, part history/part autobiography. Virago Press began reprinting her fiction and nonfiction. In one sense, she was a fixture in the literary landscape; in another, no one quite knew how to place her--as one of her best critics, Samuel Hynes, observed in his introduction to the anthology of her writing. The multiplicity of her interests and her resort to several different genres explained this neglect--as did the defects of her novels (excepting *The Return of the Soldier* and *The Birds Fall Down*), which had not matched the superiority of her nonfiction or the fiction of her greatest contemporaries.[9]

*1900*, a big picture book with a short narrative, provided the opportunity to salvage some of West's autobiography by weaving it into a portrait of turn-of-the century London and the emergence of the modern world. But finding the right tone, beginning in the right key, frustrated her. She tried at least eighteen different openings, many beginning with the premise of her as a "noticing child." She evoked her memories of Richmond-on-Thames on the outer edge of London, described the period clothes, the Boer war. One draft began with an allusion to the turmoil in contemporary Afghanistan and Iran. Another referred to her old age and sitting in her "invalid chair." Still

---

[9]Hynes, "Introduction," *Rebecca West: A Celebration* (New York: Viking, 1977), xviii.

another discoursed on the vagaries of history, assessing the differences between past and present. In Proustian fashion, she evoked the sights and smells (the burning of gas jets, for example), the aura of another age. She returned to the themes of her first book, portraying Henry James and John Singer Sargent (both Americans) as the "two butlers" to the English upper classes. They were the aliens, the outsiders, who could see "most of the game."[10]

West herself was an outsider, who could see "most of the game," and *Family Memories*, even in its fragmentary state, marks the closest she came to closure on her career. West worked on the text for nearly twenty years, and her undated drafts make it impossible to say how she would have ultimately arranged her material. Her editor, Faith Evans, has done a skillful job of selecting the most finished drafts, scrupulously pointing out (in and introduction and extensive notes) that in some cases there are multiple and contradictory versions of events. The title of the memoir captures the spirit of West's work, but it is not her choice, and no evidence has yet come to light about her intentions for the title, or about exactly how far she would have taken the history of her family and of herself. The extant drafts end with the period of West's childhood and early adolescence, with a separate chapter on her husband and his family, which is included as an appendix in the Evans edition.

The memoir aims to show how the unfortunate history of a remarkable family shaped West's character. The first chapter details the career of Alexander Mackenzie, West's uncle. A distinguished musician and composer, he became the man of the family after his father died. But he practically disowned his mother (Janet Campbell Mackenzie) and his brothers and sisters (Johnnie, Joey, and Isabella) when one of the brothers (it is not clear which one) insulted Mary Ironside, the woman Alexander wished to marry.

---

[10]West's drafts of *1900* are at Tulsa.

Consequently, Johnnie, Joey, and Isabella were deprived of support for their own musical careers that Alexander could have provided. The chief sufferer, West emphasizes, was her mother, Isabella, who as a woman had considerably fewer opportunities than her brothers to travel and to develop her genius as a pianist.

Because neither Johnnie nor Joey had much strength of character and were subject to various tubercular ailments, the women in the Mackenzie family had to make do with a lace shop and positions as governesses and teachers in a nineteenth-century Europe that severely restricted the roles women could play in society. Although there are separate chapters on Joey and Johnnie (a third brother Willie, an alcoholic painter, receives little attention), the memoir centers on Isabella's plight. After various interruptions of her career, she is dispatched by her mother to Australia to check on Johnnie, who has been sent there to recover his health. Aboard ship Isabella meets the elegant, dark-eyed, romantic looking Charles Fairfield, whom she marries sometime later in Australia.

Subsequent chapters describe Fairfield's service in the military, his travels to the United States, and his brilliant but erratic career as a journalist. West's awe of her father vies with her contempt for his abusive treatment of his mother and family. He is an unfaithful husband and a poor provider. Once again Isabella finds herself on her own, seeking to support her three daughters. As the youngest child (Letitia and Winifred were eight and six years older than her) West was in the weakest position to understand her father's wayward behavior, though even as a toddler she was aware (she claims) of his potent sexuality.

Significantly, the memoir ends at about the time of West's thirteenth year, just before her father died and her family had to move to Edinburgh. She was never able to get beyond this point and describe the painful adolescent years she endured without his presence. An added chapter on her husband, Henry Maxwell Andrews, also details the misfortunes he suffered at the hands of a mentally ill father. The implication is that like her, Andrews was never able to fully recover from the early traumas of his family life.

*Family Memories* has a very strong feminist theme. From the outset West makes it clear that she has many grievances against men. In nineteenth-century Scotland, men were given privileges largely because they were men, not because they were inherently superior to women. Her uncle, Alexander Mackenzie, for example, was no doubt a genius, but West believes that her mother Isabella's talent was just as great. Yet Isabella's mother, Janet Campbell Mackenzie, lavished all her resources on her son, not on her daughter. And when that son rejected his own family, Janet Campbell Mackenzie continued to yearn for his approval. This angers West because her grandmother had shown such strength after her husband's early death, opening up a lace shop and refusing the charity of her community. In other words, there was no reason why Janet Campbell Mackenzie should defer to the wishes of any man. Yet Alexander Mackenzie was treated like a king.

Of course, Isabella gets caught in the same pattern of male dominance when she marries Charles Fairfield. In fact, the pattern is intensified because Fairfield came from an Anglo Irish family in County Kerry Ireland which claimed aristocratic descent. He had been raised to regard himself as a gentleman. This is what gave him such a noble bearing, but it is also what removed him from the reality of making a living and supporting a family.

But *Family Memories* is not merely about the tyranny of male authority, it is about West's rebellion against authority figures, men and women. Her primary target is her sister, Letitia, eight years older, a brilliant student who became both a doctor and a lawyer. Because Charles Fairfield was unde-pendable and eventually left his family when West was eight-years-old, Letitia (her father's first born and favorite child) was given a large measure of authority over West that West clearly resented. West portrays her elder sister as rebuffing her, treating her as an unruly intruder. Similarly, at school the precocious and outspoken West is disciplined and prayed over by one of her teachers in a way that embarrasses her and increases her distrust of authority.[11]

Like the incomplete "Cousin Rosamund," the unfinished *Family Memories* is a protest against the humiliations of childhood and of family history which the child is powerless to combat or to rectify. West gives her memoir a strong theme and plot, and her editor, Faith Evans, strongly suspects West fictionalized and intensified certain events to give them a meaning that fits her design but that is not necessarily the truth of what actually happened. In part, Evans is drawn to this conclusion (stated in her introduction) because of West's style, which often has the narrative power of a novel. West's fictionalizing can also be detected in overwrought passages relating to her mother and father; some of her elaborate descriptions bear the imprint of an imagination which has worked certain events over and over again in her mind until they have a highly polished form.

At the core of *Family Memories* are unresolved feelings about the place of men and women. Although West excoriates men for usurping positions of power, and she is nearly as severe on women who allow themselves to be exploited, she is obviously attracted to powerful males and often presents them in her fiction and nonfiction as alluring figures. A good part of her finds the idea of kingship emotionally satisfying. Some feminists have taken West to task for this subservience to the male ideal. They have greeted the posthumous publication of another West novel, *Sunflower* (1986) with dismay because its heroine's imagination is so dominated by figures of her two male lovers. Yet in West's own mind, there may not have been a contradiction. Her powerful attraction to men, and her desire to have a fulfilling romantic relationship with a man, caused her to idealize the male, to be sure, but she associated this idealization with the power of love. Neither West herself nor

---

[11]West left several fictional portraits of Letitia. She is Alice Pemberton in "The Salt of the Earth, (*The Harsh Voice*), Cordelia in *The Fountain Overflows,* and Gerda in "Short Life of a Saint" (*The Only Poet and Short Stories*).

her female characters ever give up their independence of mind, even when it comes into conflict with the men to whom they wish to surrender themselves. West's insistence on women's equality, on the one hand, and her yearning for submission to male authority, on the other hand, may seem paradoxical and ironic.[12] Certainly these conflicting tendencies frustrated West as a writer and as a woman, but she thought they could be compatible, that she could give herself completely to a man and retain herself in her entirety. To be totally free and totally committed is a contradiction in terms, and yet it has been the theme of many love stories.

West can be faulted perhaps for not scrutinizing her own motives sufficiently, but as an artist she presents very human and believable dilemmas. Although her political position as a feminist is quite clear in her nonfiction, her fiction explores how difficult it is to live by doctrine; her fiction makes room for conflicting human impulses, for the desire to both exert and to surrender the will. Because women historically have found themselves in subordinate roles, and because some feminists are determined to shake off demeaning aspects of women's experience, West's work is likely to continue to be troubling. Yet the assertion of self is so powerful in virtually everything she wrote that it seems certain that she will be accorded high respect not only in the history of women's literature but in the canon of modern authors.

---

[12]See two recent studies, Ann Norton, "Paradoxical Feminism: The Novels of Rebecca West" (Ph.D. diss., Rutgers University, 1993); Loretta Stec, "Writing Treason: Rebecca West's Contradictory Career" (Ph.D diss., Rutgers University, 1993).

# ABBREVIATIONS:

## RESEARCH COLLECTIONS AND PRIVATE PAPERS

AM  Papers of Alison Macleod

BU  Mugar Memorial Library, Special Collections, Boston University, Boston

Cornell  Rare and Manuscript Collections, Carl A. Kroch Library, Cornell University Library, Ithaca, New York.

CU  Rare Books and Manuscripts, Butler Library, Columbia University, New York City

HH  Houghton Library, Harvard University, Cambridge, Massachusetts

LC  Manuscript Division, Library of Congress, Washington, D.C.

Lords  Lord Beaverbrook Papers, House of Lords Record Office, London

NYPL  The New York Public Library

PML  Gordon Ray Collection, Pierpont Morgan Library, New York City

PU          Special Collections, Firestone Library, Princeton University

Syracuse    Dorothy Thompson Collection, Syracuse University Library.

Texas       Rebecca West Collection, Humanities Research Center, University of Texas, Austin

Tulsa:      Rebecca West Collection, McFarlin Library, Special Collections, University of Tulsa

Viking      Viking Press Research Library, New York City

Yale:       Rebecca West Collection, Beinecke Rare Book and Manuscript Library, Yale University, New Haven, Connecticut

# BIBLIOGRAPHY

Except where otherwise specified, New York is the publication venue.

Adamic, Louis. *My Native Land*. Harper & Brothers, 1943.

Allen, Walter. *The Modern Novel*. E.P. Dutton, 1964.

Annan, Noel. *Our Age: English Intellectuals Between the World Wars--A Group Portrait*. Random House, 1990.

Beach, Joseph Warren. *The Twentieth Century Novel: Studies in Technique*. D. Appleton-Century, 1932.

Bell, Anne Oliver, ed. *The Diary of Virginia Woolf. Volume Four 1931-1935*. Harcourt Brace Jovanovich, 1982.

Belford, Barbara. *Violet*. Simon and Schuster, 1991.

Bogan, Louise. What the Woman Lived: *Selected Letters of Louise Bogan*. Harcourt, Brace Jovanovich, 1973.

Brown, Peter. *Augustine of Hippo: A Biography*. Berkeley: University of California Press, 1967.

Chamberlain, Lesley. "Rebecca West in Yugoslavia." *Contemporary Review* 248 (1986): 262-266.

Colquitt, Clare. "A Call to Arms: Rebecca West's Assault on the Limits of 'Gerda's Empire' in *Black Lamb and Grey Falcon*." *South Atlantic Review* 51 (1986): 77-91.

Deakin, Motley. *Rebecca West*. Boston: Twayne, 1980.

Dragnich, Alex N. *Serbs and Croats: The Struggle in Yugoslavia*. Harcourt Brace, 1992.

Ellmann, Mary. *Thinking About Women*. Harcourt Brace Jovanovich, 1968.

Ferguson, Moira. "Feminist Manicheanism: Rebecca West's Unique Fusion." *The Minnesota Review* 15 (1980): 53-60.

Ford, Ford Madox. *The Good Soldier* [1915]. Vintage, n.d.

Garner, Les. *A Brave and Beautiful Spirit: Dora Marsden 1882-1960*. Aldershot, England: Avebury, 1990.

Gilbert, Sandra. "Soldier's Heart: Literary Men, Literary Women, and the Great War." *Signs* 8 (1983): 422-50.

Glendinning, Victoria. *Rebecca West: A Life*. Knopf, 1987.

Hall, Brian. "Rebecca West's War." *The New Yorker*, April 15, 1996, pp.74-83.

Hammond, J.R. *H.G. Wells and Rebecca West*. St. Martin's, 1991.

Hardwick, Elizabeth. *Seduction & Betrayal: Women and Literature*. Vintage, 1975.

Hart-Davis, Rupert. *Hugh Walpole: A Biography*. Macmillan, 1952.

Hunt, Violet. *The Flurried Years*. London: Hurst & Blackett, 1922.

Judd, Alan. *Ford Madox Ford*. Cambridge: Harvard University Press, 1991.

Kaplan, Robert D. *Balkan Ghosts*. St. Martin's, 1993.

Kobler, Turner. "The Eclecticism of Rebecca West." *Critique* 13 (1971): 30-49.

Kramnick, Issac and Barry Sherman. *Harold Laski: A Life on the Left*. Allen Lane, 1993.

Laing, Kathryn. "Addressing Femininity in the Twenties: Virginia Woolf and Rebecca West on Money, Mirrors and Masquerade." In *Virginia Woolf and the Arts: Selected Papers from the Sixth Annual Conference on Virginia Woolf*, eds. Diane F. Gillespie and Leslie K. Hankins. Pace University Press, 1997, 66-75.

_____. "The Sentinel" by Rebecca West: A Newly Discovered Novel." *Notes and Queries*, forthcoming June 1998.

Lamb, Richard. *Churchill as War Leader*. London: Bloomsbury, 1991.

Langner, Lawrence. *The Magic Curtain*. E.P. Dutton, 1951.

Lees, Michael. *The Rape of Serbia: The British Role in Tito's Grab for Power, 1943-44*. Harcourt Brace Jovanovich, 1990.

Lindsay, Franklin. *Beacons in the Night: With the OSS and Tito's Partisans in Wartime Yugoslavia*. Stanford: Stanford University Press, 1993.

Mackenzie, Norman & Jean. *The Life of H.G. Wells: the Times Traveller*. Revised edition. London: Hogarth, 1987.

Maclean, Fitzroy. *Eastern Approaches*. [1949] Penguin, 1991.

McLynn, Frank. *Fitzroy Maclean*. London: John Murray, 1992.

Mannin, Ethel. *Confessions and Impressions*. London: Jarrolds, 1930.

Marcus, Jane. "A Speaking Sphinx." *Tulsa Studies in Women's Literature* (Fall 1983): 151-54.

_____. "A Voice of Authority." In *Faith of A (Woman) Writer*. Alice Kessler-Harris and William McBrien, eds. Greenwood, 1988

_____. "A Wilderness of One's Own: Feminist Fantasy Novels in the Twen--ties: Rebecca West and Sylvia Townsend Warner." In *Women Writers and the City: Essays in Feminist Literary Criticism*. Nashville: University of Tennessee Press, 1984.

_____. ed. *The Young Rebecca: Writings of Rebecca West 1911-1917*. Bloomington: Indiana University Press, 1982.

Martin, David. *Web of Disinformation: Churchill's Yugoslav Blunder*. Harcourt Brace Jovanovich, 1990.

Mizener, Arthur. *The Saddest Story: A Biography of Ford Madox Ford*. The World Publishing, 1971.

Mosley, Diana. *The Writing of Rebecca West*. Francestown, New Hampshire, Typographeum, 1986. Originally published in *The European*, July 1956.

Moyers, Bill. "A Visit with Rebecca West," interview transcript, *Bill Moyers Journal*, Air Date: July 8, 1981.

Nicolson, Nigel and Joanne Trautmann, eds. *The Letters of Virginia Woolf. Volume III: 1923-1928*. Harcourt Brace Jovanovich, 1978.

_____. *The Letters of Virginia Woolf, Volume IV: 1929-1931*. Harcourt Brace Jovanovich, 1978.

_____. *The Letters of Virginia Woolf. Volume V: 1932-1935*. Harcourt Brace, Jovanovich, 1979

Norton, Ann. "Paradoxical Feminism: The Novels of Rebecca West." Ph.D. diss.: Columbia University, 1992.

Olson, Stanley. *Elinor Wylie: A Biography.* Dial, 1979.

Orel, Harold. *The Literary Achievement of Rebecca West.* St. Martin's, 1986.

Orlich, Sister Mary Margarita. "The Novels of Rebecca West: A Complex Unity." Ph.D. diss.: University of Notre Dame, 1967.

Pritchett, V.S. "The Climate of Paranoia." *The New Yorker*, December 12, 1966,

Ray, Gordon. *H.G. Wells and Rebecca West.* New Haven: Yale University Press, 1974.

Ray, Philip E. "*The Judge* Reexamined: Rebecca West's Underrated Gothic Romance. *English Literature in Transition 1880-1920* 31 (1987): 297-307.

Redd, Tony Neil. "Rebecca West: Master of Reality." Ph.D diss.: University of South Carolina, 1972.

Rollyson, Carl. "Rebecca West: A Portrait," *Confrontation: A Literary Journal of Long Island University*, forthcoming.

_____. "History Brought Home: Rebecca West's Yugoslav Journey," *Bangkok Post*, February 7, 1994, p.5.

_____. "The Lessons of Nuremberg," *The Journal of Commerce*, October 1, 1996, p. 8A.

_____. "Rebecca West," in *Research Guide to Biography and Criticism Vol. VI* (Washington, D.C.: Beacham Publishing, 1991), pp. pp. 600-06.

_____. *Rebecca West: A Saga of the Century* (London: Hodder & Stoughton, 1995). Published with revisions as *Rebecca West: A Life* (New York: Scribner, 1996).

_____. "Rebecca West and the God that Failed," *The Wilson Quarterly* 20 (Summer 1996): 78-85.

Saint Augustine. *Confessions.* Penguin, 1961.

Scott, Bonnie Kime. *The Gender of Modernism: A Critical Anthology.* Bloomington: Indiana University Press, 1990.

_____. *Refiguring Modernism.* Bloomington: Indiana University Press, 1995.

Secor, Robert and Marie Secor. *The Return of the Good Soldier: Ford Madox Ford and Violet Hunt's 1917 Diary.* University of Victoria, 1983.

Secunda, Victoria. *Woman and Their Fathers.* Delacorte, 1992.

Showalter, Elaine. *A Literature of Their Own: British Women Novelists From Bronte to Lessing.* Princeton: Princeton University Press, 1977.

Smith, David C. *H.G. Wells: Desperately Mortal.* New Haven: Yale University Press, 1986.

Spender, Dale. *There's Always Been a Women's Movement in This Century.* London: Pandora, 1983.

Stec, Loretta. "Writing Treason: Rebecca West's Contradictory Career." Ph.D. diss.: Rutgers University, 1993.

Stetz, Margaret Diane. "Drinking "The Wine of Truth": Philosophical Change in West's *The Return of the Soldier.*" *Arizona Quarterly* 43 (1987): 63-78.

_____. "Rebecca West's 'Elegy': Women's Laughter and Loss." *Journal of Modern Literature* 18 (Fall 1993): 369-80.

_____. "Rebecca West and the Visual Arts." *Tulsa Studies in Women's Literature 8*, #1 (Spring 1989): 43-62.

Swinnerton, Frank. *The Georgian Scene: A Literary Panorama.* New York: Farrar & Rinehart, 1934.

Taylor, A. J. P. *The Habsburg Monarchy 1809-1918* [1948]. Penguin, 1990.

_____. *A Personal History.* London: Coronet, 1984.

Taylor, Telford. *The Anatomy of the Nuremberg Trials.* Knopf, 1992.

Teachout, Terry. "A Liberated Woman." *The New Criterion* 6 (1988): 13-21.

Thomas, Sue. "Rebecca West's Second Thoughts on Feminism." *Genders* 13 (Spring 1992): 90-107.

Tillinghast, Richard. "Rebecca West & The Tragedy of Yugoslavia." *The New Criterion* 10 (1992): 12-22.

Todorovich, Boris. *Last Words: A Memoir of World War II and the Yugoslav Tragedy.* Walker, 1989.

Urie, Dale Marie. "Rebecca West: A Worthy Legacy. Ph.D. diss.: University of North Texas, 1989.

Watts, Marjorie. *Mrs. Sappho: The Life of C.A. Dawson Scott, Mother of International P.E.N..* London: Duckworth, 1987.

Wells, H.G. *Boon, The Mind of the Race, The Wild Asses of the Devil, and The Last Trump Being a First Selection from the Literary Remains of George Boon, Appropriate to the Times Prepared for publication by Reginald Bliss, with an Ambiguous Introduction by H.G. Wells.* Doran, 1915.

_____. *H.G. Wells in Love: Postscript to An Experiment in Autobiography*, ed. G.P. Wells. Boston: Little Brown, 1984.

_____. *Marriage* [1912]. London: Hogarth, 1986.

_____. *The New Machiavelli* [1911]. Viking Penguin, 1985.

_____. The World of William Clissold. London: Ernest Benn, 1926.

West, Anthony. *H. G. Wells: Aspects of a Life.* Random House, 1984.

_____. *Heritage.* Random House, 1956.

West, Rebecca. *Black Lamb and Grey Falcon: A Journey Through Yugoslavia* [1941]. Penguin, 1986.

_____. *Cousin Rosamund.* Viking Penguin, 1986.

_____. *Family Memories.* Viking Penguin: 1988.

_____. *The Fountain Overflows* [1957]. London: Virago, 1984.

_____. "Goodness Doesn't Just Happen." In *This I Believe*, ed. Edward P. Morgan, Simon and Schuster, 1952, pp. 187-88.

_____. *Harriet Hume.* Doubleday Doran, 1929.

_____. *Henry James.* Henry Holt, 1916.

_____. *The Harsh Voice* [1935]. London: Virago, 1982.

_____. "I Regard Marriage With Fear and Horror." *Hearst's International*, November 1923, pp. 67, 207-09.

_____. *The Judge* [1922]. Dial, 1980.

_____. *Lions and Lambs*. With David Low. Harcourt Brace, 1928.

_____. *The Modern Rake's Progress*. With David Low. London: Hutchinson, 1934.

_____. "My Religion." In *My Religion*. D. Appleton, 1926, pp. 19-25.

_____. "The Necessity and Grandeur of the International Ideal." In *Challenge to Death*, ed. Storm Jameson. E.P. Dutton, 1935, pp. 241-60.

_____. *1900*. Viking, 1982.

_____. "The Novelist's Voice," BBC Broadcast, September 14, 1976, Tulsa.

_____. *The Only Poet & Short Stories*, ed. Antonia Till. London Virago, 1992.

_____. *Pablo Picasso: A Suite of 180 Drawings*. An Appreciation by Rebecca West. Harcourt, Brace, 1954.

_____. "The Private and Impersonal Notebooks of Braque." *Harper's Bazaar*, November, 1955, pp. 123-25, 193-95.

_____. *This Real Night*. Macmillan, 1984.

_____. *Rebecca West: A Celebration*. Viking, 1977.

_____. *The Return of the Soldier* [1918]. Carroll & Graff, 1990.

_____. "On "*The Return of the Soldier*." *The Yale University Library Gazette* 57 (1982):66-71.

_____. *Selected Poems of Carl Sandburg*. Harcourt, Brace, 1926.

_____. *The Strange Necessity: Essays Reviews* [1928]. London: Virago, 1987.

_____. *Sunflower*. Penguin, 1988.

_____. *The Thinking Reed* [1936]. Penguin Books, 1985.

_____. "Tradition in Criticism." In *Tradition and Experiment in Present-Day Literature*. London: Oxford University Press, 1929, pp. 179-97.

_____. *War Nurse: The True Story of A Woman Who Lived, Loved, and Suffered on the Western Front*. Cosmopolitan Book Corporation, 1930.

_____. "Woman As Artist and Thinker." In *Woman's Coming of Age: A Symposium*, ed. Samuel D. Schmalhausen and V.F. Calverton. Liveright, 1931, pp. 369-82.

_____. "Women as Brainworkers." In Women and The Labour Party, ed. Dr. Marion Phillips. London: Headley Brothers Publishers, 1918, pp. 57-65.

Wexler, Alice. *Emma Goldman in Exile: From the Russian Revolution to the Spanish Civil War*. Boston: Beacon, 1989.

Wolfe, Peter. *Rebecca West: Artist and Thinker*. Carbondale, IL: Southern Illinois University Press, 1971.

Wolff, Larry. "Rebecca West: This Time, Let's Listen." *The New York Times Book Review*, February 10, 1991, p. 1.

# INDEX

RW's break with, 42
RW's criticism of, 14, 18, 63, 193
in RW's fiction, 35, 48
RW's first meeting with, 14-15
RW's quarrels with, 43, 78
on RW's work, 19, 28-30, 36, 40,
  63-64, 72
Werfel, Franz, 154
West, the, 135, 139, 149, 153, 157,
  180, 208
West, Anthony, 78, 85
  birth of, 23
  childhood of, 23
  education of, 43
West, Rebecca (Cicily Isabel Fairfield):
  acting of, 9
  American lecture tour of, 43
  anti-Communism of, 5, 89-90,
    105, 175, 181, 191
  attitude toward authority of, 184,
    223
  as book reviewer, *see book reviews*
  childhood of, 4 n.5, 74, 220
  conservatism of, 51, 105
  education of, 9
  as feminist, 12, 23-4, 28, 146, 148,
    209
  fictional self-portraits of, 35, 41,
    47, 113, 119, 122
  independence of, 200
  isolation of, 189
  lack of critical attention to, 1
  marriage of, 87
  name change of, 1n
  playwriting of, 107-110
  rebelliousness of, 223
  reputation established, 220
  reputation problems of, 220
  romanticism of, 76, 94, 103
  Serbo-Croatian studies, 128
  as socialist, 19
  as suffragist, 4

Williams, William Carlos, 62, 74
Wilson, Edmund, 75
Wolfe, Peter, 1, 100
*Woman Adrift*, 7
"Woman As Artist and Thinker,"
  82
women:
  idiocy of, 133, 14
  women's suffrage, 35
Woolf, Virginia, 31, 67, 76, 78, 91,
  105
Woollcott, Alexander, 89, 107, 129
Wordsworth, 111
World War I, 21, 197, 206
  in *Black Lamb and Grey Falcon*,
    133, 135, 150, 154-55, 162
  in *Cousin Rosamund*, 201
  in *War Nurse*, 47
*World of William Clissold, The*
  (Wells), 64
"World's Worst Failure," The, 23
*Wound and the Bow, The* (Wilson),
  194
Wylie, Elinor, 73

*Yorkshire Post*, 53
*Young Rebecca, The*, 7, 220

Yugoslavia:
  Alexander, king of 132, 135, 155,
    165
  Andrews in, 128, 130, 135, 138,
    141, 143-45, 150, 152, 154,
    159, 161, 165
  Communism in, 170, 175
  Easter ceremony in, 156
  history in, 130, 132-35, 137-143,
    145, 148-49, 152-55, 161-62, 165
  Peter, king of, 155, 171
  and Soviet Union, 170, 176

Zagreb, 136, 140